BASIC HORSE CARE

BASIC HORSE CARE

Eleanor F. Prince and
Gaydell M. Collier

Drawings and photographs by the authors
unless otherwise credited

DOUBLEDAY
NEW YORK LONDON TORONTO SYDNEY AUCKLAND

PUBLISHED BY DOUBLEDAY
a division of Bantam Doubleday Dell Publishing Group, Inc.
666 Fifth Avenue, New York, New York 10103

DOUBLEDAY and the portrayal of an anchor with a dolphin
are trademarks of Doubleday, a division of Bantam Doubleday
Dell Publishing Group, Inc.

Library of Congress Cataloging-in-Publication Data
Prince, Eleanor F.
    Basic horse care.
    Bibliography: p.
    Includes index.
    1. Horses.   I. Collier, Gaydell M.   II. Title.
[SF285.3.P75   1989]   636.1   88-33400

ISBN 0-385-26199-3 (pbk.)

2 4 6 8 9 7 5 3
BVG

to the memory of
Ellin K. Roberts
who helped us to get started and to keep on keeping on

Acknowledgments

Our sincere thanks
to the following for their professional help in reviewing the manuscript, correcting errors, and making suggestions:

Dr. John Ismay, D.V.M., Sturgis Veterinary Hospital, Sturgis, South Dakota—"Health, Ailments, and Restraints" (Chapter 8); J. W. "Jim" Waggoner, Jr., Ph.D., C.A.S., Livestock Management and Nutrition, Division of Animal Science, University of Wyoming, Laramie—"Feeding, Feeds, and Pastures" (Chapter 5); Jerry Banks, farrier—"Hoof Care and Farriery" (Chapter 7) and to:

Dorothy R. Feldman and Barbara E. Wallace for reviewing other parts of the manuscript and helping in so many ways; Freda Weaver and Jenny Carpenter for their help with art and graphics; Dave Ellsbury for photography, and Mary Jean Wilson and Frank R. Collier for processing photos; Gail Stuchlik, Leslie Turner, Lana Brokau, Arlowe Hulett, and Kathryn H. Dennison for their help and support; our intrepid typist, Judy R. Johnson, for review, suggestions, and typing of the manuscript; the many people who supplied advice, photos, or other assistance; our editor, Jean Anne Vincent, for her suggestions and patience; and our husbands, Bill and Roy, for their help and encouragement, for making suggestions and finding information, and for putting up with us throughout the project.

CONTENTS

INTRODUCTION

Horses are naturally nomads. Their evolution, through geologic ages, fitted them so well for the wandering, grazing life that it is nearly impossible to imagine the wild horse without vast, open country surrounding him.

As he evolved, the horse adjusted totally to his environment. His four-toed foot developed into the hoof, better for traveling rapidly across the drier open steppes of an emerging world. He was always on the move. His digestive system developed to handle quick, light feedings; he cropped grass while traveling, spending most of his day eating. He became wary and alert, ever ready to begin instant flight to outrace his enemies, and his entire physical makeup developed to make this flight possible and natural.

And then, in an incredibly short span of time, he was domesticated by man. The horse was plucked from the environment that suited him to perfection, plunked down in a totally alien one, fed strange foods in an odd way, restricted in exercise, and subjected to extraordinary mental and physical demands. He has been expected to almost instantaneously adjust to total change affecting every aspect of his being.

And amazingly, he has done so, almost in spite of us. But his basic instincts and pastoral characteristics remain; they are so much a part of him that only one generation is needed to effect a complete return to a wild (feral) horse.

And so now horse owners must be responsible for their horses' physical and mental well-being. But often, today, because they have not grown up with horses as working partners, new owners are unfamiliar with the horses' needs —possibly even unaware of them.

Aside from his interest in and affection for his horses, the horse owner's responsibilities fall into three distinct areas:

Education. He should learn and understand the factors involved in care, feeding, health, training, riding, breeding, and specialized fields. This knowledge may be gained through books and magazines, apprenticeship, schools, and observation and participation in shows, 4-H and other youth programs, and clinics—as well as by homegrown experience.

Finances. Very few people make their living with horses; usually the horse must be supported with outside financial resources. These must be adequate to care properly for the horse's board (feed and pasture), facilities, training (if not done at home), farriery, veterinary care, parasite control, immunizations, and exercise.

Time. The horse owner must have time each day for regularly feeding his animal, keeping the stall clean, grooming and training, exercising, and companionship. If his time or physical abilities are insufficient for these tasks, he must pay someone else to do them.

Inadequacies in these three areas of responsibility lead directly to the main pitfalls of ownership and are the cause of most of the problems that are encountered in keeping horses.

The purpose of this book is to present guidelines for good horse management, including hints and ideas we have picked up from over sixty years of combined personal experience. We hope it will prove a useful tool in helping any horse owner care for the most wonderful of all animals. The old saying is still true that "there is something about the outside of a horse that is good for the inside of a man."

Part I

THE HORSE HIMSELF

The copartnership of form and function—conformation and performance—is one of the factors affecting a horse's usability. (Courtesy Wyoming Travel Commission)

CHAPTER 1

THE USABLE HORSE

From earliest historical times, man has valued the horse because of his usefulness—whether packing man's burdens, pulling his carriages and plows, carrying him into battle, helping him work his stock, or aiding him to compete in sports. That the horse has provided man with pleasure, inspiration, and companionship as well, is as delightful as it is unarguable.

There are three main factors affecting a horse's usability. The first is the copartnership of form and function—conformation and performance. Ideal conformation is based on performance: the best conformation allows the best accomplishment of a desired function or task. Together, form and function constitute the main characteristics of a breed.

The second important factor is soundness. When a horse is unhampered by any fault or defect and is in good health and good condition, he is able to perform adequately—even superbly—any normal task asked of him.

Third, an agreeable temperament is a vital factor in usability. Temperament includes intelligence, disposition, and the qualities of willingness, confidence, and courage. Such a horse will be more valuable (even without ideal conformation) than the near-perfect individual with poor temperament.

These factors are interrelated and have considerable bearing on each other. A fault in conformation may predispose a horse to an unsoundness, such as cow hocks tending to curbs or splints, which in turn will affect his performance. Conformation that causes faulty gaits will affect the horse's willingness, attention span, and ease in learning, just as an unsoundness or ailment causing pain or discomfort will make him irritable or miserable.

Basic Horse Care and the Usable Horse

The way we care for the individual horse—in the broad sense of the words "care for" that includes training, working, and riding—serves to increase or decrease his usefulness by affecting his soundness, disposition, health, condition, and willingness. Good care includes proper facilities, good nutrition, attention to health and hoofs, proper exercise and rest, and a pleasant atmosphere resulting from balanced discipline, respect, and love. Such care tends to make a horse mannerly and willing, as well as strong and healthy; it enables the animal to approach his potential in conformation, temperament,

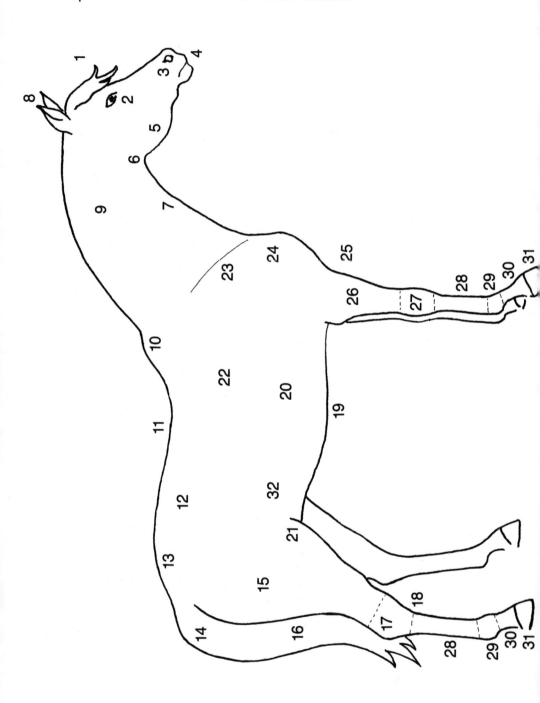

1. Head: comparatively small, good carriage, features well defined — contributes to style, balance and quality
2. Eyes: for better vision, should be large, low-set, prominent, set apart, dark, and uniform in color; look of intelligence
3. Nostrils: big and full to take in large amount of air
4. Teeth: meet when biting
5. Jowl: deep
6. Throatlatch: fine and clean to allow maximum flexion
7. Windpipe: detached, for generous air passage
8. Ears: placed close together, short and fine, display alertness
9. Neck: long, for maximum mobility; set on high, blending well into the shoulder to allow agility; slightly arched to affect action; length and shape of neck affect balance, style, and maneuverability
10. Withers: well defined, for holding saddle well; extend deep into back for strength
11. Back: short, for strength
12. Coupling: short and strong, for easy "keeping qualities"
13. Croup: long and rather level, to accommodate more muscling and increase style and balance
14. Tail: carried well and straight
15. Thigh and gaskin: muscular development extensive, for power
16. Hip to hock: long for leverage
17. Hocks: large, clean, strong
18. Angulation: sufficient in hind leg for driving
19. Underline: long—keeps forelegs and rear legs farther apart
20. Girth and barrel: deep, for strength, weight-carrying

21. Stifle: wide, for free motion
22. Ribs: well sprung
23. Shoulder: 45-degree angle with length, to help raise head, give easy ride with less shock and more extension in stride, reduce stumbling, move elbows away from body
24. Chest: good width, depth, for stamina and strength
25. Legs: correct and fine, for good circulation and soundness; hocks well let down
26. Forearms: powerful, long muscles to increase length of stride, contributes to style
27. Knees: straight, large, flat; deep, to absorb concussion; pisiform bone (behind knee) is prominent
28. Cannons: short, flat bone, for leverage and strength
29. Fetlocks: smooth, well-defined
30. Pasterns: moderately long, well sloped, same as feet (45 degrees)
31. Feet: large enough to hold body, hard, tough, set squarely on ground, toes straight ahead, heels round, open, and spread; shapely
32. Flank: deep

Overall: Bone is hard, sharp, clean; proud carriage, to contribute to style and physical fitness; alertness; substance (muscle and bone); style, fineness; sex character; sharp, chiseled features; squareness of stance; well-defined tendons; quality; smoothness; glossy, fine hair coat

Action: free, easy, true, straight stride, collected stride, stylish way of going

Features of stride: length, trueness, height; rapidity (snap, promptness); regularity; balance, spring; folds and lifts knees; works and drives hocks; straight arc (highest point in center)

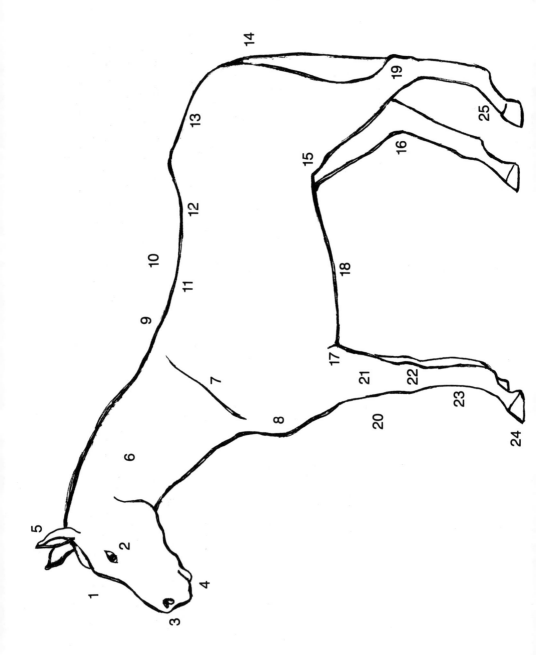

1. Head: large, overbalances forehand; heavy, hard to collect and maneuver
2. Eyes: small and poorly set, poor vision, contributes to poor disposition
3. Nostrils: small, with thick throatlatch, limits intake of air
4. Teeth: parrot mouth and monkey mouth (congenital conditions) reduce intake of food, thus a "poor keeper"
5. Ears: large, no style
6. Neck: short and thick, no flexion; ewe-neck is weak and can overbend; set on low, no agility
7. Shoulder: steep angle contributes to shock and wear of forelegs and feet; less extension of stride; stumbles
8. Chest: too wide, rolling gait; too narrow, weak and horse lacks substance
9. Withers: mutton, won't hold saddle; high and sharp, saddle will rub
10. Topline: rough, lacks style and smoothness
11. Back: too short, with long legs, contributes to forging; too long, weak, tires easily under weight; roach back, weak
12. Loin: too long, weak
13. Croup: short, steep, rough, no room for muscling, loss of style and balance, cannot perform off hocks; lack of strength
14. Tail: low-set, no style
15. Stifle: too close to body, restricts free movement
16. Angulation: too straight, contributes to crampy, hard ride
17. Elbows: too close to body, restricts free movement
18. Underline: short, contributes to short strides; tucked up, unthrifty, hard keeper
19. Hocks: sickle, bear more weight, contributing to spavins and curbs; wide hocks or bandy legs deter collected action and predispose to unsoundness
20. Legs: coarse, meaty legs reduce circulation, tend to stock, puff, bog; base narrow and base wide cause dishing and winging
21. Forearm: short, no extension, short stride
22. Knees: calf knees, increase concussion and pounding gait; buck knees, weak, tend to stumble; tied-in, weak, inadequate tendon and ligament development
23. Cannons: long, weak, tend to bow
24. Feet: splayed, cause paddling, winging; pigeon-toed, paddling; long toes cause stumbling and unstableness; feet too small for body help legs break down
25. Pasterns: long, weak, cannot stop well; irregular stride predisposes to ringbone; short, straight, contribute to rough, trappy stride, stiffness, sidebones

Physical handicaps cause horse to be clumsy, use excessive energy; contribute to rough riding, lack of strength and speed; decrease potential usefulness and length of life; are aesthetically unpleasant and soundness. The well-cared-for horse is best able to reach the peaks of performance.

There are few so-called rogues, and they are usually man-made. Mismanagement and mistreatment, ranging from ignorance and neglect to overseverity and cruelty, have diminished the usefulness of many a horse. Give your horse the best chance to achieve his full potential by giving him the best of care.

Is There an Ideal Conformation?

Although conformation may vary according to the function of the horse, there are some basic standards that we look for in any horse, regardless of breed. An ideal conformation refers not so much to a given outline, as to a structure that is free of any defects that might lead to unsoundness or weakness in any part or the whole. This can best be shown by comparing a good conformation with a poor one.

Soundness, temperament, and conformation are ideals that any horseman should consider carefully—but he should balance his ideals with common sense. Excellence in any one or two of these factors is worthless if the horse cannot perform his function.

Eyesight

The focusing mechanism of the horse's eye is unique in the animal kingdom. Horses cannot focus by altering the shape of the lens, as humans do. Instead, they compensate with their long, flexible neck, powerful extraocular muscles (behind the eye), and the peculiar shape of the eyeball—focus is determined by the position of the head, as shown in the illustration. They have a wide, panoramic vision, allowing them to see nearly all the way around their bodies.

Horses can see quite well in the dark, but they have little stereoscopic vision—that is, they do not see things in three dimensions. They learn to judge distance through trial and error (as is evident when teaching a horse to jump), and they have a keen perception of movement.

Color and Markings

As a rule, a horse's true color is shown by his muzzle; a horse that looks black at a distance may really be dark brown. When foals are changing hair coats, their true color may be seen on the muzzle and above the eyes.

Generally considered, there are five basic coat colors: bay, black, brown,

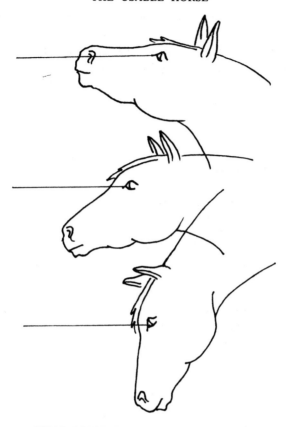

HEAD POSITION AND FOCAL DISTANCE

Because some parts of the retina are closer to the lens than others, the horse changes focal length by changing the angle of view. The horse raises his head to see objects close to his nose. In natural head position, he can see objects farther away; he can see where his forefeet will land, not where they are landing. With head down in grazing position, he has maximum distance vision and can see about 340 degrees around him (not directly behind).

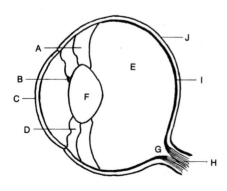

Cross Section of the Equine Eye

A. ciliary muscle	F. lens
B. corpora nigra	G. blind spot
C. cornea	H. optic nerve
D. iris	I. retina
E. vitreous body	J. sclera

chestnut (sorrel), and white. Common variants of these include dun and buckskin, gray, palomino, pinto, and roan. Within these classifications lie dozens of variations, some of which have conflicting names in different places. The distinctive coat of the Appaloosa is more a characteristic of pattern markings than of color.

White markings or spots are often seen on the head and legs, and occasionally under the body in the flank area. True white markings are indicated by white hair growing from white or pink skin; they are evident at the time of birth and do not change throughout the horse's life.

The hoofs of all foals are white at birth, but darken as the foal grows if the skin hair immediately above the hoof is dark. If the foal has a white marking (pink skin) above the hoof, the hoof will remain white. Hoofs can also be striped, depending on the color of the hair and skin immediately above the hoof.

The terms for head markings include star, spot, stripe or strip, blaze (over width of nasal bones), bald face, snip, race, lip markings, and white muzzle. Horses that have no pigmentation in the eyes (light blue or pink iris) are referred to by the terms walleye, watcheye, glass eye, and china eye. The horse with such an eye is able to see fully as well as the horse with normal eye

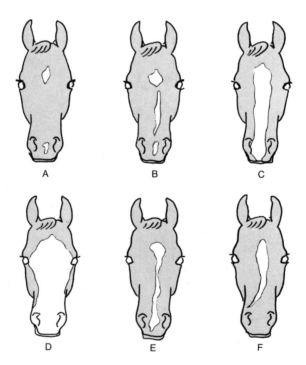

HEAD MARKINGS
A. Star and snip. B. Star, strip, and snip disconnected. C. Blaze. D. Bald face. E. Star, strip, and snip connected. F. Race.

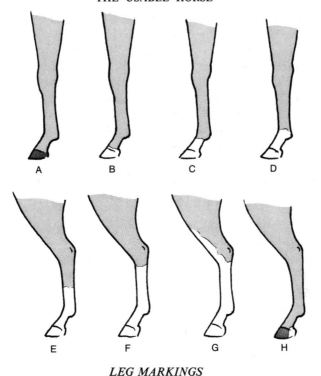

LEG MARKINGS
A. Unmarked leg. B. Coronet. C. Pastern. D. Fetlock. E. Sock. F. Stocking. G. Full stocking extending in front into gaskin. H. Heel.

coloring. Usually, the walleyed horse has a bald face and may have trouble with snow blindness due to more reflection from the light. Coloring the hair around the eye with dark, solid-wax shoe polish will alleviate this condition.

Leg markings are shown in the illustration. To remember easily how to describe lower-leg markings, state the highest part of the leg that includes white. For instance, if the fetlock, or part of it, is white, refer to the marking as "fetlock." Higher white markings are referred to as "socks" and "stockings."

Breed associations expect owners to accurately describe the locations and sizes of white body spots. Where there are scattered white hairs mixed in the coat, as in the flank on bays or chestnuts, they should be recorded.

Measuring Height and Weight

Horses are measured in hands (4 inches) from the highest point on the withers to the ground. The figure following the decimal point represents inches: a horse standing 15.2 hands is 62 inches high at the withers. Riding horses average out to be around 15.1 hands and 1,100 pounds. A horse's weight-carrying ability usually depends on his conformation, rather than on his height.

It is important to know your horse's weight, for the purpose of administering medicine and wormers (directions for medication usually give so many cc's per hundred pounds). Some feed companies give complimentary tapes that are marked not only for measuring height but also for finding the approximate weight. To be completely accurate, however, a livestock scale should be used.

Age

The life span of the horse is relatively short compared to that of man. One year of a horse's life equals three of man's.

Although most foals are born in the spring months of April, May, and June, an occasional foal is born later, even in September or October. Some breeders push to have early foals (January and February), which gives them a size advantage when racing or showing. After a foal is weaned, usually from four to six months, he is known as a weanling. On January 1 of his first year, the weanling becomes a yearling (late in the same year, he may be termed a long yearling); then, on each succeeding January, regardless of actual birth date, he becomes a two-, three-, and four-year-old. At four years of age, the filly is termed a mare and the colt a stallion or a gelding. The stallion can be termed a sire if he has "get" (offspring). A mare's offspring is termed "produce."

A horse is considered mature from six years of age on and is termed "aged" from ten to the end of his life (not "agèd," meaning senile). Some horses have lived thirty-five to forty years or more. Many horses that have been stressed by hard usage or lack of supplemental feed live only into their teens, but most horses that are properly trained and well cared for can live useful lives well into their twenties. Ponies seem to be longer-lived than larger horses. The traditional method of ascertaining the age of a horse is by examining his teeth.

Identification

Because horses are sometimes switched or stolen, for any number of nefarious reasons, systems of positive identification have been developed over the years which limit such activity and protect the owner. These include the hot-iron brand, the tattoo, the freeze mark, and pattern records of "night eyes," or chestnuts.

The upper lip tattoo is used officially by the American Paint Horse Associ-

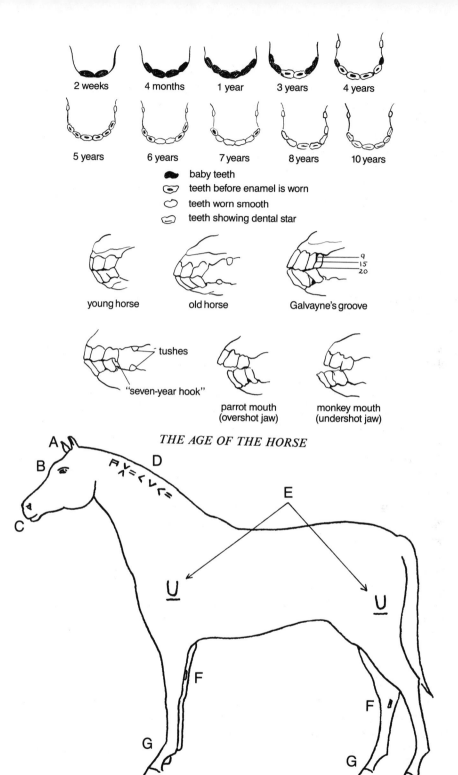

2 weeks	4 months	1 year	3 years	4 years
5 years	6 years	7 years	8 years	10 years

baby teeth
teeth before enamel is worn
teeth worn smooth
teeth showing dental star

young horse   old horse   Galvayne's groove

9
15
20

tushes
"seven-year hook"

parrot mouth
(overshot jaw)

monkey mouth
(undershot jaw)

THE AGE OF THE HORSE

MEANS OF IDENTIFICATION

A. Whorls. B. Face markings. C. Lip tattoo. D. Freeze mark. E. Hot brands. F. Chestnuts, or "night eyes." G. Leg markings.

ation and on Thoroughbreds, especially racehorses. Unfortunately, the tattoo can disappear as the horse grows older.

Hot-iron branding was the West's answer to cattle rustling, and most ranches also have a smaller iron of the same brand, which they use on horses. Most horse brands are placed on the hindquarters, but also may be found on the cheek or shoulder. Most Western states require a brand inspection (whether or not the horse carries a brand) when moving horses from one county to another within a state, or from one state to another. A brand inspection is also required when there is a change of ownership. In Wyoming, a lifetime brand inspection may be purchased for a horse as long as he remains under one owner who does not move his residence to another state. In some states, the brand-inspection papers may count as proof of ownership, replacing a bill of sale. Stiff fines are imposed if horses in transit are found without brand-inspection papers, and the animals may be required to return to their starting point.

Utilizing the chestnuts (night eyes) is a relatively new system of equine identification. The chestnuts—the horny growths on the insides of the horse's legs—are as individual to the horse as fingerprints are to a human. The chestnut is photographed in cross section, and the data are converted into audio signals that are recorded on a cassette tape. The recorded data can then be transmitted over ordinary telephone lines to a national computer data bank.

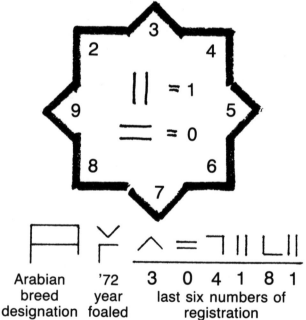

How to read a freeze mark. Freeze marking is permanent, painless, and unalterable.

Freeze marking was introduced by the Arabian Horse Registry in 1972 as a voluntary method of identifying horses. The mark is administered by a technician sent out by the registry. (Some other breeds are now admitting this kind of identification, and may have different requirements.) The marks are made under the mane in an area two by seven inches (smaller on foals—a smaller marking iron is used). The iron is chilled to -109 degrees F and placed on the clipped area for about twenty seconds on dark horses and somewhat longer on grays. The nerve ends are made insensitive by the super cold, so little restraint is needed. Freeze marks destroy the pigment-producing cells that color hair, so the mark shows up white. On grays, a hairless mark occurs.

Identification is an important aspect of usability, and the wise horse owner takes whatever measures are necessary or available in his locality to make sure his animals are protected.

What to Do if Your Horse Is Stolen

1. Contact local law enforcement and make sure a report is filed.
2. Contact neighbors and friends concerning the theft.
3. Notify saleyards, horse auctions, veterinarians and slaughterhouses within two hundred miles.
4. Put up posters in feedstores, tack shops, and public stables.
5. Tell your story to local newspapers, horse magazines, or other pertinent publications.
6. Contact your registry.
7. Contact your insurance company.
8. Contact organizations: shows, fairs, racetracks, Humane Society, Department of Agriculture.

CHAPTER 2

BUYING AND SELLING HORSES

CHOOSING AND BUYING A HORSE

Questions to Ask Yourself Before Buying a Horse

When you are seriously considering buying a horse, zero in on what you're really looking for. How do you want to use the horse? To some extent, price will always be a determining factor in selection. Registered, fully trained, specialty trained, and proven horses will cost more. However, the novice horseman can often buy an older, well-trained, experienced gelding (twelve to sixteen or even older) for a very reasonable sum, and be well satisfied.

Although many experienced horsemen buy young horses and train them themselves, this is usually not a good idea for novices, especially children. Their first horses should be their teachers, and their first experiences should be pleasurable. Unfortunately, the "wrong" horse can spoil future interest in horses and horsemanship.

Geldings are often more stable temperamentally than mares, but there are many mares with fine dispositions. It is true, however, that some mares in estrus may be cranky and not willing to perform to their potential.

As to size and weight, horse and rider should be well proportioned to each other. Very large people should opt for large, well-built horses, just as petite individuals should usually select smaller, finer animals. For specialized work such as jumping or dressage, choose a horse with the conformation, size, and weight to perform best at that specialty.

Buying a breeding or show animal entails knowledge of pedigrees, breed type, standard conformation, and breeding record of the individual and his sire and dam. Naturally, the "best" usually cost relatively more.

Sometimes the more expensive horse may be the least expensive in the long run, because the factor of safety must be considered. The untrained horse requires a more experienced horseman to properly develop his potential; trying to do it yourself because the untrained horse is cheaper can be costly from the standpoint of safety.

You want a horse with a good disposition and one that is consistent day after day. Buy a horse as an individual, not just for breed or color, and buy a horse that can be resold if necessary; inferior, unreliable horses will be difficult to sell.

When buying a horse, look for a bright, alert expression, a good eye, and an intelligent appearance.

Are You Ready to Buy a Horse?

The more exposure you have to the various aspects of the horse world, the better able you'll be to make knowledgeable decisions and avoid disappointment.

Visit your local breeding farms, riding schools, vet clinics, and farriers. If possible, take a horse-wise friend with you and talk shop. Go to shows, clinics, and horse auctions to become familiar with local interests and prices. Subscribe to a breed or all-breed magazine, and frequent your local library for horse books and magazines. Apprentice yourself to a local trainer or horseman and learn such basic procedures as routine feeding, grooming, cleaning stalls, and other unavoidable chores—are you willing to take on the work as well as the pleasure? Horsemanship schools that include courses in training and stable management are valuable. For young people, there is no better training than the 4-H program.

Without proper facilities, you and your horse will not enjoy a happy relationship. Your horse should always have shelter from the elements, whether a windbreak, shade, open shed, or barn. The new horse owner must provide space for the horse to exercise himself, or else budget plenty of time to exercise his animal. When specialized training is involved, specialized facilities should be provided—these might be a jumping course and equipment, a roping arena, or some other facility.

Stable equipment and tack are still another consideration, and feed (hay, grain, and minerals) is a big item requiring space for storage, as well as adequate finances. Further considerations may include insurance, farrier care, health care, and other local or specific items.

Where Can You Buy a Horse?

Horses for sale are advertised in general equine market mailings, in printed nonpersonal circulars, in breed associations' newsletters, and in letters from breeders and dealers. You will find horses listed for sale in classified advertising under "Horses" or "Livestock" in newspapers and other publications. You may also find horses for sale at a riding school. In rural areas, horse farms and ranches publicize with ranch signs. Advertising livestock is encouraged on bulletin boards in feedstores, tack shops, boarding and training stables, horsemanship schools, and some veterinary clinics.

By attending horse shows, whether breed shows or open events, the prospective buyer can see a horse fitted out at his best, and can observe him performing in competition with others. If you visit the stable area at a show, you will find stall placards noting horses for sale, with pedigrees and show records prominently displayed. This is ideal, since you can see the horse and talk with the owners at leisure.

If a buyer is inexperienced, and especially if he is unable to round up a knowledgeable horseman to advise him, his best bet would be to purchase from a breeding farm where the owners depend on their good reputation, stand behind their stock, and guarantee the horse in question. When buying from dealers or at auctions, the buyer should be especially careful to obtain professional advice.

Hazards in Buying a Horse

It is true that some horses may end up at a sale every few months because the new owner discovers that the horse did not live up to his expectations. When sold, the animal may appear to be a fat, shiny, healthy horse, but the fat might cover a multitude of conformation sins. And there may be other problems that diminish his working ability, such as poor legs, feet too small for the bulk of the animal, or lack of flexibility due to a short, fat neck.

Buying a horse in poor condition may make the price of the animal attractive, and this may be acceptable if he is not later found to have serious problems.

Poor disposition and inadequate or imperfect training are unseen bugaboos when buying a horse at any time. Vices such as bucking, rearing, kicking, and biting may become evident; with breeding stock, severe problems involve the inability to breed (stallion) or to conceive (mare). Conscientious breeders guarantee their stock's breeding ability.

Another hazard is equine infectious anemia (EIA). The seller should provide papers proving a recent negative Coggins test, since a horse found with a positive test must be isolated and quarantined on the owner's premises, or euthanatized.

Use the checklists in this section to help you avoid the hazards in buying a horse.

Buying a Horse at an Auction

Honest auctions give the small breeder an opportunity to market his animals without putting out expensive advertising. Breeders selling at quality breed auctions will generally guarantee their animals, provide pedigrees, sometimes provide financing, and in general endeavor to make the buyer satisfied. All-breed "Saturday night" auctions are entirely different, however; here each horse is sold "as is" (once the horse is sold, problems and faults belong to the buyer). These sales often sell the bulk of their consignments to slaughterhouses.

If you intend to buy a horse at an auction, find out about the reputation and intent of the sale, and be sure to take a knowledgeable friend or veterinarian with you. Arrive early enough to look the horses over well and talk with owners. Before attending any auction, know your price range and stick with it; be aware of local pricing, as well as of the individual horse's worth. During the sale, be sure you understand the bidding system.

Checklist when going to an auction:

1. If the horse is offered as a registered animal, ask to see the registration papers; make sure the papers match sex, age, color, and markings.
2. At high-quality sales, a veterinary health certificate will be available for each horse. It will be not more than forty-eight hours old and will include Coggins papers, which will have been prepared previously. The breeding status of the mare (open or bred) should be verified by a veterinary certificate. A pregnant mare should also have a registration application for the unborn foal signed by the mare owner, and a statement signed by the stallion owner that the mare was indeed bred to his stallion, with stud fee and board charges paid. If the mare has a foal at her side, the application for its registration should be complete.
3. The auction should have clear, fair rules of procedure written in the catalog (not usually true of a Saturday-night everything-goes sale), and the rules should be followed, without exceptions or sloppy procedure.

4. Prior to or during the quality sale, each horse declared trained should be exhibited with rider or driver.

How to Buy a Horse for Your Child

Often, parents who know little or nothing about horses are unwilling to buy a superior, safe mount for their child, because they feel "the horse craze" may be a passing fancy. Unfortunately, an inferior, unreliable mount discourages and scares a child, and may be downright dangerous. The superior horse may cost more, but in the long haul not only encourages the child's confidence and love for horses, but also is readily salable if the animal proves indeed to be a passing fancy, or if some other reason develops.

Do be sure of your own motives in buying a horse for your child. Are you simply indulging the child's whim, and really want nothing to do with the horse yourself? Then, consider buying an inanimate toy instead—a horse must be cared for daily whether or not anyone is interested in him at the moment. When you buy a horse for your child, you are making a serious commitment: It is your responsibility to see that the horse is well cared for and that the child assumes whatever responsibilities you have assigned to him. Further, it is your responsibility to ensure the safety of your child, other children, and the horse. If you are willing to accept the responsibilities and encourage your child, his relationship with his horse can teach him a great deal, help him mature and accept responsibility, and bring lasting pleasure and benefits.

Be careful in selecting a child's mount (see other checklists in this chapter). Make sure that the horse is small enough for the child to handle and mount, and that the animal is consistent in performance day after day. If you buy a horse that is temporarily out of condition, it is very possible that he will become more spirited as he picks up physically and mentally. He may then be "too much horse."

Should you choose a large horse or a pony for your child? Unfortunately, many ponies tend to be balky, herd-bound, or barn-sour. A willing, tractable pony might be the ideal size for your child. A small horse would still allow for some growth of the child and could be excellent due to temperament and better training. The safety aspect of any pony or larger horse should be a prime concern.

Children need help, instruction, and supervision. If you as parent are unable to provide this yourself, it is wise to send youngster and horse to a school, or to arrange for a series of lessons not only in riding instruction, but also to help in the basic care and handling of horses. If your child's horse is stabled where other children keep their horses and adults are present, this is usually an ideal situation, as duties, riding opportunities, and shows spark interest and promote knowledge.

Select tack for safety and proper fit for both horse and child. Halter shanks should be sturdy, with large, strong snaps; halters and girths should be strong; and bridles should be made of strong, pliable leather. Stirrups on Western saddles should be covered (so that a small foot cannot go through and become caught), or the youngster should ride bareback. Most English saddles have safety stirrups, but Western saddles are not so equipped. The habit of wearing a helmet or hard hat should be encouraged, as well as developing the child's safety sense for himself, his mount, and others in the vicinity.

Checklist When Buying a Horse

1. With a veterinarian or knowledgeable friend along, give the horse an allover look in his normal surroundings. When you have your overall impression, check his conformation, keeping qualities, teeth, feet, eyes, manners, breed type if he is to be used for breeding, size, blemishes, and unsoundnesses. Is he cut proud? Watch his actions among other horses—is he timid or a bully? Has he been kept in pasture, corral, or stall? Find out whether he will relate easily to the facilities you plan for him. Ask the veterinarian to give him a thorough health check.

2. Watch the owner catch, halter, lead, tie, groom him (including handling his hind legs and feet), saddle, bridle, mount, and ride the horse at all gaits. Observe whether he is a smooth ride, good on transitions of gait, stabilized in gait (cadenced), whether he reins well, and whether he takes his leads. Observe his tack, and if there is anything out of the ordinary or questionable, such as a tie-down or a gag bit, ask the reason for its use.

3. Handle the horse yourself, duplicating the actions listed in paragraph 2. If you plan to use him for specialized work, observe his training as well as his physical and mental ability to learn to perform that task.

4. Why does the owner wish to sell? Some valid answers may be reduction of herd, his child has grown up, "too much" or "too little" horse, age of horse, health of owner.

5. Is the horse guaranteed for the purpose he is sold for? This might be for breeding ability or show record. Anything for which the owner guarantees the horse should be in writing.

6. Beware of owners (with horses for sale) who run down other people and horses.

7. Don't aspire to train or retrain this particular horse if you are not prepared for it.

8. Does the horse load, trailer, and unload well? Try it! Take nothing for granted.

9. Do you like the horse, and vice versa? You should have an immediate rapport with your potential new horse.
10. Will the owner provide you with a health certificate and negative Coggins papers?

SELLING YOUR HORSE

Advertising

When you have decided to sell your horse, for whatever reason, you must advertise and put extra work into him. See "Where Can You Buy a Horse?" earlier in this chapter for suggestions on where to advertise.

When writing copy for an ad, you should state the breeding (perhaps showing part of the pedigree), age, sex, height, color, performance ability, any show wins, price (optional), your name, address, telephone number, and sometimes directions or a map. If stating a price that you will not negotiate, be sure to put "firm" after it; if you are open to negotiation, you may state this fact. Mention any tack or other benefits you are including in the purchase price, such as free stud fee for a mare, or free riding lessons. If you are preparing a large ad, you may wish to have a halter or performance photo included. Photographs catch the eye, and they should be excellent, without busy, distracting backgrounds. Use a clear, flattering picture of professional quality or none at all; amateur snapshots often show the horse at his worst.

Take a good photo to advertise your horse. Compare these two: Poor picture (left) for advertising. Hand too close to nose; lead rope bunched up; horse stepping forward instead of standing quietly; background good, but shadows distracting; too windy— blowing mane and tail. Good picture (right) for advertising. Shows good conformation and proportions; background plain, doesn't interfere with subject; lead shank loose (tight shank pulls, interferes with muzzle); horse relaxed and alert; shows all four legs, with horse standing well; horse clean and well groomed (mane should be recombed); lighting good, showing detail on black horse; handler back far enough that she can be cropped out of photo.

If your horse is an older grade horse that is gentle with children, be sure to advertise the safety aspect. If the horse should be sold to a more experienced horseman, you may state "for experienced rider." Talk enthusiastically about your horse, but be honest.

If you advertise your horse in a national magazine, have several good photos immediately available for mailing, as well as copies of his pedigree and show or breeding history. Using these to accompany a descriptive letter, you will be replying to inquiries in a professional manner.

Effective advertising should gain attention through headlines, pictures, design, color, and name recognition. Create interest by introducing yourself and what you are selling; inspire the potential customer's desire by promoting the benefits your product can offer and by motivating him to ask for more information. Beware the use of humor, as it can sometimes backfire. Keep your ad short and precise, be honest, and proofread your copy several times.

Large breeding farms give out business cards, ranch brochures, and flyers, as well as using distinctive stationery with attractive logos. Many national magazines will supply you with copies of your ad that may also be used in mailing.

Showing Your Horse to a Buyer

Set up an appointment with your potential buyer, and prepare your horse ahead of time. Your animal should be groomed as for show, with halter and tack enhancing his appearance. Assemble his health papers, pedigree, and some good photos showing him performing or winning a show class.

When the buyer arrives, greet him promptly and show your horse at halter and under saddle, or otherwise performing to his ability. Demonstrating special on-the-ground training, such as longeing and driving, will make your horse more salable. Always ride your horse yourself (or have your assistant do so) before letting the prospective buyer ride him. Not only will the buyer observe your methods, but also he will find out whether he feels he can handle your animal well enough.

Be cautious about selling to a novice or mounting one on a horse that is difficult or too spirited. You are liable for injuries. Selling to a novice, in any case, should involve some lessons and advice in care and handling your animal.

When Your Horse Is Sold

Upon the sale of your horse, you must usually provide a health certificate (in most states good for at least ten days), Coggins test papers (in some states good for six months, in others for a year), a bill of sale, or, if sold on contract, a sale agreement with terms of payment specified, and finally, a brand inspection (even if the horse has no brand), necessary in many Western states. Check laws (through your brand inspector or veterinarian) for the state to which the horse is going, because some states do not require a Coggins test but do require a permit.

BILL OF SALE

TO WHOM IT MAY CONCERN:

 Know all men by these presents: That I, _____

_____, of _____(address), have this day sold to _____(name), of _____ _____(address), a _____(sex), _____ (breed) horse, foaled _____(date), _____(color), for the sum of _____ Dollars ($_____), the receipt of which is hereby acknowledged.

 IN WITNESS WHEREOF, I have hereunto set my hand and seal this _____ day of _____, 19__, at _____ (city), _____(state).

_____(Seller)(Seal)

A Bill of Sale Without Warranty

 It is necessary to correctly record the small but important details in the negotiations and the closing of any sale or agreement (sample forms are shown in the Appendix). Word-of-mouth agreements can lead to misunderstandings, which in turn may lead to litigation. Extra copies of written agreements should be kept for tax purposes.

 When selling a horse "on contract," it is usual for the buyer to insure the animal for at least the selling price. The seller usually keeps the registration papers until the horse is paid for in full, and the seller must sign any necessary breeding papers while the contract is in force.

Taking Your Horse to a Sale

Before considering taking your horse to an auction, be sure you are familiar with the kinds of sales and the mechanics of a horse sale. See "Buying a Horse at an Auction," in this chapter, for some guidelines applicable to sellers as well as buyers. It is wise to attend some horse auctions to see how they operate.

Breeders' sales require the most preparation on the part of the seller but also bring better prices. Most breeders' sales allow outside consignments. Let's suppose you have one or two horses to sell and have been allowed to fill out another breeder's sale. When the date has been set, write to the sale manager for pertinent information, requirements, and necessary forms. Some usual policies, terms, and conditions of sale for both sellers and buyers are as follows:

1. The seller must obtain a veterinarian's certificate attesting to the state of the horse's health. A veterinarian's certificate should also be obtained when a mare is guaranteed to be in foal (provided she has been bred at least fifty days). Give a copy of the health certificate to the sales office prior to the sale.
2. A veterinarian will examine the horses prior to sale, and any defects (such as blemishes or injuries) will be noted so that they can be announced during the sale.
3. The seller warrants each horse's pedigree as represented.
4. Registration certificates must be signed and in possession of the sale management before the sale. The registration certificates do not pass to the buyer until the horse is paid for in full (and the check has cleared the bank). Certificates are then mailed to the buyer, who pays for the transfer and obtains a new or authorized certificate from the registry (in some registries, transfer costs are paid by the seller).
5. Most horses are offered for sale under the laws of the state in which the sale is held. Some states have sales tax on livestock, which is not included in the sale price. Nursing foals are usually sold with their dam as part of the lot. Registration applications for the foal are furnished and duly signed by the seller.
6. Credit purchases must be approved before the sale.
7. The sale is advertised *with* or *without* reserve. This means that with reserve the owner may put in the highest bid and keep the horse. In other words, the horse is a "no sale," and the seller often will do this if he feels the price is not commensurate with the quality of the horse. When the sale is advertised as "without reserve," the seller must sell no matter what the price. Be sure to check this condition of the sale if you are a seller!
8. If the buyer defaults, the seller has the right to resell the lot or pursue

any other legal remedy permitted by law, with the buyer agreeing to pay all costs of any suit or costs of resale.

9. Immediately after each horse is sold, the buyer has the sole risk and responsibility of the horse. The buyer must transport at his expense each horse purchased from the sale, or, if stalled in the sale area, must be responsible for the horse's care.

10. The sale management (owner, manager, employees, and auction staff) publicize that they will not be responsible for any loss, personal injury, or damage to a horse purchased, as well as loss of any article or for personal injury while on the grounds.

11. Immediate full mortality insurance coverage is effective upon "fall of the hammer" for the amount of the purchase price in most breed sales. This arrangement is made by the seller with a certain insurance company and remains in effect until an insurance contract is signed by the new owner or until midnight of the night of the sale. When a horse is bought on contract, it is usual for the seller to be included, stipulating the seller as joint loss payee.

12. If a potential buyer is unable to attend the sale, he may usually send in a sealed bid with a certified or cashier's check for the amount of his bid. The auctioneer must keep the bid in confidence.

13. Because time will be set for an inspection of horses before the sale, you must send the sale management a copy of health certificates, signed agreement with consignment fee, and signed registration papers (if the horse is not sold, these papers will be returned to you). It is wise to arrive a day or two before the sale, with your horse prepared as if for the show ring. Young horses should be halter-trained, have good manners, and be used to being handled (including feet and mouth).

14. Stall signs, photos, pedigrees, and show or performance records should be available at the stall area. If possible, you, an employee, or a friend should stay at the stall to answer questions, show your horse, and give out written information to possible buyers.

15. In the case of an all-breed or grade sale, the buyer takes more risk; however, you as a seller can obtain a better price if you adhere to the guidelines of the breeder's sale. Sometimes a few extras—lessons offered, a free breeding, or assistance with training—are good ways to help sell your horse.

Buyers attend many of these sales to purchase horses for slaughter. If you do not wish your horse to go to the killer market, find out ahead of time if you can sell "with reserve," and be prepared to set a minimum price well above current slaughter-market prices.

Part II

KEEPING HORSES

CHAPTER 3

FACILITIES

FARMSTEAD PLANNING

In areas of rapid growth, it is wise to envision future development: If most of the new residents have horses, the area will probably remain free of provisions against the horseman. On the other hand, if most of the residents of an area have no horses or livestock, even if there are no ordinances or regulations against horses at the present time, you may have problems in the future. Although it is not always possible to foresee the shifts of urban development, foresight and planning will improve your chances for harmonious horse ownership.

To find zoning restrictions for your area, look in the zoning ordinances under Agricultural Uses. Ownership and sales of horses are controlled by laws governing personal property.

Stable Sites

A good arrangement of pastures and corrals in relation to the stable area can make horse ownership pleasant and productive. Ideally, the horse should have the opportunity to graze and exercise during good weather and have adequate shelter when necessary. Horses on pasture, with access to shelter and extra feed during bad weather, have the best of both worlds.

When you plan your stable and corral or paddock area, arrange convenient access to the pasture. This should have good footing, be relatively straight, and be strongly and safely fenced, since horses have a tendency to become exuberant on the way to and from a pasture.

The stable should be convenient to your house, but no closer than one hundred feet. There are sometimes restrictions set on this distance by local zoning laws and by your own insurance. Be sure to check both before building.

A good stable site will allow for dry foundations, free drainage, good lighting, adequate water supply, and pure air. Avoid damp and marshy soils; the best site would have a subsoil of gravel or deep sand, giving a firm base with consequent free drainage and dryness.

Plan the arrangement of buildings and loafing sheds to give protection from

Quarter Horse youngsters grow up in good arrangement of buildings, corrals, and pastures on the Redwater Hereford Ranch, Beulah, Wyoming. (Courtesy Dave Ellsbury)

Good planning, combined with safe fencing, can make a convenient, labor-saving arrangement. This tank provides water for three paddocks or pastures on the Ellsbury Brothers Ranch, Aladdin, Wyoming. (Courtesy Dave Ellsbury)

prevailing winds, to benefit from adequate sunlight, and to permit a free supply of air. Buildings should have plenty of room between them; when they are crowded, there is less free air circulation and less opportunity to separate sick horses from healthy ones, thereby increasing the danger of contagion.

Loafing sheds are usually situated in, or adjacent to, pastures. Their main purpose is to protect animals from wind and weather, or to provide shade on hot summer days. Because of their structure (usually two or three sides and a roof), they let in plenty of light and air and allow the animals free access to shelter. Since loafing sheds are normally used by several horses, manure should be cleaned out often to minimize parasite infestation and for insect control. If horses are fed within this area, raised hay mangers should be provided. The loafing shed has the added benefit of protecting horses without the necessity of haltering and leading each one into the stable or barn, thus keeping individual care to a minimum. If the shed is not open on at least two sides, there must be several wide gateways with good spacing to avoid danger spots where a horse might be trapped by others.

Corrals, Fences, and Gates

Barbed wire. Most of the West is fenced with barbed wire, which of course is dangerous for horses. Few pastured Western horses are free from wire-caused scars and blemishes. Besides the danger of scraping against it and ripping long cuts in the skin, horses tend to paw at a fence, and may catch a pastern over the wire. It is hard to believe the amount of damage a barbed-wire fence can cause—wire wounds often look as though they had been inflicted by a dozen jagged knives.

In the West, where pastures can be measured in miles, finances and lack of wood often necessitate using barbed wire rather than other kinds of fencing, especially when horses share pastures with cattle. To minimize injury:

1. Replace the two bottom wires of a five-wire fence (or the bottom wire of a three- or four-wire fence) with smooth wire. The upper barbed wires are effective in stopping cattle, and horses are less likely to injure or catch themselves when pawing over the smooth wires on the bottom.
2. Build several panels of a safer kind of fence in corners, next to gates, and in other places where horses congregate, or where conditions are particularly hazardous.
3. When first turning out young horses (or horses unused to barbed wire), hang white cloth strips on the wires to make the fence more visible (wire can be hard for horses to see, especially when they are running).

Sheep fence and wire mesh. Some mesh or woven wire fences are hazardous, as well. The pattern of wire should be either too small for foal feet, or so large that a foal or mature horse cannot get a hoof caught. Unfortunately, with time and wear, sheep fencing can get out of shape or broken, becoming dangerous for this reason.

Where use of barbed wire is unavoidable, the danger for horses can be minimized by using smooth wire on the bottom one or two strands. Horses pawing at the fence are far less likely to become caught and injured. (Courtesy Dave Ellsbury)

Mesh fencing can be good for young horses if flush to the ground and if the top edge is not sharp. Boards added to this fence improve strength and safety, but a finer mesh would keep a foal's feet from getting caught. Ellsbury Brothers Ranch. (Courtesy Dave Ellsbury)

V-wire, or diamond mesh.

Heavy-gauge "V" or diamond wire, on the other hand, is excellent, since it is very durable and there is no way a hoof (either foal or mature horse) can become entangled. It is better than chain link, as it does not have the same tendency to bend over and has no dangerous projections at top and bottom. Also, "V" or diamond wire cannot be climbed by unwanted persons.

Any type of *mesh fencing* should be four to five feet high. It can be hung on wooden posts a foot above the ground, making a high, safe fence. However, if foals are expected to use the pasture, the fence should be flush to the ground. It is too easy for a foal to lie down close to a fence, roll under it, and rise on the other side.

Metal pipe fencing is strong, safe, and relatively maintenance-free. Of course, it is expensive. In warm, humid climates, however, it may prove less expensive in the long run, since a wood fence will decay quickly and is subject to insect assault, and wire will rust and need replacing.

Buck fences, as found in the West, are both attractive and safe. Since there are no poles in the ground to rot off, they are also durable when constructed from the proper wood (lodgepole pine is excellent).

Post and pole, post and board, and *split cedar rails* all make good, safe fences for horses. Split cedar rail fences are durable, though expensive. Posts used for these fences (and for wire mesh fences, as well) should be four inches in diameter and at least eight feet in length. The ground end should be treated with creosote, Penta, or old engine oil to deter rotting; set them three feet deep. Both wood and metal posts can be set in holes in which cement has been poured—especially good in humid, hot climates. In some wet areas,

Interlocking metal panels can make an extra paddock when needed. (Courtesy Dave Ellsbury)

Buck fence.

Board fences make suitable, sturdy, and attractive fencing for corrals, paddocks, and farmstead areas. Ellsbury Brothers Ranch. (Courtesy Dave Ellsbury)

cement posts can be used; heavy wire loops are set into these posts so that wire can be attached.

When building board fences, use 2 × 6 inch or 2 × 8 inch boards 16 feet long, with squared posts set 8 feet apart; boards should meet at the center of the post (2 × 10 inch boards are also used). Attach boards or poles on the inside or on the side of greatest use. Horses push on fences and can loosen boards that are nailed to the outside; ring-shank nails hold better than common nails, and using long bolts instead of nails can prevent this problem altogether.

Wood fences are safe if they do not splinter easily. Horses do enjoy chewing on wood, however, especially if confined with little to do. Wood posts, poles, and boards can be treated with engine oil or preparations such as Carbolineum to discourage chewing. Be careful not to use preparations such as creosote above the ground, since this can cause allergic reactions in both horses and humans.

White *plastic fencing* is a relatively new development. Although expensive, it is maintenance-free and considered very safe for horses, since it never needs paint and will not splinter, crack, rot, or peel.

Stone walls. These are excellent for horses when built high enough to discourage jumping (poles or wire may be used in conjunction with them to attain sufficient height). Because horses dislike bumping their knees and legs on stone walls, they generally stay well away from them.

Horses are not likely to chew or crib on this white plastic fencing. Rancher Lloyd Geweke of Ord, Nebraska, reports no damage to the fence after three years of use. (Courtesy Nebraska Plastics, Cozad, Nebraska, and Lloyd Geweke)

Electric fences. A single-wire electric fence, used in conjunction with other fencing, can often be effective and useful for problem areas or problem horses. The horse should be introduced to the fence under some control until he understands and respects the shock.

Some *rubber and nylon-rubber fencing,* although safe for horses as far as contact is concerned, has one drawback: if horses chew on and ingest some rubber, impacted bowels and colic can result. Make sure of the quality of any rubber fencing you buy.

Gates. Corral and paddock gates can be made of poles, boards, aluminum, steel frame and wire mesh, or metal pipe. They should be wide enough to allow passage of several horses without crowding and to allow machinery to pass through for cleaning corrals. Well-constructed and well-hung pole or board gates are attractive and sturdy, and have the added bonus of being easily opened from horseback. They should be kept in good repair and not be allowed to sag. Pasture gates must be wide enough for farm machinery— usually ten feet, although some haying equipment requires sixteen-foot gates. Longer gates could best be made of aluminum or of "V" wire framed with steel.

Barbed-wire gates are found throughout the West, and as with barbed-wire fences, are dangerous for horses. However, they are inexpensive and quickly constructed. The hazard can be reduced somewhat by replacing the bottom strand or two with smooth wire. Wires should be kept taut to minimize possibility of injury—a running horse is more likely to bounce away than to become entangled.

In high-wind areas of the northern plains and mountains, fences and gates must be designed to minimize drifting of snow. Wire fences and gates allow snow to blow on through. Drifting snow not only blocks gates but breaks down fences and permits livestock to walk out of their pastures over the hard drifts. Each area has its own problems, and the fence builder must use materials that are available and financially feasible.

STABLES AND ARENAS

Building Safety

Stables may be constructed of a number of different materials, including wood frame, log, and cement block, or they may be of pole construction with wood or metal siding; cost is often a major factor. When possible, it is pleasant to have the outer design and construction in harmony with your house or other buildings. In any case, safety should have priority.

Complete plans for horse barns and stables, stalls, and other facilities may be had at little or no charge from your county extension office, or write to Agricultural Engineer, Extension Service, U.S. Department of Agriculture, Washington D.C. 20250.

Learn to "think safety" and keep aware of possible dangers: spaces where a horse could catch his head or foot, protrusions where he could injure himself, and so on. Plan your stable with recessed or flush fittings, and check for projections such as nails or protruding latches and hinges. Electric light fixtures should be on the outside of the stall, where the horse cannot reach them, and of the special type designed to prevent electrocution. In areas where severe electrical storms are prevalent, use wood instead of metal for buildings, stalls, and fences. In tornado areas, stables can be constructed of solid concrete.

Fire safety. When planning your barn and surrounding area, be sure to provide easy access and exits. Stall latches and other fastenings should work easily. Keep passageways free from obstructions. "No smoking" signs should be prominently placed and stringently enforced. Provide adequate fire extinguishers and inspect them regularly. Make sure that everyone working regularly in the stables knows how to use the fire extinguishers, knows where hoses and buckets are kept, and knows what to do in case of fire. Fire drills should be held periodically.

What to do in case of fire.
1. Call the fire department (the number should be pasted on the phone).
2. Get the horses out. Be quiet and calm, to keep the horses from becoming frightened. Cover the horses' eyes if necessary (horses can be trained

to lead blindfolded—a good precaution for stabled horses). If they can't be led, try to drive them well away from the stable—because horses feel secure in their own "homes," they may run back to their stalls if not prevented.
3. Use fire extinguishers and hoses. Saturate other nearby buildings. Saturate as much of the burning building as possible. If there is a lot of smoke, cover your face with a wet cloth.
4. Get out if the fire is beyond your control.

Floors

Floors should give good traction, and be level, durable, and waterproof (not allow dampness to seep up from underneath). They should be laid on a solid foundation, level overall, but with a gentle, one- or two-degree slope to ensure good drainage. It is difficult to find flooring that is satisfactory in all respects. In some areas, zoning laws limit the types of flooring that may be used: be sure to check if you are building a new stable.

Concrete. Although excellent for general flooring of a stable, concrete has drawbacks when used in a stall. It can be slippery, unless the surface has been given a rough facing. It is hard on feet and legs, and can be cold in winter—ample bedding must be provided to prevent leg problems.

Wooden planking, although easier on feet and legs, is absorbent and becomes slippery when wet. Stalls with wooden floors must be dried out and limed often to keep them sweet. *Earthen* floors are easy on feet and legs but must be kept level, since holes develop either by horses moving in a certain pattern or from frequent cleaning. They may be difficult to keep dry and are sometimes prohibited by zoning regulations. *Asphalt* is affected by heat and becomes slippery when wet. *Clay* and special *cork-type paving bricks* make good flooring but are expensive and not often used; clay needs relaying at regular intervals.

Roofs and Walls

Buildings should be high enough for free access and comfortable movement within, but not so high that body heat is wasted near the roof. Roofs should be durable, fireproof, and as quiet as possible, and should help maintain an equable year-round temperature in the building. In most areas of the country, sloping roofs are best, as they offer ample ventilation, prevent snow buildup, and allow rapid runoff (gutters should be installed to take moisture runoff to the proper site). Less slope is required in areas of high wind. In heavy snow areas, especially without high winds, a steeper slope is needed to keep roofs clear.

Translucent fiberglass panels in the side of this arena allow plenty of light inside (an excellent alternative in areas where roof panels may be broken out by hail). Ellsbury Brothers Ranch. (Courtesy Dave Ellsbury)

Galvanized iron is popular today, not only for the roof, but also for the entire building. It is easy to transport, quick to assemble, and fireproof; it is noisy, however, and not always esthetically pleasing. Metal buildings must have adequate ventilation, since the walls and ceiling will sweat when several horses are enclosed within them. Also, they can become ovens in summer, freezers in winter. With metal roof and plexiglass skylights, heat from the sun will melt snow from the roof quickly, or cause it to cascade off (scaring livestock inside). Although insulation in metal buildings reduces extremes of heat and cold, condensation may be a problem even if there is adequate ventilation.

Wood frame buildings can be comfortable and attractive, though extra precautions should be taken for fire protection, and wood roofs should be well fireproofed. Slate or composition shingles make good roofs. Plastic or fiberglass roofing may be worth considering. In some areas, small stables constructed from logs (or from precut log kits) can be very attractive and economical; they are well insulated and comfortable but again, require adequate fire protection.

It is not necessary to heat stables. Horses do very well even in the coldest weather if they are dry, have plenty of fresh air, and are free from drafts. A tightly constructed and well-ventilated stable or barn is adequate for most horse-keeping situations.

Windows

Stables should have plenty of natural light. This may be provided by skylights or by windows. Windows that are accessible to horses should be covered with mesh wire or iron bars (on both sides, if accessible to horses on both sides). They should fit flush with strong wooden frames, and should be hinged to open inward from the lower edge or from the center, thus creating an upward slant that deflects fresh air toward the ceiling, minimizing drafts, or they can be hinged from the top to open outward, creating much the same effect. Each stall should have its own window or two—kept open on the leeward side, closed on the windward side. In hot weather, all windows should be open to allow free circulation of air.

Aisles

Aisles should be ten to twelve feet wide, to allow two horses to pass without conflict, and so that there is room for a small tractor to help with stall cleaning if construction allows. Electrical outlets can be conveniently situated for clipping horses. Install crossties in areas where traffic is not a problem. Rubber mats can be used on slippery floors.

Straight and Box Stalls

Most horses should be kept in box stalls, where they can move around freely and have room to lie down. Straight stalls have their place, however, keeping horses temporarily separated in riding schools, for instance, or separated for feeding. Straight stalls should be five feet six inches wide and approximately eleven feet long, with a manger divided into separate compartments for grain and hay.

Box stalls, especially when the horse lives in one day in and day out, should be at least twelve by fourteen feet; fourteen feet square or sixteen feet square would be better. Anything much larger than this is difficult to clean and keep bedded.

Stalls should be as draft-free as possible, with good ventilation. They should be of strong construction, designed so that a horse cannot kick over a partition, or rear up to put his forelegs over the top. He should be able to look out, however; metal bars or grills on the upper part of the partition can provide the necessary strength and separation. If the horse has a good view of the stable and other horses, he is less likely to become bored, and thus less likely to develop stable vices.

All gates and doors should open outward, allowing the door to be opened even if the horse is cast in his stall against the door. Sliding doors are excellent (these should be hung so as to slide along the outside of the stall—see photo). Dutch doors are great favorites for horse barns, allowing ventilation and visibility. The lower half must be high enough to discourage jumping.

Doors and gates should be wide enough to permit free passage (at least four feet). If a horse knocks his side or hip when going through a narrow opening,

A straight stall. Notice large hay manger in front, pegs for hanging halters and lead ropes. Redwater Hereford Ranch, Beulah, Wyoming. (Courtesy Dave Ellsbury)

Box stalls with well-hung sliding doors. Note overhead hay storage, and fiberglass roof panels for ample lighting. Redwater Hereford Ranch, Beulah, Wyoming. (Courtesy Dave Ellsbury)

he may balk the next time, or rush through. Such an experience might encourage balkiness when entering any gate, especially that of a horse trailer.

Be sure that all gate latches are "horse-proof." Provision for a blanket rack and a place to hang halter and lead are useful on the outside of each door.

Stable Fittings

Mangers should be placed three and a half to four feet from the floor. Grain mangers should be large, broad, and shallow, with smooth surfaces; narrow, deep mangers are difficult to clean, and allow greedy horses to gouge out overlarge mouthfuls of feed.

Overhead or high-hung hayracks offer an unnatural eating position and allow chaff and dust to fall into a horse's eyes and nose. Usually the best and most economical arrangement is a hay manger with a grain compartment, as less hay is wasted or soiled. Hay nets are efficient if positioned properly: high enough so that a foot cannot be caught in them when they are empty, and low enough to keep chaff from eyes and nose.

Water

Keep water pails readily accessible for filling and cleaning. Fix them in place (a snap attached to the pail can clip into a ring set in a corner) so that they can't be accidentally or deliberately upset. Automatic waterers save labor, but they should be placed away from the manger to keep them from becoming stuffed up with feed.

The source of water should be convenient, preferably in a central area. Hydrants, hoses, and individual waterers should be part of the plan of any stable.

Tack Room

The tack room should be convenient and easily accessible, making it unnecessary to carry tack very far. You should be able to lock it: tack is expensive and can be easily resold. Mark each piece, and lock it up when it is not in use. Plan plenty of windows for light and ventilation—necessary for preserving leather—but make sure they can't be reached through or entered.

Provide a saddle rack for each of your saddles, with an extra rack or two if there is room. Western saddles will take up more room than English. Standing racks should be three to four feet high, and if space is at a premium, hang wall racks for lighter saddles above the standing racks.

A handy bridle rack should be high enough to allow the reins to hang

A convenient and attractive tack room. Redwater Hereford Ranch, Beulah, Wyoming. (Courtesy Dave Ellsbury)

straight without touching the floor, but low enough to reach easily—long, Western reins may have to be looped. Always hang your bridle over a rounded fixture (a two-inch section of wood post is good, or a tunafish can), rather than a nail or narrow hook that will bend and weaken the leather. Since bridles and halters are very individual, the horse's name can be printed on each bracket, or fancier nameplates can be made.

Extra fixtures will be needed to hold driving harness, longeing equipment, bits, and extra halters and bridles. Racks, shelves, and cabinets should be provided for orderly storage of grooming equipment, farrier tools, blankets, sheets, electric clippers, veterinary supplies, and other equipment. You may want to keep books, notebooks, and records available in a convenient place also. A table, chairs, and space for trunks and show boxes are a good idea. (A show box is a large wooden box, often decorated with farm logo or brand, that most exhibitors use to carry equipment—blankets, small tack, grooming tools, etc.,—and keep it organized at shows.) A small refrigerator will allow you to keep all your vet supplies handy. A large-space wall calendar on which to jot down estrous cycles, vaccination dates, breeding dates, and so on will be a great help in record keeping.

The most utilitarian tack room is nearly square, rather than long and narrow, allowing several people to move in and out carrying saddles and equipment without developing a bottleneck. The space in the center can be used for cleaning tack.

Grain Room

You'll thank yourself many times over if you plan your grain room so that it is conveniently situated, both from the standpoint of delivering feed and from the standpoint of convenience in feeding your horses. You should be able to back a truck up to a wide door to minimize lifting if you buy your grain in sacks, or to unload it conveniently into bulk bins.

The grain room should be dry and well ventilated, with provision made for rodent control. Metal or wire-mesh lining is sometimes used, or grain can be stored in mouse-proof bins and barrels. Grain sacks are hard to measure from and are prone to attacks by rodents; if possible, empty the sacks into metal barrels (sometimes, used fifty-five-gallon drums can be bought cheaply— make sure you know the drum previously contained nothing harmful) or large metal or plastic garbage cans with lids. A good barn cat serves double duty as a mouser and a cheerful friend to horses and humans.

One of the most dangerous hazards in feed-room predation is your own horse—if he is wandering loose, he will soon work out the secrets of a loose catch on the door. If not found quickly, he could eat enough to founder or become colicky. Keep your grain room well secured.

You may prefer to keep some equipment and supplies in the grain room rather than the tack room; some smaller stables combine the two rooms to good effect.

Hay Storage

Situate hay and straw as close as possible to the stalls for convenience in feeding and bedding. In a large stable, overhead hay storage is desirable, with an individual "drop through" above each stall. In the very dry West, most hay and straw can be stacked outside and may or may not be covered. Damper climates require some kind of protection if the hay is not stored in a barn.

Keep the ever-present hazard of fire in mind, and try to make your arrangement as safe as possible. Some insurance regulations may require storing hay a certain distance from house or other buildings. In any case, water and fire-fighting tools should be handy and accessible.

Converting Existing Buildings to Horse Stables

Converting an existing building may or may not be worthwhile. Compare the cost of converting an older building with that of constructing a new facility. Make sure foundations are solid and construction sturdy; there's no point in building a palace over a sinkhole. Consider water sources, hay and grain storage, access, and fire hazard. Rebuild doorways to be at least four feet wide and eight feet high; examine their location and distance from your house in regard to fire codes, insurance, and zoning laws. In addition to the usual considerations of ventilation, light, and so on, make sure that the previous use of the building has not contaminated walls or floor with paints, oils, or chemicals that may be either hazardous to your horse's health or conducive to increased fire danger. Electrical outlets and fixtures should be examined carefully and replaced or adequately protected. If a building is to do double duty as stable and shop or garage, the problems of fumes and noise may be added to the other considerations; in any case, such double duty is rarely a good idea and may be dangerous.

Arenas, Rings, Jumping Lanes

Even if most of your riding is on roads and trails or over open country, it's helpful to have a training ring or arena. For serious schooling in dressage, a ring is a necessity. Roping arenas are just as necessary for serious training in roping and cutting.

An ideal size for an indoor or outdoor arena is 80 or 100 feet by 250 feet. This will allow plenty of room for a dressage ring, a fair-sized jumping

A sample jump course constructed for a show class: Open Equitation Under Fourteen. This course is designed to help the judge evaluate the basic qualities and abilities of the rider. The course must have:

- *a combination jump,*   • *jumps not to exceed three feet,*
- *change of direction,*   • *wings thirty inches wide.*

(An oxer is a jump with a guard rail set about three feet in front of it on one side.) A. Combination. B. Rail oxer. C. Gate and rail oxer.

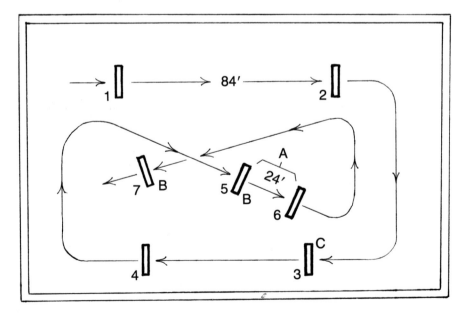

ARENAS FOR DRESSAGE COMPETITIONS

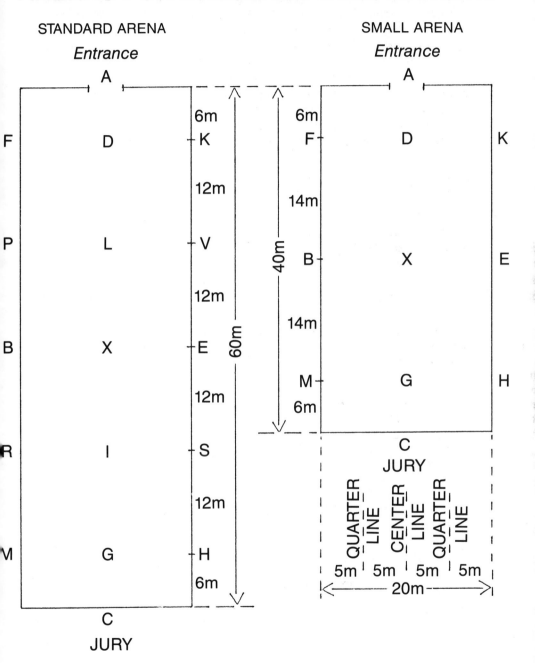

The public must be at least 20m (66 feet) from all sides.

course, and gymkhana events. When planning arenas larger than this, the problem of hearing an instructor or hearing show class directions becomes difficult without a public address system. Smaller rings should be at least 60 by 120 feet if at all possible.

An outdoor riding arena need not be sturdily fenced, but there should be one or two rails to mark its boundary, and it is helpful when working young or fractious horses to be able to close the entranceway with a gate or rails. The arena should be level and free from stones. Because hard-packed ground is hard on feet and legs, the surface should be plowed or otherwise broken occasionally to loosen the soil. It may be necessary to lay a surface of sand or sawdust over the arena to provide good, springy footing (except in high-wind areas).

Dressage rings are of two sizes: the smaller is 66 feet by 132 feet (20 meters by 40 meters), and the larger, official size is 66 by 198 feet (20 by 60 meters). Levels up to Level Two may compete in the smaller ring. The dressage ring should be fenced, but no higher than 16 inches. Markers are placed at exact intervals as shown in the diagram.

Most indoor arenas are designed so that the stable is either attached or at least incorporated into the plans. Where wind, snow, or cold is a factor, it is helpful to have everything under one roof or connected by a covered passageway. An outdoor arena should be available, as well as the indoor facility— sunshine and good air are helpful to both horses and riders. Cavalletti and jumps, jumping lanes, and so on can be built into one section of a large arena, or they may be movable. There should be adequate storage space for jumps and cavalletti, sawdust, and bedding.

COMMERCIAL BOARDING STABLES

Commercial stables can run the gamut of types, from the large boarding stable incorporating a riding academy to someone with a few empty stalls who may consider taking boarders. In general, there are two major kinds of boarding stables: 1) where the horse owner provides feed, exercise, water, and full care of his horse (in other words, the stable only provides the space); and 2) where the management provides the feed and does all the work, with perhaps the exception of exercising the horse.

There are advantages and disadvantages to both kinds. If you are providing full care of your own horse, you know he is well cared for; however, since this type of establishment is less expensive, it will cater to the undesirable horse owner as well as to the desirable one. Everyone feeds at different times (making horses resentful and nervous if they are not fed also). Some horses will have adequate water, others will not; some owners clean the stalls daily, others do not, making the stable smell and become a haven for disease and flies. People borrow tools or tack, which inevitably get "lost." Feed sacks dumped anywhere and hay piled in the aisles increase fire hazard and the danger of colic or founder if a horse should get loose. The cruelest treatment of all is when horses are left stalled for long periods of time—they develop vices such as weaving and cribbing that they pass on to their stablemates. This type of public stable tends to have more unauthorized people wandering through the buildings, feeding tidbits, opening stalls, and looking at horses. Many times, young children and nonhorsemen can be hurt or cause harm from their ignorance.

The more expensive, full-board public stable is only as good as its management. Conscientious professional ownership will assure your horse of good clean feed (at regular times), clean stalls, adequate water, and a professional eye kept on your horse each day. Some large stables also offer to groom, graze, and exercise the horses. Naturally, these added services add to the cost per month, but for many busy people, the extra care is well worth it. Their facilities often include roomy box stalls, corrals, pastures, grooming areas, tack rooms with individual lockers for patrons, an indoor and outdoor riding ring with jump courses, and riding trails. Use of the facilities may be included in the monthly board fee or there may be an added charge.

In any public stable, you will find horses coming and going constantly, providing conditions in which distemper, pneumonia, and external skin problems can run rampant. Stables that have a block of stalls away from the others for a ten- to twenty-day quarantine period will lessen the likelihood of spread of contagious disease.

Legally, the boarding stable is not an ensurer of the safety of a horse left in its care, but is bound to take normal care of the animal. However, if negligence is proved, the stable is liable. The boarding stable should notify the owner if the horse becomes ill or injured; if not able to locate the owner, the management should contact a veterinarian to treat the horse, and charge the fees to the owner. Owners are generally required to pay the fees of the farrier, veterinarian (for shots, parasite control, injury, and sickness), extra training, and perhaps use of certain facilities not included in the board (these should be indicated). The boarding stable is liable for the actions of its employees, including negligence, within the scope of their employment.

In order to make the boarding-stable idea work for you, you must realize that the individual horse owner and the owner of the stable are equal partners in the care and well-being of the horse. Duties of both should be written out and understood by both parties. The following checklist may help you and the boarding stable to a mutually happy agreement:

Boarding-Stable Responsibility Checklist

1. Keep surroundings clean and neat, with a special area designated for parking.
2. Post the rules of the stable.

3. Dispose of manure in designated areas.
4. Keep the stable itself neat and clean, and clean feed tubs, water tubs, and mangers regularly.
5. Clean stalls daily.
6. Make sure stalls, runs, and paddocks are safe (no projecting nails, barbed wire on the ground, cans, etc.).
7. Provide feed that is bright, clean, and adequate (extra vitamin and mineral supplements are usually provided by the owner). Keep feed and grain storage rooms and tack rooms locked.
8. Make adequate safety provisions for the stable. Fire extinguishers should be evident, with instructions posted for their use. Take precautions against unlawful entry, with adequate locks, sturdy doors, and a night watchman if necessary.
9. As management, be calm, professional, and pleasant; hire (and train) knowledgeable and courteous employees.
10. Post feeding, farrier, and parasite-control schedules. Most good boarding stables require their boarders to have—and pay for—the latter services. One horse with parasites infects another.

Ownership Responsibility Checklist

1. Pay bills promptly for board, farrier, parasite control, veterinarian, and other agreed-on expenses.
2. Give your horse enough exercise and attention, including grooming.
3. Don't leave tack around, and don't borrow tools, tack, or feed.
4. Don't arrive to exercise your horse at feeding time; your horse's well-being comes before your pleasure.
5. Park in authorized areas.
6. Don't run through the barn, being noisy or obnoxious, or allow your children (or children in your care) to do so.
7. Don't expect stable personnel to cool out your horse or give him special attention due to your thoughtlessness.
8. Be as knowledgeable about horses as possible, so that you can notice when something is wrong with your horse or wrong at the stable.

CHAPTER 4

STABLE MANAGEMENT AND TACK

Stable Routines

Horse lovers enjoy taking care of their horses as much as they enjoy riding them, and there is a great deal of satisfaction in keeping your horse healthy and comfortable. Since horses are creatures of habit and thrive on a fairly strict routine, their health and well-being depend on their people's adhering to a reasonable schedule.

Although horses generally do better with small, frequent feedings, a variety of feeding schedules are acceptable. Many of us feed and water our horses before breakfast, then clean stables and begin work or training after breakfast. Someone else may prefer to feed, clean, and exercise in one morning time block.

Here are two suggested feeding schedules (to figure total daily rations, see Chapter 5, on feeding):

Schedule 1

A.M. 1/2 daily grain ration (with supplements), 1/3 hay
P.M. 1/2 grain, 2/3 hay

Schedule 2

A.M. 1/3 grain (with supplements), 1/3 hay
NOON 1/3 grain
P.M. 1/3 grain, 2/3 hay

Clean water should be available for your horse at all times, except after strenuous exercise, when it should be withheld or given in small quantities until body temperature returns to normal. Horses drink approximately twelve gallons a day, so at least two large bucketfuls each day (more during hot weather) are necessary.

Routines change as the seasons change or conditions warrant, and horses in training need special consideration. Although one graining (or none) may be sufficient for mature idle horses on good pasture, up to four grainings may be needed for horses at hard work or for poor keepers.

Here is a suggested daily routine for the stalled horse:

EARLY A.M.   Feed, water, check for injury, check droppings
                 to see if normal

AFTER FEEDING	Clean stall, groom, including picking out feet, exercise
NOON	Feed (if in routine), refill water bucket
EARLY EVENING	Feed, refill water bucket, clean stall
EVENING	Check to see that horse is comfortable, gates are secure, blankets are in place

KEEPING A CLEAN, COMFORTABLE STALL

Stable tools include a hayfork, manure fork, rakes (fine-tooth and wide-tooth), shovels (spade-type and large-scoop), a plastic or wicker basket for manure, wheelbarrow, and stable broom. These should be stored conveniently for you and safely out of your horse's reach. Other tools and accessories include hay hooks for handling bales, rubber grain pans, fencing tools, jack-knife, and wire cutters.

Bedding

Bedding is important for the comfort of your horse, helping to prevent injury, to keep him clean, and to prevent foot and leg problems. It should be absorbent and provide drainage, as well as being dry, soft, financially feasible, easily disposable, and nontoxic and not injurious if eaten. It should also have a good appearance (not moldy straw) and be free from dust.

Good dry oat straw is the best choice of straws. Others are wheat and barley, although barley straw can cause itching from the awns and can cause colic if eaten. Straw is a good heat conductor, but keeps feet cooler than sawdust.

Sawdust should be dry; it is deodorizing and has a pleasing smell, but can clog drains. Shavings are less dusty. Horses do not ordinarily eat sawdust or shavings, but stalls should be cleaned often: Soggy, overheated sawdust can ball up in a horse's feet and result in thrush. Sawdust derived from any nut-bearing tree, especially the walnut, is very toxic (a pound is lethal). Black walnut—especially newly milled shavings—invites an attack of acute laminitis by skin contact alone. Check sawdust for walnut-wood content before using.

Bedding should be laid evenly or higher at the sides than in the center of the stall. Lay bedding deep enough to accomplish its purpose.

Cleaning the Stall (Mucking Out)

When the stall is bedded with straw, take the hayfork and shake the straw to one side or to the back. Use the manure fork to pick up the dirty straw and droppings and place them in the center, or pile them directly into the wheel-barrow or manure basket. With the rake, clean up the scattered pile, and use the scoop shovel to finish cleaning completely. If the stall is wet, it should be dried out before new bedding is laid. If considered dry enough, the straw at the sides of the stall can be forked back over the clean area and more clean straw added. Picking up droppings and damp straw several times during the day will help save straw (keep good straw from being wallowed and wasted), keep your horse more comfortable, and keep the stable from smelling of urine.

When using sawdust or shavings, fork the droppings and very wet sawdust or shavings into a wheelbarrow or basket. Rake the dry material over the clean floor and add more as necessary.

Wooden and clay floors should be sprinkled with lime two to three times a week to keep the stall sweet.

The manure should be disposed of in a convenient place, but an appropriate distance from the stable. Straw manure heaps should be close-packed and squared off, as this assists decomposition, and the heat generated inhibits fly breeding. Shavings and sawdust should not be spread on pastures, as they do not break down like straw.

Deep-Litter System

A warm, labor-saving method of preparing a stall, especially good for broodmares and foals, is the deep litter system. This consists of a six- to eight-inch base of sawdust or straw that is well packed; another deep bed of straw is laid on top. No complete mucking out is done—remove only the droppings from the top layer and add clean straw each day. Complete cleaning should be done at least twice a year (aided by use of a tractor, if convenient). Care must be taken if sawdust is used as a base layer, as this can heat up and become maggoty. Horses' feet need frequent cleaning and checking for thrush with this bedding method; however, in damp, cold climates, this system can be a good one.

GROOMING

Grooming is essential to the health and appearance of all horses, and especially to stalled horses that don't have the opportunity to exercise themselves and roll. Grooming removes dirt and impurities from the coat, stimulates circulation, helps to prevent disease, improves muscle tone, and contributes to the general well-being of the horse. Also, it is an intrinsic part of the training of young horses.

Show grooming is a more thorough operation than the standard daily grooming procedure. It includes washing, clipping, use of coat conditioner, and the final polish of coat, hoofs, mane, and tail. However, thorough daily grooming, properly balanced with a high-quality diet, regular exercise, scheduled parasite control, and veterinary care, is necessary for any halter and performance horse and should be practiced year-round.

The electric groomer, a labor-saving device for large stables, is thorough and quiet (though expensive), but does not stimulate circulation, as hand rubbing will do. Various grooming tools and instructions for using them are explained in *Basic Horsemanship: English and Western,* pages 25 to 32. For information on handling the feet, especially of young and green horses, see *Basic Training for Horses: English and Western,* pages 46 to 48.

Restricting Your Horse for Grooming and Washing

Safety and convenience are the factors to consider when restricting your horse. In stall or alleyway, the crosstie is efficient and comfortable for the horse, and allows room for the handler to move around him safely. It is especially valuable when you are washing or bandaging your horse.

Never tie your horse to a horizontal pole unless it is stout and solid, such as a large, strong, green tree limb. Poles and boards may break, or may be pulled away from their uprights, leaving the horse loose and dragging a long pole with nails protruding at the ends—obviously a danger to himself and any other animal or person in the vicinity.

Tying a horse to a sturdy fence post or to a tree is the usual alternative, although it does have the disadvantage that the horse can move sideways, crowd into the wall or fence, or rotate almost a full circle. Also, after strenuous workouts, horses like to rub their heads against the post, often ducking under the rope and then panicking and pulling back, or injuring their eyes. Rings for tying should be attached to the posts about level with the withers.

When grooming and tacking up several horses at a time (as for a family ride or in a riding school), leave plenty of room between them to limit the opportunity of kicking and maximize safety for the handler.

When designing a wash rack, think of it in terms of a straight stall, without solid walls. There should be a stout post in front of the horse to tie him to, a bar across his chest, and parallel poles from the chest bar the length of his body. Most wash racks are made for two horses, but for a small operator, one is sufficient. Usually there is nothing behind the horse; however, a detachable butt rope or bar can be installed. This design enables the handler to move around the horse easily and tends to keep the horse quiet when being hosed.

Bathing Your Horse

A thorough washing, leaving a shiny, spotless coat and bright white markings, makes any horse more attractive. Even though washing strips some of the natural oils from the coat, these are replenished quickly in a healthy horse, especially with vigorous grooming, and frequent baths for show horses and other hard-working horses are generally beneficial. Frequent warm, clear-water baths after hard work will get salt and sweat out of the coat; if no soap is used, body oils are not affected. "Brace" or muscle toner can be added to the water. Give your horse a good grooming before washing, as bathing will make tangles in mane and tail worse, rather than removing them.

Restrain your horse at a wash rack, if available; if not, use a crosstie or ask an assistant to hold him securely. A nylon web halter is usually best: leather stains and stretches, and damp rope halters will shrink. Be organized. Gather towels, scrapers, plastic brush, sweat scraper, and cooler, sheet, or light blanket. Grooming tools you intend to take to the show can be washed at the same time.

Your shampoo can be the animal or human variety (baby shampoo is excellent for the head, as it will not irritate the eyes). Use only plastic containers around horses.

Bathe your horse only on a warm, sunny day or in a warm, draft-free stable. You will need a supply of lukewarm water, either from a hose or in six or more full twelve-quart buckets. Proceed calmly and slowly, especially with an inexperienced horse, starting at the top on the near side and working down and back.

Moisten a sponge and wet the whole face with clear, warm water, bringing the forelock back between the ears. It can then be soaped with the mane and neck without getting soap in the horse's eyes. Also, avoid getting water in the ears.

The mane should be washed on the side it falls on. If it is split between two sides, comb it all to one side, preferably the right. After lathering the forelock and mane from the roots to the end of the hair, rinse thoroughly and comb it out carefully with a wide-tooth comb. Do not brush a wet mane, as this causes the ends to split (wet hair loses its elasticity).

Work up a lather with your hands or a sponge, so that you are massaging as well as cleaning. Scrape off excess lather, and rinse several times with a low-pressure hose, scraping between rinses. Proceed toward the tail, doing one section at a time (shoulder, chest, barrel, hindquarters). This will keep the soap from drying on the body. Soap left in the coat irritates the skin and encourages the horse to rub.

Wash legs completely, rinse, and squeeze your hands down them to scrape off excess water. Wash hoofs with soap and water, cleaning with a plastic brush or pad. After washing the tail (lather it in a bucket of warm water and rinse very well), proceed to the off side and repeat. Finish by giving the horse several allover rinses, and scrape.

After washing, put on a cooler and walk your horse on grass. He should be stabled in a freshly bedded, draft-free stall.

You may wish to braid the mane to give it body or to keep an unruly mane on one side. Large sections of mane will make gentle waves; tiny sections braided tight will make a frizzy mane. The tail may be braided into one big plait, which you may encase in a pillowcase or cloth wrap to keep clean. Braiding the tail loosely stimulates growth and keeps the tail hairs from breaking off, allowing it to grow longer and thicker.

Avoid stains by thinking ahead. Use colorfast horse clothing (saddle blankets and sheets). Encase cinch rings in fleece chafe guards, and cinches with fleece tubes. Spot-washing can be done often: use mild hand soap to remove grease and some grass stains; laundry soaking solutions (two to three tablespoons per gallon of water) work on grass and manure stains, and lemon or other citrus fruit juice (full strength) will bleach out latigo stains. Do not use laundry bleaches. Nontoxic laundry bluing in the rinse water makes white and gray areas more silvery and less yellow.

Clipping Your Horse

A horse's hair is there to protect him—a hairy coat shields him from the weather, natural oils prevent rain from penetrating to his skin, and his mane and tail defend him from insects. The hair on his fetlocks protects his pasterns, and long coronet hair protects his heels from getting sore and cracked. Whiskers and eyebrows are feelers, especially in the dark, and hair in the ears keeps out dirt and insects, as well as protecting the inner ear from cold.

When horses are used year-round, however, a heavy coat can be a drawback. Clipping helps the working horse avoid heavy sweating, permits longer, faster workouts, saves time in grooming, and keeps him clean and dry, thus helping to avoid chills. An allover body clip is used by sellers or those who show their horses at halter in winter.

The hunter clip protects legs against cold, mud, scratches, and injury. The clip can be made with or without the saddle patch. When the blanket clip is used, the horse need not be blanketed when turned out in reasonable weather. Although the trace clip (originally used for harness horses) is not attractive, it is useful for horses hunted or worked strenuously in winter.

Do not clip whiskers and the insides of ears unless necessary for show. Ears can look neat if you fold the ear together and clip the edges; the inside hair will still do its job. The body clips should be left until the winter coat has come in (early October); a second clipping can be done in December or early January, depending on the rate of hair growth. Do not clip a horse after he has started to shed, as this is detrimental to his new coat growth.

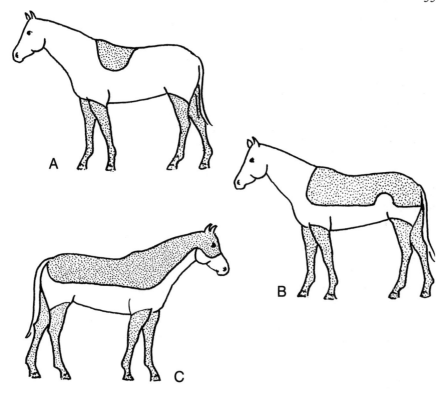

KINDS OF BODY CLIPS
A. Hunter clip. B. Blanket clip. C. Trace (high) clip. White areas indicate parts to clip.

If you wish your horse to look neat, yet keep his winter coat, clip a bridle path, and keep the hair trimmed under the chin and cheek up into the throat-latch.

For a smoother clip, bathe your horse before beginning (dirt and oil on his hair dull clipper blades quickly). Bathing also stands the hair up, making it easier to clip evenly; however, dry the hair thoroughly. When preparing for a show, we generally clip about five days ahead of time, touching up the day before the show. This lets the hair appear more natural and shiny, and any small mistakes have a chance to grow out. Be sure to start on a day when you have plenty of time.

How to clip. If your horse has never been clipped, thoroughly accustom him to the sound and vibration of the clippers before actually beginning to cut. Let them run for short periods while you are in the stall. Then lay the clippers (while running) gently on the flat of the shoulder and stroke him with them (not clipping); in the same fashion, move to the neck and legs. Several sessions of this are usually adequate.

Keep clippers in good repair so that they do not pull hair instead of cutting

—blades should be clean, sharp, and well oiled (keep a spare set of sharpened blades at hand). Beware of machines that become hot, especially on the sensitive muzzle and the ears. Small clippers (usually more quiet) can be used around the head, while larger clippers can be used on body and legs. Work in an area with good lighting, and arrange all cords so that your horse (or you) won't become entangled. Have an assistant help you, especially if you anticipate problems, and be prepared to use a twitch or other restraint if necessary.

Start clipping on less sensitive areas, such as the shoulder, and clip with long sweeps against the growth pattern of the hair. Clip the hollows and indentations surrounding the muscles by pulling the skin tight with your free hand. If you hold your free hand on the horse's legs to steady him, he'll be less likely to pick his feet up.

The bridle path varies with the breed and conformation. It is usually four to six inches long, starting at the poll. A longer bridle path makes the neck appear slimmer and the throatlatch finer. The forelock is never shortened; if narrow, it makes the forehead appear narrower; if wide, wider.

"Hogging" (cutting mane off completely) or "roaching" (cutting mane very short so that it stands erect) is done by clipping the top of the mane from withers to poll, and then trimming up the sides to give it a rounded look (not flat on top). With hogging and roaching, it is usual to leave a lock on the withers, which tends to make the withers look less broad and flat. The appearance of a horse with slight ewe-neck can be improved by leaving the roached mane a little longer in front of the withers.

To do the ears, start from the tip. Hold the ear with your free hand, being ready to lift the clippers away if the horse should toss his head. Hold clippers flat and parallel to the horse's skin to keep from nicking him.

After clipping, wash the horse with clear, warm water; this will remove any scurf and hair, as well as fluffing up spots you missed. Cover him with a clean blanket; the rubbing of the material will help activate the oils in his skin, creating a nice shine. In severe weather, he may need two blankets to equal the protection of his natural coat. Scissors can be used to finish the legs (fetlock scissors are curved to work well here), any long hairs on the head, and stray hairs at the top of the tail.

Mane and Tail

The halter show horse should have special care taken with the mane and tail. Since continued brushing can thin the mane, we suggest only picking the hairs apart with your fingers, especially for Arabians, Morgans, and five-gaited American Saddle Horses. Before a show, put a little oil on your fingers as you pick the hairs to give the mane added sheen.

When brushing the tail, stand to one side of the horse instead of directly behind him. Pull part of the tail toward you and brush straight down as the tail fans out, to make brushing easy.

Depending on the breed, final polishing of the show animal may include pulling the mane, thinning or shortening the tail, or braiding mane and tail. To cut the mane and tail would produce a choppy, bushy look—hand pulling, although tedious, gives the best finish. Do a little at a time, well before the show. Section off the mane into braids, and untie one or two braids (starting behind the bridle path) each day. Hold several hairs between thumb and forefinger of your right hand, stretching them straight down. With the same fingers of your left hand, take hold above your right and push some hairs up. You will still have a few hairs in your right hand; wrap these around a metal-tooth comb and give a short, sharp pull. By removing just two or three hairs at a time from each part you pull, you are equalizing the amount, making a smoother appearance.

To get the mane to lie properly on one side of the neck, coat-conditioner, Vaseline, hair spray, or baby oil can be applied and neck wraps put on. Some hoods with satin linings help lay the mane also. Daily brushing with a damp brush (this will not pull out hairs) will work, if you prefer not to braid or wrap.

Length of tail is controversial. In judging Quarter Horses and Appaloosas, it should usually be short and thin enough for the judge to obtain a good view of the hindquarters, gaskins, and hips. Following the trend for length and thinness in your area is important when showing. The short hairs around the top of the tail need to be hand pulled, leaving no hairs sticking out to the side. To thin the tail all the way through, hold it out behind the horse to one side so that some of the hair hangs down and separates; pull a small section at a time. Shorten and taper as for the mane. Use the current rule books of the AHSA and the AQHA to find out the latest official requirements for grooming.

Oiling and Whitening

To make the muzzle look fine and small and the eyes large and luminous, take a small amount of baby oil or Vaseline in your hands, rub them together, and then gently rub on the muzzle and around the eyes. Take care not to overdo it and make the horse look greasy. Because dust and dirt can adhere easily and ruin the effect, do this only just before going into the show ring. Never leave your horse alone to paw or put his nose on the ground. After oiling the muzzle and around the eyes, rub the excess on his body coat in light slapping motions in the direction the hair grows, to give a finished, satiny look to his coat, especially over shoulders and neck.

To make his white markings whiter, dampen them and pat on corn starch or rice powder. Be sure to do this before you tend his hoofs, because when your brush out the whitener it will fall over the feet. There are commercial whitening sprays that can also be used.

Braiding

It is correct to braid the tail and mane when showing hunters. Many short braids will give the neck a longer look, and fewer thicker braids tend to shorten a horse's neck. In today's competitive showing, such nuances in show grooming may make the difference between winning and losing. Traditionally, the mane lies on the right.

BRAIDING THE FORELOCK
One way to braid the forelock is to divide it into three equal parts and proceed as for a mane braid. Saddle-horse forelocks are braided with long, colorful ribbons. If you braid a hunter's mane, his forelock and tail should also be braided.

On breeds such as the Arabian and the Morgan, the manes and tails should be naturally long and flowing. Some breeds are shown with braided forelock and three long braids woven with ribbon ahead of the natural mane. In dressage and hunting, many patterns, such as the French braid, scalloping, and Continental braid, are attractive and effective. Traditionally, mares wear an even number of braids; geldings and stallions, odd.

There are also many ways to braid tails for hunters, saddle horses, draft horses, dressage, and polo. One method, called over-braiding, is somewhat easier than the others to do. To begin, be sure the tail is well brushed and free from snarls.

Other Finishing Touches

Trim the excess off the chestnuts (horny growths on legs) and ergots (growths on backs of fetlocks). If Vaseline is rubbed on for several days, these growths will be easier to remove or will drop off by themselves.

Coat conditioners put the finishing touches on the show coat and are good for the horse, helping to maintain a moisture level in the hair. We like sprays, such as Grand Champion, that also contain a fly repellent. Anything you use should be tried out at least a week before the show to make sure your horse is not allergic to it. Coat-sprays on manes and tails make them glisten. When manes and tails are damp-braided with spray and then combed out, the waves come out beautifully bright and glossy.

For general hoof care, see Chapter 7. Here we are concerned with show-grooming the foot. Use of hoof black is controversial; under some AHSA rules, white hoofs cannot be blackened. This makes sense, as it would be

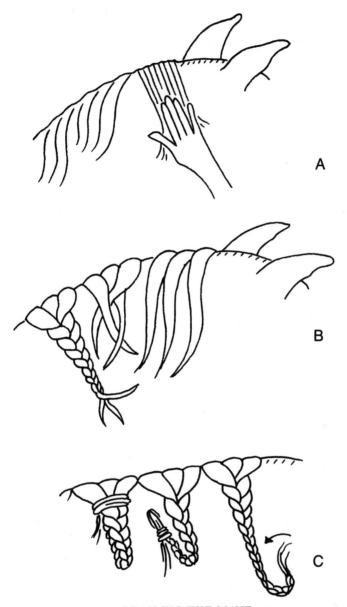

BRAIDING THE MANE

To braid, dampen the mane and start behind the ears (or behind the bridle path) with a well-combed section of hair about three inches wide (A). Divide in three parts, braid tightly to the end of the hair (keeping it tight and close to the neck) (B). Fasten with a rubber band, fold the braid underneath itself to the root of the mane, and fasten in place with a second rubber band or by sewing with colored thread or yarn (C). Tape is sometimes added for dressage. Keep braids even.

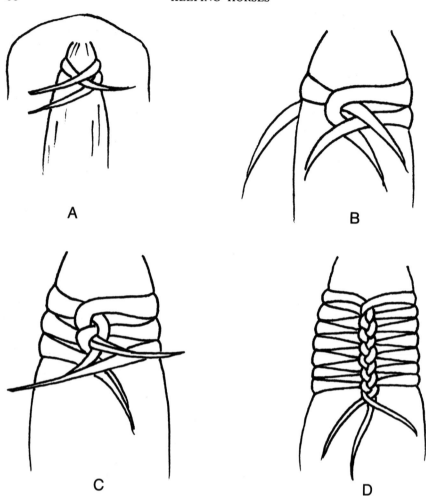

A

B

C

D

BRAIDING THE TAIL

To under-braid the tail, dampen around the dock and separate small sections of hair on either side. Taking one strand from the left and two from the right (A), proceed as for the mane (or a human braid), except bring each new strand under (from behind) instead of over (B and C). This will form a raised braid down the center of the tail (D). Keep braid straight and centered by applying tension evenly on both sides as you braid; keep added strands small, even, and tight. At end of dock, pick up no more new strands, but continue center braid for six to eight inches. Finish off as a mane braid by looping back under itself and sewing together.

unnatural for a horse with white on his lower leg to have a black hoof. Hoof black is easy to apply—brush it on a clean, dry hoof and it dries almost instantly. Removing it, however, is another story—fine sandpaper, steel wool, fine wire brushes, and soap and water can be used.

Leaving commercial preparations on the hoof eventually seals the hoof and causes drying, chipping, and cracking as the protective outer layer is destroyed. Did you realize that 25 percent of the hoof wall is water? Decreasing moisture content will lessen the cushioning effect of the hoof, and sanding destroys the moisture-retaining veneer, or periople. Acetone and alcohol-based polishes form a shield against the moisture. Be sure to use hoof conditioner to keep the hoof pliable, and remove polish immediately after the show, before it bonds on completely.

One method that we have found to work well is to hand-rub black wax shoe polish on the hoof and then use a light hoof oil over the top (for white hoofs, a white wax and oil). However, the hoofs must be very clean for this to work well. Too much oil will attract dust and dirt.

Rubbing the outer wall of a clean hoof with a cut onion imparts a shine on both light and dark hoofs.

BANDAGING

Bandages are among the most versatile articles of your horse's clothing and the most misunderstood. Although bandaging may look easy, improper bandaging can damage your horse. Especially when it comes to bandaging wounds, you should proceed under the instructions of your veterinarian (see Chapter 8).

There are several reasons for bandaging. Stable or shipping bandages are used for warmth, support, and protection. A sick horse or one that is tired from very hard work has less resistance to chills; the warmth of a leg bandage can help speed recovery, especially if the horse must be stalled in a cold, drafty place. When a horse must stand quietly for long periods of time, such as when trailering, he will be kept more comfortable and will not stock up (have lower legs swell) when supported by bandages. "Track" or "roller" bandages are used for this purpose. They often come in sets of four, are usually made of flannel or wool, and are about four to six inches wide, seven to nine feet long. They may be set over four to six layers of sheet cotton or quilted cotton leg wrapping.

Exercise bandages support back tendons or reinforce weak or strained tendons while the horse is working. They may also protect the leg from external injury, such as striking against rocks or being pierced by thorns. They are shorter and narrower than stable bandages and are applied from above the fetlock to just below the knee. Exercise bandages should be used only when necessary, perhaps when the horse is soft or tired. If they are overused, he may become dependent on them. Wide adhesive tape wrapped over the bandage will help to keep it from slipping or becoming snagged.

New products keep appearing, some of which may take the place of bandaging. Shipping boots that cover the entire leg are made in tough vinyl with thick fleece lining and Velcro closing. Other equipment includes hock boots of lined leather Naugahyde, tail wraps of Equiprene (neoprene rubber with nylon shell), tendon wraps, and kneecap boots. Because much of this convenient, ready-made equipment heats up when left on for several hours, many horsemen prefer to roll their own bandages. Head bumpers for protecting the poll, rubber poultice boots, ice boots, and shoe-boil boots are other convenient products.

How to Apply a Bandage

Bandaging can harm your horse if it is not done correctly. Adequate padding can reduce the danger, and the following principles will help you to avoid problems (for bandaging wounds, see Chapter 8):

- Keep pressure even—snug but not too tight. Use one hand to manage the roll, the other to smooth the bandage.
- Wrap from the bottom up. Although tradition and many books advise starting from the top, a nonexpert will have far fewer problems with circulation impairment if he keeps this rule, especially if padding is not used.
- Work from front to back when unrolling the bandage, tightening pressure on the shinbone, rather than on the back tendon.
- Tie off or fasten with the same pressure as applied in wrapping; never make the fastenings tighter.
- Fasten on the outside of the leg.
- Check: The bandage should feel firm and even over the entire area. It should not be so tight that a finger can't be inserted at the top.

Applying a stable bandage. Wrap cotton padding or quilted cotton around the lower leg, making it slightly longer than the anticipated bandage. The padding should be smooth, without lumps or holes that might cause uneven pressure.

Begin by taking one wrap around the pastern. Then wrap snugly up pastern and fetlock, keeping pressure even. An extra wrap may be taken under the fetlock to add support. Continue to wrap up the cannon, overlapping by one third to one half the width of the bandage, to the edge of the padding, just below the knee. Come back down with slightly less pressure. Fasten on the outside.

Shipping bandage. Follow the directions for the stable bandage, except: Begin by wrapping around the coronet band, and take several wraps under the bulb of the heel. It is important to come under the heel, even though bandage will be stepped on—otherwise it will creep up.

Exercise bandage. When bandaging over cotton padding, start just above the fetlock, and continue to wrap firmly up the cannon to just below the knee, then back down with slightly less tension, and fasten on the outside.

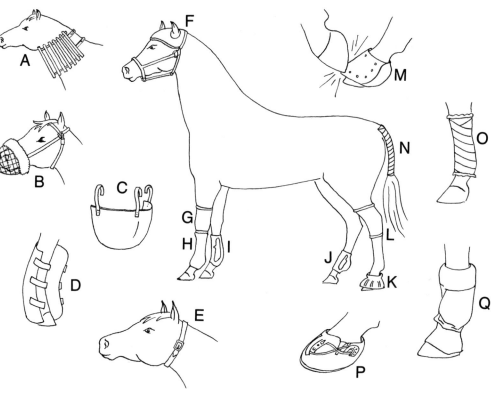

PROTECTIVE, SUPPORTIVE, AND BANDAGING EQUIPMENT

Wood neck cradle (A) and wire muzzle (B) prevent gnawing of wounds and blankets.
Leather bib (C) prevents tearing of blankets and bandages but allows feeding and
watering. Shipping boot (D). Cribbing strap (E) applies pressure on throat when horse
cribs, but allows him to eat comfortably.

F. Head bumper, or poll guard	L. Hock boot
G. Knee bandage	M. Calking boot
H. Tendon boot	N. Tail wrap
I. Galloping boot (splint boot)	O. Track bandage
J. Ankle boot	P. Easyboot
K. Bell boot	Q. Skid boot

With padded elastic bandage, start by running a strip down the back tendon from the knee to just above the fetlock, turn it and proceed as above. When starting back down just below the knee, turn down the loose end of the bandage and cover it with wraps. Fasten on the outside.

To help keep the bandage in place while the horse is moving, tape around the top and the bottom as well as around tie tapes or closures.

Wrapping the tail. When trailering, it is wise to wrap the tail to protect it from rubbing, especially in hilly country, where horses tend to ride the tailgate or butt strap. (see p. 194) You may use disposable gauze, track wraps, elastic bandages, or Velcro tail bandages. Since tail bandages may be left on for long periods of time during shipping, it is essential that they be wrapped so as not to restrict circulation or contribute to loss of hair. Start at the base of the tail and continue to the last tail vertebra. Turning a few hairs back as the tail is wrapped keeps the bandage from slipping.

When wrapping a mare's tail for cleanliness during foaling, first braid the tail into a three-strand length and double it back on itself.

HORSE CLOTHING

A blanket is a replacement for a horse's natural winter coat; it is needed only under special circumstances when that coat is no longer adequate. Use a blanket:
- when the winter coat has been clipped and the horse is turned out of a warm barn,
- when transporting a horse, to protect him from dust, chill, drafts, and insects,
- for mares after foaling,
- for weak, ill, or thin horses in cold weather or to keep them from drafts.

Heavy blankets with hoods are used to keep show horses from growing their winter coats.

For versatility, buy a good-quality, medium-weight, water-repellent blanket; in rough weather, a blanket liner (fleece, quilted, or wool) may be used underneath. Two light layers are warmer than one heavy layer.

If you blanket your horse, do it consistently and in tune with weather changes. Once you begin blanketing a horse in winter, you must continue, as blankets discourage hair growth. Clipped horses should also be equipped with hoods. Use your older blankets on young horses, as the youngsters tend to be hard on them.

Avoid improper blanketing:
- Torn or broken buckles may injure a horse by rubbing or poking him, or they may allow him to become tangled and fall as the blanket twists. If the blanket comes off in severe weather, he could catch a cold or pneumonia.
- A poorly fitted blanket can rub raw, bare spots on the skin.
- Using one blanket for several horses may spread skin disease.
- Constant blanketing causes sores and skin irritation, especially on bony horses. Remove blankets daily to groom and check your horse, watching for signs of wear or chafing, especially around the shoulders.
- A blanketed horse must be checked frequently, as any equipment left on a loose horse is a hazard.

Coolers envelop the whole horse; they can be made of wool, cotton, duck,

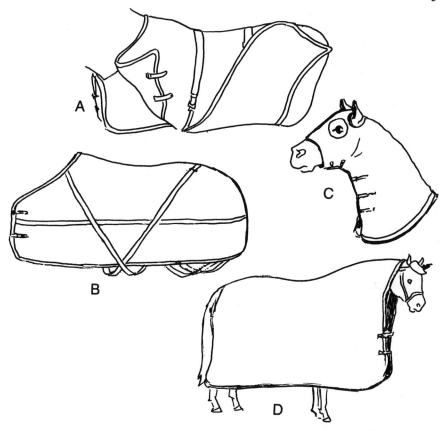

HORSE CLOTHING

A. Standard stable blanket for indoor use (32–45 degrees F), with liner (10–32 degrees).
B. Turn-out blanket (waterproof and wool-lined) can be used with liner blanket as
temperature drops (32 degrees to 0). C. Winter hood. D. Wool cooler (lightweight) keeps
horse from cooling down too quickly after stress.

or woven acrylic yarns, and they come complete with browband, front tie straps, and a tail strap. They are used for cooling out a horse after a bath, either while on a lead or on a mechanical hot-walker—they are not designed for use on loose horses. Warm air from the hot horse circulates within the confines of the cooler, helping to cool and dry him and prevent chills.

Sweat sheets capture body warmth and prevent the horse from cooling out too rapidly and becoming stiff.

Other horse clothing includes sweat hoods, full and partial neck wraps, and jowl wraps. These are used to trim a show horse's throat and neck by inducing sweat (most are washable), although allowing flexibility and freedom of movement. They should not be left on for long periods, and care should be taken to wash and air the skin under the wraps after each use.

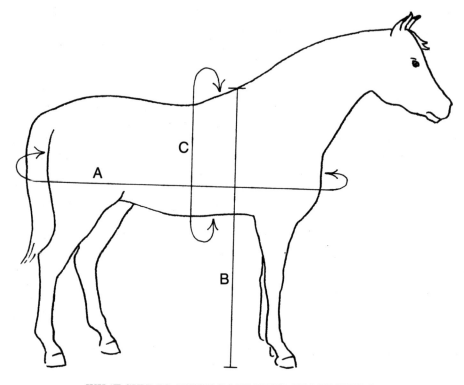

WHAT SIZE BLANKET DOES YOUR HORSE NEED?

Measure your horse as shown. A. Center of chest to edge of tail (this will give you the inch measurement shown on the size chart). B. Withers to ground (hands). C. Girth circumference (for adjusting straps).

SIZE CHART

Small pony	10 hands	48 inches
Foal or medium pony	11–11½ hands	56 inches
Yearling or large pony	13–13½ hands	64 inches
Average horse	15–15½ hands	72 inches
Large horse	16–16½ hands	80 + inches

TACK

Selection, Care, and Cleaning of Leather

Leather has always been first choice with horsemen. Nylon or other synthetics can sometimes be substituted, but leather is smooth, strong yet flexible, lasts indefinitely with proper care, enhances appearance, and even smells good. Good leather is more expensive every year, so it is wise to know how to care for your investment. The condition of your equipment reflects the kind of horseman you are.

When selecting leather goods, feel both sides of the leather. The flesh side (inside) of better leather should feel smooth on surfaces and edges, with no loose or rough fibers. Quality leather will feel thick and a bit greasy when new, and it will bend easily; however, there should be no creases or bubbles on the skin of the top side.

New tack is very stiff, and may be uncomfortable for your horse. Before using new tack, saddle-soap both sides of the leather and be sure to get off any waxy finish, as oil cannot penetrate wax (be sure that excess soap doesn't dry in the indentations of carved leather). Just before leather is completely dry from washing, rub in oil or leather dressing sparingly to keep it pliable. The USDA recommends a mixture of cod oil and tallow, neatsfoot oil and tallow, or neatsfoot and castor oils with wool grease (make a paste the consistency of butter and work it in by hand). Synthetic preparations may also be used.

Better-quality old tack will be flexible but have life and substance, whereas less-expensive grades of leather will be either lifeless or brittle. Used tack should be pliable and free from cracking or splitting, and repairs should be made before using.

Regular cleaning and conditioning will keep your saddle in proper condition. Wipe off dust and dirt after each use and clean with saddle soap once a week. Depending on the frequency of use, oil and conditioner should be applied every few months. Overconditioning and overoiling will damage leather.

To clean your saddle and tack, gather your materials and arrange your saddle and other tack on newspapers or a saddle rack. You will need: two sponges, two containers of warm water, chamois, glycerine saddle soap, soft clean cloths, conditioning pastes or liquid synthetic conditioners with proper applicators, and metal cleaner for stirrup irons, buckles, and other hardware. English saddles should have girth and stirrup leathers removed (noting which one is left and which right and putting the irons to soak in cool water).

If your saddle is very dirty, damp-sponge the entire saddle before soaping with castile, endeavoring to remove as much scurf as possible. With a clean, rinsed sponge, work up a "dry" lather with glycerine saddle soap; avoid getting the leather too wet. Use the sponge in a circular motion. As the dirt is worked up with the lather, take a clean rag dipped in clean water and wash the dirty lather off before starting on a new area. Keep the dirt away as you go. All small accumulations of grease and dirt ("jockeys") should be removed.

This is a good opportunity to check your billet straps, stirrup leathers, and leather girths for wear and safety. Check the parts of your bridle, too, which also should be taken apart for cleaning. Remember that dirt on bridles will be from sweat on the *inside* of the leather, where it rests on the horse.

If marks from the irons are deep on the stirrup leathers, either replace the leathers or have a saddlemaker shorten them about an inch on the buckle end, so that your irons will rest on a different area. Black marks where metal

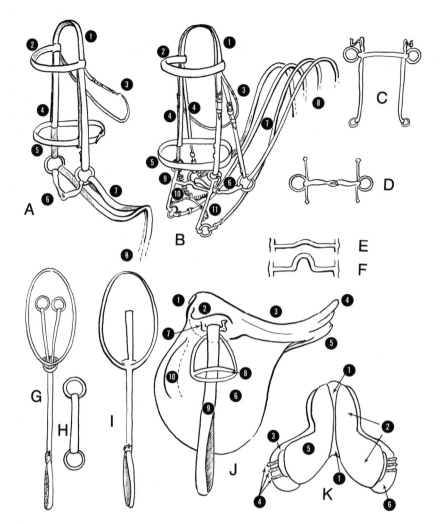

ENGLISH TACK

A. Snaffle bridle   B. Double bridle
    1. Crown piece or headstall
    2. Browband
    3. Throatlatch
    4. Cheekpiece
    5. Noseband or cavesson
    6. Snaffle bit
    7. Reins
    8. Bight of reins
    9. Weymouth (curb) bit
    10. Curb chain
    11. Lip strap
C. Pelham half-moon bit
D. Snaffle with full cheek bars
E. Low-port curb
F. High-port curb
G. Running martingale
H. Irish martingale
I. Standing martingale

J. English saddle
    1. Pommel
    2. Skirt
    3. Seat
    4. Cantle
    5. Panel
    6. Flap
    7. Stirrup safety bar (under skirt)
    8. Tread or stirrup iron
    9. Stirrup leather
    10. Kneepad or knee roll

K. Underside of English saddle
    1. Gullet
    2. Lining (part of panel)
    3. Buckle guard
    4. Girth strap or tabs
    5. Panel
    6. Saddle flap

presses against leather should be scrubbed. Readjust girths on the off side so that different holes can be used. Irons can be cleaned with metal polish.

Western saddles are cleaned in the same manner, with the off latigo, stirrups, and cinch removed. Use silver polish for silver trim and wash and scrub the cinch with laundry detergent, letting it dry in the sun.

After all pieces are cleaned with saddle soap, rinse and dry off the excess with a chamois. Brush or wipe on oil or conditioner lightly, and remove excess.

Storing and Transporting Tack

Tack that you do not intend to use for several months should be covered with Vaseline, wrapped in burlap sacks or sheets, and stored in a dry place. Saddles should be hung up or placed on saddle racks and covered, allowing stirrup leathers and fenders to hang down naturally. Avoid heat and dampness. Cats, mice, and rats can damage leather; mice love Western string cinches, especially if dyed, and cats enjoy climbing (with claws) onto the seats. All saddles should be stored so that the tree is not stressed, and covered to protect from dust and bird droppings.

Dumping your saddle and other leather equipment into a car trunk or pickup is a serious abuse that takes the life from your tack. When transporting your saddle, either put it in a saddle-carrying case or wrap it well in soft, clean saddle blankets. Stand it on its gullet against the back seat, or packed well among other soft goods. The motion of a vehicle will rub large spots in leather set against hard surfaces and not adequately protected.

When carrying your saddle, latigos should be wrapped on cinch rings and girths over the horn, never dragged along the ground. If the saddle is not put directly on the horse's back, but set down first, it should be set on its gullet, with a blanket over the saddle and off the ground. If you ever tie knots in Western open reins, be sure to untie them before you put them away; if knots are left to set, the reins become twisted and difficult to manage, and their life is shortened.

Extra Tips on Tack Care

1. If a saddle is exposed to excess water by rain or snow, leave it alone and let it dry at least twenty-four hours. Proceed as in cleaning and conditioning, but use very little soap. Oil it lightly.
2. Rotate the use of the third billet strap occasionally to give a "rest" to the straps.
3. Wax the linen threads on the buckles of the girth with beeswax to protect them from water and eventual rot.

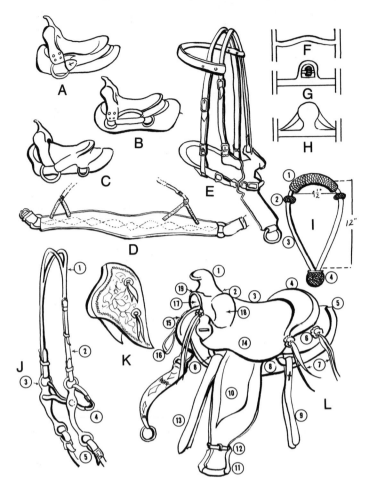

WESTERN TACK

A. Three-quarter standard rig
B. Full double rig
C. Three-quarter double rig
D. Leather breast collar
E. Easy stop hackamore
F. Port (low) bit
G. Half-breed bit   A spade bit may
               be used with a
H. Spade bit   halfbreed
               roller.

I. Standard bosal
   1. Nose button
   2. Side button
   3. Noseband
   4. Heel knot
J. Split ear bridle
   1. Crown piece
   2. Cheekpiece
   3. Curb bit
   4. Curb strap
   5. Reins
K. Tapaderos (taps)

L. Western saddle
   1. Horn
   2. Fork
   3. Seat
   4. Cantle
   5. Skirt
   6. Rear housing
   7. Saddle strings
   8. Rigging dees or dee rings
   9. Rear cinch billet
  10. Fender
  11. Stirrup with tread cover
  12. Stirrup leather
  13. Long latigo, cinch strap, or
      front tie strap
  14. Seat jockey
  15. Wool lining
  16. Rope strap
  17. Gullet
  18. Swells
  19. Pommel

4. Use steel wool on raw steel (but not on plated metal). Stainless steel does not rust.
5. Dirty, worn pads, blankets, or saddle linings cause sores; caked or worn cinches can cause sores and accidents. Wash pads, girth covers, and Western cinches regularly. Felt can be brushed vigorously—do not wash.
6. The fenders of new Western saddles can be so stiff you can hardly get your feet into the stirrups. Before using the saddle (and between uses until the leather has softened), put it on a saddle rack and thoroughly dampen the fenders. Twist the fenders into riding position and keep turning them until you can hold them in place by putting a heavy pole (such as a crowbar) through both stirrups. This will greatly improve the comfort of your "break-in" rides.

Saddles

Saddles have a frame called the "tree" (the key to good design, determining shape and size), which may be made of traditional beechwood (for lightness) or laminated wood. Some are now available in aluminum and fiberglass, and most are reinforced with metal for strength.

Saddletrees should be shaped to help the rider sit in the center of the saddle —the lowest part. Early Western saddles tended to push the rider toward the cantle, but recent modifications present a better-balanced saddle with free-swinging fenders (set farther forward than the older saddles). Saddles should be sensibly suited to both horse and rider.

Buy the best-quality saddle you can afford, not only for your own satisfaction, but also for the comfort of your horse. In general, it is better to buy a good used saddle than an inferior new one.

When buying a used saddle, first check the tree: a broken one will cause injury and pain to your horse. Check the stitching, the padding, curling flaps (English) or skirts (Western), stirrup-leather wear, and the security of the rigging. Check latigos and cinches, off billet and tabs. Any part of the leather that touches metal should be checked for weakness. True, many of the above can be repaired or replaced, but take care that the price will be reasonable and acceptable.

Checking for saddle quality

1. Push and press on the swells, twist on the horn cap, push on back of the cantle and seat. You should feel no give. The pieces should fit tight against the tree.
2. Check the right and left sides of the saddle. They should have identical weight and balance—similar thicknesses of leather, with the stitching even and professional-looking.
3. Are the rigging screws (into the tree) brass? Nonstainless, or raw, steel

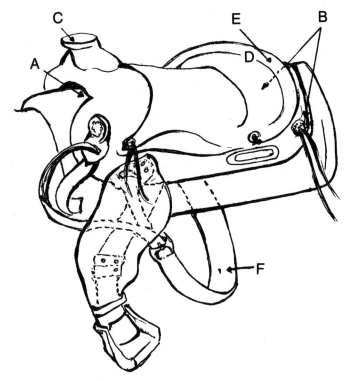

FITTING THE WESTERN SADDLE

*Front of gullet (A) must be wide enough to fit the conformation of the horse.
Quarter Horse bars (also suitable for Arabians and Morgans) conform to
round, low withers: 6¹/₄–6¹/₂ inches wide (extra-wide are 6³/₄–7 inches). Semi
Quarter Horse bars, for higher-withered, Thoroughbred type, are six inches
wide. Regular bars are 5³/₄ inches wide. Heavy riders should have wider bars
for back of gullet (B). The higher the horn (C), the more leverage that can be
exerted against it; thus a roping saddle needs a wider gullet to help prevent it
from turning or sliding. A low cantle (D), allowing more maneuverability, is
good for roping; a high cantle is good for fast events. The Cheyenne roll (E) is
solid, with no give. Western cinches (F) run from pony size (22 inches) to large-
horse size (36 inches).*

will rust, and rot leather and wood. Nails should also be brass, copper,
or resin-coated.

4. Leather on the skirts should have good-quality, one-inch genuine sheepskin or pile lining.

5. Quick-change buckles should be stainless steel, not chrome-plated. Also,
all hardware should be made of stainless steel, brass, or nickel to prevent rotting of leather. Nonstainless (or raw) steel will rust and rot
leather and wood.

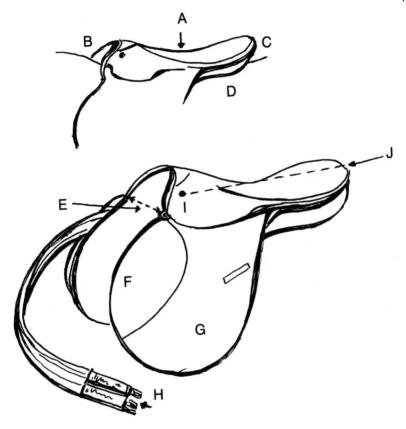

FITTING THE ENGLISH SADDLE

Do not use a saddle pad when making these tests and measurements. Make sure the saddle sits level; sit in its center (lowest part) (A): two fingers should fit between pommel and withers (B), and there should be a few inches to spare in front of and behind you. Daylight should be observable through the gullet (C). Center of padding should rest on back muscles (D). Front arch "spread" (gullet) should be wide enough over the withers (E). Panel (F) should be well stuffed for support of knee and tilted to prevent the rider from sliding backward. Flaps (G) should be long enough that boot tops do not catch on the bottom edges, short enough to allow direct calf contact with the horse's sides. Girth size is measured from the tip of one buckle to the other (H): 36 inches pony size, 48 inches average size, and 54 inches large-horse size. Measure tree size from center of saddle nail (I) to center of cantle (J).

6. Girths should be made from mohair, which can be washed and dried without hardening.
7. Conchas and latigo keepers should be tight, not roll around.
8. The saddle should look and feel good to both horse and rider.

Fitting a saddle. A saddle should be comfortable for the horse, with the weight bearing equally along the bars and no pressure spots or protrusions to

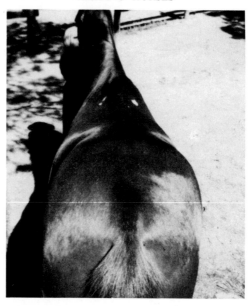

*Spots of white hair over the withers indicate for-
mer saddle sores.* (Courtesy Woodson Tyree)

rub or gall. There should be a clear air channel along the spine—not only no
pressure or weight on the spine, but ideally not even any contact—so that the
backbone is free to move. The saddle must also allow absolute freedom of the
shoulder blades.

Occasionally faults of an English saddle may be temporarily alleviated with
a pommel pad, which allows air to circulate and keeps withers cool and well
protected, or a foam seat riser (placed between saddle and pad at the rear to
raise the cantle). It should be stressed that these are temporary measures
only; steps should be taken immediately to procure a properly fitting saddle.

A saddle that is a poor fit for the horse will quickly cause sores, galls, and
fistula of the withers. The withers should be neither pinched nor pressed. The
biggest problem occurs when the tree is either too wide (sitting down on the
withers and causing fistula) or too narrow for the horse (riding too high on
his back, with too much pressure on only a few points). A badly fitted saddle
can also cause deep muscle-tissue damage; bruising, inflammation, and mis-
shaping of vertebrae; bumps (cellulite or furuncles); as well as other problems.

When fashioning a custom saddle, the saddlemaker will try bare trees on
the horse until he finds one that gives full contact along the bars at the proper
places on the horse and that clears the gullet properly. Before buying, you
may check whether a new or a used saddle will fit your horse without taking
the horse with you by using the method shown in the illustration. This will
also help your saddlemaker if it isn't possible to take the horse to him.

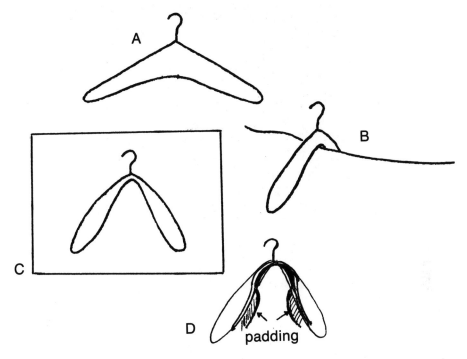

CHECK FOR PROPER FIT BEFORE BUYING A SADDLE

A. Bend a large, lightweight metal coathanger or a 24-inch piece of 12-gauge indoor-outdoor wire, or use other material that molds easily and holds its shape. B. Set the hanger or wire over the withers approximately where the nail head of the English saddle would be. Conform the wire exactly to the shape of the horse's back. C. Trace the shape on paper immediately. Even if you take the wire with you, the drawn pattern can be used to check that the wire has not changed shape on the way to the saddle shop. D. Hold the hanger or wire in position against the front of the saddle—it should fit into the seam between padding and flap.

Saddle Accessories

Breastplates and crupper straps (or cruppers) are used to keep the saddle from moving backward or forward when riding in mountainous country. When fitting the breastplate (breast collar), allow enough room to admit a hand at the withers on the neck strap, or beneath each shoulder strap. It should neither be too low to restrict shoulder movement nor too high to interfere with breathing.

The crupper is attached to the back dee of the saddle and passes under the tail. It is attached when the girth is loose or undone. Stand close to the near hind leg, lift the tail, and pass it through the crupper (or unbuckle the crupper, pass it around the tail, and rebuckle), and draw it well up to the top of

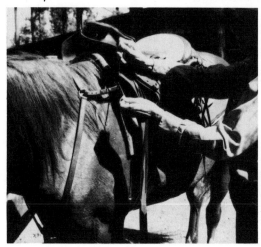 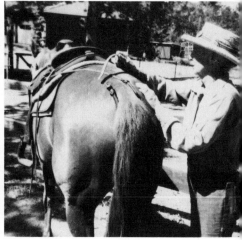

Breast collar   *Crupper*

The late Ruth Tyree used breast collar and crupper with a Western saddle for endurance riding. (Courtesy Woodson Tyree)

the tail. It should be adjusted so that it stabilizes the saddle but does not pull the tail up.

The most important reason for the use of saddle pads and blankets is to protect the horse's back. They absorb moisture and protect the saddle from sweat, as well as enabling you to use the same saddle on different horses.

In the show ring in English classes, the saddle pad is usually not used; it is used, however, for ordinary riding. The English saddle pad is specifically designed to fit a certain style of saddle and is equipped with sewn-in leather loops that slide over the billet straps to keep the pad from slipping. There are many materials available, among them quilted cotton fabric, fleece, felt, and covered foam.

Western pads are not generally designed to fit a specific style of saddle. They are usually thirty by thirty inches and one inch thick. Some have a cut-back head for the high-withered horse. They are made from wool, felt, foam rubber, polyester fleece, or a combination of these. Foam rubber tends to heat up and irritate the skin. Most good pads are reinforced with leather for longer wear.

Indian-woven Western saddle blankets are colorful, with original designs; they're both colorfast (100 percent virgin wool) and durable. Usually thirty by sixty inches, they are folded and used double—or a thirty- by thirty-inch blanket can be used over a protector pad or cotton blanket. This double protection absorbs moisture and helps to prevent chafing, as well as producing a pleasurable, colorful effect. Because imitations of the Indian blanket may not be colorfast and can shrink, it is wise to shop with care.

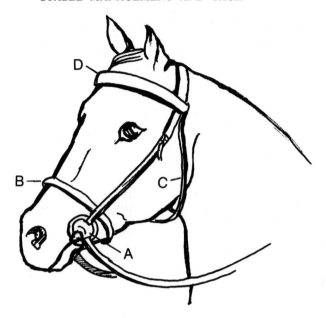

FITTING THE SNAFFLE BRIDLE

1. Jointed mouthpieces shift pressure from bars to lips and have a nutcracker effect; the thinner the bit, the more severe. 2. The snaffle should be placed up into the corners of the mouth, so that one well-developed wrinkle appears (A). 3. The bit should be wide enough to just touch the corners of the mouth. 4. The cavesson should lie halfway between the cheekbone and the corners of the mouth and should admit two fingers between noseband and nose (B). 5. The throatlatch should allow the full width of an adult hand between it and the side of the jawbone (C). 4. The browband lies flat and even, below the ears (D). When fitting the double *bridle, the bridoon rests above the curb, fitting closely into the corners of the lips, but with no wrinkle. The curb (Weymouth) rests below the bridoon on the bars. The curb chain lies flat in the chin groove and acts when the cheeks of the bit are drawn back at about 45-degree angle to the mouth.*

Packsaddle pads are larger than riding-saddle pads, coming down farther on the sides for more protection.

Bridles, Reins, and Accessories

Bridles come in many styles, generally designed to fit the kind of activity to be performed. The specific uses and effects of bits, bridles, and hackamores are discussed in both *Basic Horsemanship: English and Western* and *Basic Training for Horses: English and Western.*

Each horse should have his own, well-fitted bridle. See the illustration for details on fitting.

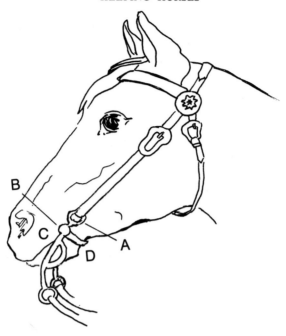

FITTING THE WESTERN BRIDLE

A. The upper cheek should be wide enough not to rub and pinch behind the mouth. B. The mouthpiece should be no more than 1/4 inch wider than the mouth. C. The bit should fit right up against the corners of the mouth. D. The upper cheek should be the correct length for the curb strap to fit into the chin groove at all times. The curb bit does not function correctly without the curb strap, which should be 3/8–1/2 inch wide.

Reins may be made of leather, rubber, nylon, webbing, rope, or cotton. Leather reins may be plain, rolled, laced, or plaited. Special reins include hunt-type (covered in the hand-grip area with pimpled rubber for good grip) and schooling reins (web with leather grips and strong elastic at the bit ends).

Accessories include leather rein stops (which keep the running martingale in place when added to the reins) and the Irish martingale. Unlike other martingales, the Irish type does not affect the horse's head carriage; it is simply a short strap with rings at either end that slip onto the reins to keep the horse from flipping both reins to one side of his neck.

The running martingale and the standing martingale do affect the horse's head carriage. The running martingale, whose rings work freely along the reins, is the more versatile: When the hands go forward for jumping, the running martingale frees the head to stretch; in normal hand position, the head is restricted from being raised. The running martingale works on the snaffle rein to keep the bit in place on the bars of the mouth. *Fitting the running martingale:* When attached to the girth, take both rings up one side of the horse's shoulder. They should reach to the withers. The neck strap should admit a hand at the withers with the buckle on the near side.

The standing martingale is fixed and restrains the horse from stargazing and throwing up his head. It applies pressure to the horse's nose when he attempts to raise his head. *Fitting the standing martingale:* when the horse's head is in the correct position, place a hand underneath the martingale and push up to reach just into the horse's throatlatch.

The sidecheck martingale does not affect head carriage but restricts the horse from lowering his head and grazing, by means of a strap that is attached to the pommel and to the top of the cheekpiece on the bridle. This is useful for young children in controlling a horse or pony.

Bits

There are so many bits available that the beginning horseman may well feel frustrated and confused. As a rule, the bit to use should depend upon the horse's stage of training, his temperament, and the kind of riding that the owner does. Generally, a bit is milder when it is thicker, heavier, has large, loose-fitting rings, has short or curved-back shanks, and has a low port, or mildly arched mouthpiece. A bit is more severe when it is lighter, has a thin or twisted mouthpiece, has a looser snaffle joint, has fixed rings, long or straight shanks, or a high port.

Most bits are made of metal, though some of these may be covered with hard or soft rubber or nylon for young, sensitive mouths. The best (finished-horse) bits are made of stainless steel; these will not flake, rust, or break, as cheaper bits do, and they are easier to keep clean. Chrome-plated and nickel-plated bits are often made from malleable iron; they may flake with age but are stronger than the older, easily bent, solid-nickel bits. Aluminum is light-weight and easier to warm up on below-freezing days; however, aluminum tends to dry a mouth out, and therefore harden it. A moist mouth is usually a soft mouth, since the moisture stimulates nerve endings. Care should always be taken to encourage salivation.

Because copper encourages a moist mouth, many bits have copper mouth-pieces—a combination of metals may be used in one bit. Solid, hard-rubber bits, along with rubber and nylon-covered bits, are popular for training the tender, uneducated mouth. In order to make any mouthpiece less severe, the bit may be wrapped with SealTex, a latex bandage that sticks to itself. This is self-sealing, three inches wide and thirty-eight inches long, which should be enough for wrapping two mouthpieces.

Curb straps and chains should not cause discomfort (shown by the horse's raising his head), and so should be neither too tight nor too loose. There should be room for three fingers to be inserted flat between strap and chin groove. Chains should be flat and never twisted.

Accessories include bit converters (convert the Pelham double bridle to a single rein), bit loops (used on full cheek bits to keep them in the proper position), rubber curb chain guards (slip over any curb chains to prevent chafing), rubber bit guards (keep the bit from pinching, or narrow a bit that is slightly too wide), and rubber bit ports (attach to the mouth of any bit to keep the horse's tongue from getting over the bit).

Various kinds of nosebands are other accessories that some horsemen add for more effective control. A dropped noseband, used in conjunction with a snaffle bit, is buckled below the bit and fitted with the front well above the nostrils, the back sitting in the chin groove. It should be tight enough to prevent the horse from crossing his jaw, but not so tight as to prevent flexing of the jaw.

The bosal hackamore can be used like a dropped noseband; others include the figure-eight cavesson, the hinge-dropped noseband, and the Kineton noseband.

Theft-Proof Your Tack

The large investment we make in tack should be protected. Stolen tack is easy to sell, and when it is unmarked, the chances of recovery are very poor. Many times, tack is worth more to the owner than just the dollar value—perhaps it has been given by a loved one, passed down for generations, or won in competition.

1. On saddles, brand or leather-stamp the undersides of the fenders, gullet, and skirts. You may also put your registered brand prominently on horn cap, skirt, or fender. Use initials, Social Security number (although Social Security Administration will not help locate owners), or brand.
2. Mark all tack in your stable and display a sign to that effect. This will alert burglars that your tack can be traced—marked tack is hard to sell.
3. Good locks, strong doors, barred windows, sufficient lighting, and watchdogs are helpful.

CHAPTER 5

FEEDING, FEEDS, AND PASTURES

FEEDING BASICS

Horses today are raised primarily for a long life of performance, rather than for quick production of meat, milk, or wool. How we feed our horses, more than any other single factor, determines how well they grow, how healthy they stay, how adequately they perform, and how long they remain energetic and useful.

Over thousands of years of evolution, the horse developed a specialized digestive system that fit his nomadic lifestyle—a lifestyle dependent on unlimited natural grazing. Today, new demands (fast growth and early maturity), stresses (competition and trailering), and artificial living patterns (stalls or corrals, with limited feeding times), play havoc with the horse's natural inclinations, as well as with his digestion.

Since state of mind and digestion affect each other, a well-adjusted, contented horse will be healthier, with fewer digestive upsets, than a miserable one. Proper feeding is the best kind of preventive medicine—and goes a long way to ensure emotional well-being.

How the Horse's Digestive System Works

The horse's alimentary canal is, in effect, a hundred-foot-long food tube. Sensitive, mobile lips select the food, which is bitten off by the incisor teeth and ground up by the molars. Because the horse is intended to eat slowly, thoroughly chewing his food before swallowing, the condition of his teeth is vital. Digestion begins in the mouth, and liquefied food passes through the five-foot-long esophagus to the stomach. A horse may choke if the food is too dry or not well-enough chewed; to reduce this possibility, check his teeth regularly as he gets older, and have them floated if necessary to improve the grinding surface. A horse that bolts his food (swallows without proper chewing because of greediness) may be slowed down by putting several large, smooth rocks in his grain pan.

The horse's stomach has a capacity of only two to four gallons (a cow's rumen holds forty gallons). The stomach functions best when two-thirds full, and takes over twenty-four hours to empty if no more food is added. When overfull, due to eating too much at infrequent intervals, fermentation and swelling can occur, resulting in colic. Some absorption of nutrients takes place in the stomach, but most occurs in the seventy-foot-long small intestine, especially absorption of proteins and carbohydrates.

Food not absorbed in the small intestine passes on to the cecum (four feet long, with a ten-gallon capacity). This first part of the large intestine has been likened to a cow's rumen, a septic tank, or a fermentation vat. It is here that bacteria and protozoa break down the crude fiber (mainly cellulose) into glucose. Because the main nutritive value of roughage (carbohydrate), then, is not absorbed until the food has passed all the way through the stomach and the small intestine into the cecum, digestion of fibers is not as efficient in the horse as in, for instance, the cow (where this fermentation process takes place in the rumen, at the beginning of the digestive tract). If the horse is fed mainly grass hay (especially if it is weedy, late-cut, or otherwise of poor quality), most of the digestion must take place in the cecum, which can become enlarged, producing "hay belly." If the horse's diet is changed suddenly, or if he overeats or gets too much spring grass (grass tetany), the balance of bacteria can be upset, causing colic, intoxication, diarrhea, or founder.

Remaining food matter passes into the large and then the small colons, which absorb the nutrients and moisture that were missed earlier. Finally feces are formed and exit through the rectum. By careful observation of the quality and quantity of your horse's urine and droppings, you will have a good indication of his health: the condition of his teeth (undigested grain will show in droppings) and of his digestive tract. The amount of urine depends on the amount of water ingested and whether sweating has occurred. Normal urine in the horse is a somewhat viscous yellowish fluid, sometimes cloudy.

Horses defecate eight to ten times every twenty-four hours. Normal droppings should be fairly well formed, free from offensive odor and mucous slime, and colored from yellowish to greenish according to the kind of feed. Hard droppings may be caused by insufficient water, lack of exercise, or feed that is dry and indigestible (sometimes all of these in combination). Bran mashes, adequate water, and daily exercise should alleviate this.

Soft, watery droppings are caused by too-hard work, fatigue, stress, legume hays, grazing lush green pasture, or excessive use of bran. To help this condition, reduce exercise, omit bran and grazing (or change to drier pasture), and if it continues, withhold feed for twenty-four hours and then feed grass hay for a day or two before gradually going to routine feeding. Irritation of the intestine and highly concentrated feed can produce mucus-covered droppings or offensive odor. Again, reduce feed and give bran mashes and plenty of water.

Feeding in tune with the horse's specialized digestive system makes for good health, good digestion, and fewer problems. Learn and practice commonsense feeding habits.

Understanding Nutrients

Just as important in proper feeding is to understand how nutrients affect the horse. Nutrients are the basic components of food, essential to life and health. These six elements are proteins, fats, carbohydrates, minerals, vitamins, and water. Fats and carbohydrates are sometimes considered together as "energy components."

Proteins are essential for growth and for the building and repair of body tissues. They are made up of amino acids, some being of more use to horses than others. Feeds that do not have the right amino acids—the right kind of protein—are said to have "poor-quality protein." Horses must have sufficient protein of good quality for growth, maintenance, reproduction, and work.

Protein accounts for 20 percent of the horse's body weight—a most important part of the body tissue, especially for young, growing horses and pregnant mares. Lack of sufficient protein can result in poor growth, unthriftiness, loss of weight and stamina, poor development of hoof and hair, irregular estrous cycles, and poor milk production.

Good sources of protein include soybean-oil meal and similar supplements, and animal products such as dried skim milk or fish meal. Legume hays have more protein than grass hays.

Fats, or lipids, are a source of energy and heat and are digested in the small intestine. They yield more than twice as much energy as carbohydrates, increase the palatability of food, condition the hair coat and skin, and help a horse put on weight. Fats also aid in the absorption of vitamin A and may help in the absorption of calcium. If there are not enough fats and carbohydrates in the diet, protein will be used for energy instead of for building and maintenance of tissue—a situation that is inefficient and expensive and can lead to poor health.

Corn and oats are good sources of fat; many horsemen add corn oil to the grain ration, especially in the spring. Other oils and oil meals do the same. Horses get used to fat in the diet; if changed suddenly to a low-fat diet (barley, for instance), they may not eat as well.

Carbohydrates are the chief source of energy for the horse, since they make up 60 percent or more of most grains and hays. They are the "fuel" burned for normal body maintenance (temperature, heartbeat, respiration, and so on) and for work and stress. Their digestibility and nutritive value differ greatly in various feeds. While glucose is highly digestible, cellulose, or fiber, needs the bacteria in the cecum and large intestine to digest properly. These facts can be used in feeding. The newborn foal doesn't have enough bacteria in the cecum to digest cellulose efficiently, although he can digest concentrates (grain). As he grows, the bacteria increase; older horses, therefore, can utilize the roughage more efficiently.

Minerals are inorganic elements, found mainly in bones and teeth, that act as vital building substances as well as catalysts for various body functions.

While some are needed only in very small (trace) quantities, others, such as salt, calcium, and phosphorus, are needed in larger amounts and are most often added to a horse's ration.

Lack of sufficient minerals shows up most often in bone and growth disorders, weakness, and eventual death. An excess, on the other hand, may also be toxic and fatal. Some minerals, especially calcium and phosphorus, affect each other and must be kept in balance (see Calcium-Phosphorus Ratio, in the Mineral Chart, in the Appendix).

The mineral intake of horses on pasture depends on the fertility of the soil nourishing the plants; the mineral content of hay would depend not only on the quality of the soil, but also on whether the hay is aged, weathered, or improperly harvested and cured. Mineral supplementation other than trace-mineralized salt or fertilization of pastures should be done with care: check with your county agent and have soils and feeds analyzed if necessary.

Vitamins are essential to the proper utilization of other nutrients, are believed to have a catalytic (accelerating) effect on metabolism, and are required for various body functions. Also, vitamins are essential components of various body fluids; some are synthesized in the intestines, while others must be present in the diet.

There are two groups of vitamins: fat-soluble (A, D, E, and K), which are stored in the body (liver or fat cells), and water-soluble (C and B-complex), which dissolve in water and must be eaten or manufactured daily to meet the body's needs. A deficiency of fat-soluble vitamins does not show up immediately, since they are used up from the stored fat. A deficiency of water-soluble vitamins, however, shows up right away. Water-soluble vitamins are found in true form in plants, whereas the fat-soluble vitamins have precursors, or provitamins. These substances are changed in the horse's body to yield true vitamins; for instance, carotene (found in green plants) is converted in the body to vitamin A. See more on vitamins in the Appendix.

Laboratory analysis for determining deficiencies. How can we tell for sure if symptoms in our horses lead us to suspect a deficiency or excess in some vitamin, mineral, or other nutrient? There are five different laboratory analyses all with the purpose of determining a diet nutritionally adequate for an individual or group of horses. Feed, soil, and water tests determine deficiencies and toxicities and help the horseman determine and correct his ration. Hair analysis gives an estimate of the mineral levels in the body; deficiencies as well as toxic levels can be determined, especially if the analysis is made periodically. Blood analysis is done routinely on some horse farms (race and show horses especially), but others find it adequate to take a blood test only on ill or seemingly deficient animals.

Water is perhaps the most vital of all nutrients, since a horse deprived of it will live only a few days. Water constitutes about 50 percent of a horse's body weight (varying considerably with age and condition), and about 80 percent of his body chemistry is water-based. A loss of 20 percent of the body fluid is usually fatal.

An average horse needs a minimum of eight to twelve gallons of water a day for his body processes, but this need is influenced by factors such as temperature, activity, function (for instance, lactating mares need more), food intake, and type of food (the drier the food, the more water needed). If a horse is pastured on succulent green grass, he'll need less water than if he is fed dry hay. Feeds that have a high fiber content produce a greater fecal excretion of water, and therefore require a greater water intake; the same is true for feeds high in minerals. Horses deprived of water eat less and less, eventually stopping altogether.

Ideally, a pure, fresh supply of water should be available at all times. If this isn't possible, water should be offered, checked, and changed at least twice a day—more often in hot weather and areas of low humidity. Keep water tubs clean: dirty or stale water causes the horse to drink less than he should.

Understanding Feeds

TDN (total digestible nutrients) is a system of measuring the energy value of feed, expressed as a percentage of the ration. Another method of measuring energy is the calorie system.

TDN is the sum of all digestible organic nutrients (protein, fiber, nitrogen-free extract, and fat—the fat is multiplied by 2.25 because it has a higher energy value than carbohydrate or protein). The percentages of TDN represent the approximate heat or energy value of the feed. Grains usually range from 65 percent to 80 percent TDN, and hays from 40 percent to 55 percent TDN. Pasture grasses vary according to kind, water content, and stage of maturity.

Nutritive ratios are used to measure digestible protein—the tissue-building nutrient—in relation to the heat and energy-building nutrients. Nutritive ratios are expressed thus: the nutritive ratio of dent corn is 1:10.9 (1 to 10.9), for instance. This means that for each pound of digestible protein in corn, there are 10.9 pounds of digestible carbohydrate and fat (with the fat multiplied by 2.25). A nutritive ratio of 1:11 is adequate for idle horses; about 1:7 for horses at hard work.

Roughage: Grasses (Pasture) and Hays

Good-quality grasses and hays contain plenty of nutrients. When the mature horse at rest grazes on young, tender, good-quality grass, or is fed quality hay (cut before going to seed), he needs little else for supplement. Because older plants are made up of more indigestible fiber, a horse must eat much more of them to obtain fewer nutrients. Late-cut hay, weedy grass or hay, and pastures damaged by overgrazing or weather, provide little nutritional value and must be supplemented, if used.

One alternative to feeding on the ground in ranch situations where the animal concen-tration is heavy and specialized horse equipment may not be available. Some horses never will put their heads into a calf feeder, but most will get used to it. (Courtesy Dave Ellsbury)

Look for hay that is leafy (a good percentage of leaves to stems) and green, indicating that it has been cured well and contains an adequate amount of vitamin A. Hay that is dark, dry, or yellow may have been cut late or else have been rained on, and in either case suffered loss of nutrients. If hay smells fresh, sweet, and clean, it is normally good hay; softer hay is preferred (indi-cating that it was cut younger than coarse, stemmy hay), and is much more palatable. Look for stems that are fine, rather than large and coarse.

When you pull hay apart, it should not be hard or dry, white or bluish, have dust flying out, or be moldy. Mold can kill a horse. How can you tell whether the inside of a bale is as good as it appears on the outside? Lift the bale; if it seems heavier than a normal bale of that size, it probably has more moisture due to improper curing, and this in turn can cause fermentation and mold inside. Also, you can insert into the bale a small stiff wire with one end bent into a hook and pull out some pieces of hay to inspect. When buying hay by the ton, check several bales at random in each ton.

Hays are divided into two main classes: legume, such as clover and alfalfa (48–51 percent TDN) and grass or nonlegume hays such as timothy, prairie hay, bromegrass, Bermuda, bluestem (47–49 percent TDN). Legume hays are generally richer in calcium, phosphorus, and vitamins A, B, and D. Good legume hay can provide all the protein a mature horse needs, although lactat-ing mares, foals, and other youngsters will need supplements. Although they

An old water tank can make a useful hay feeder, as on the Moeller Ranch, Sundance, Wyoming. (Courtesy Dave Ellsbury)

are high-yielding, legume hays may be harder to cure, since they grow densely and are therefore more susceptible to mold. When mixed with grass hays, they are not too rich or as apt to mold and cause colic. Legume hays are also more laxative and encourage growth.

Grass hays should be cut early, either before blooming or in early bloom, after which they drop sharply in quality, eventually becoming tough, fibrous, and unpalatable (also true for legumes). They are more likely to be free of dust and mold than legume hays, and are not "washy" (laxative)—an advantage for race and show horses. Although rich in carbohydrates, grass hays are somewhat lacking in digestible protein; generally they are best when mixed with a legume hay.

Remember that the fertility of the soil has a direct bearing on the quality of the plant and the amount of minerals in that plant. Generally, hay should be bought in large quantities for economy, but not more than can be fed in one year, since nutrients are lost during storage.

Pellets vs. long-stem hay. Pelleted feeds—a complete hay/grain ration—are composed of ground-up, dehydrated hay, often alfalfa, sometimes mixed with grain or corn molasses and vitamins. They are usually sold in fifty-pound bags or in bulk, and should not be confused with grain-supplement pellets and cubes (called "cake" in some areas). Nor should they be confused with hay cubes or wafers, a haymaking process alternative to baling (these are larger than pellets and consist solely of compressed hay, with the nutritive value of hay).

"Complete-feed" pellets are the "fast foods" of the horse industry, and of course have both advantages and disadvantages. They can be stored in a small area, are easily transported, and consist of a stable, well-balanced ration—

therefore less total feed is required and less manure is produced. Because less bulk and fiber are consumed, horses stay trimmer and won't contract "hay belly," but this lack of bulk creates other problems. If the contents of the pellets are too finely ground, impaction of the bowels may result. Choke can be another problem. Also, since the entire day's ration can be eaten quickly, there is nothing to occupy the horse's normal grazing time, and boredom (and a craving for bulk) may lead him to chewing wood and other behavioral problems. These problems may be alleviated if some long-stem hay is fed in combination with the pellets. Although the ration is well balanced, young stock, broodmares, and working animals will need special supplementation that does not conflict with the pellets. If a change to all-pelleted feed is contemplated, it should be made gradually.

Cereal-grass hays (47 percent TDN) have high nutritive value, are palatable, and are popular, in the order of oat, barley, and then wheat hay. The stems and leaves become coarse and unpalatable as the grain ripens and are lower in calcium than other hays—check the calcium-to-phosphorus ratio when feeding these hays. All cereal-grass hays should be tested for nitrate levels that are too high, and the beards in barley and wheat hay (depending on maturity) can cause sore-mouth problems similar to those of foxtail (see p. 92).

Haylages and silages (15–20 percent TDN) are not recommended as a feed for horses, since spoilage and the presence of molds and toxins cause digestive disturbances. If it is of excellent quality, fresh, and not frozen, it can provide a nutritious alternative to hay for winter feeding; but even so, it should not replace more than a small portion of the normal feed.

Straw (oat, barley, wheat) is principally used for bedding, but some can be used as filler when wintering horses. Oat straw is the best, as it has a bit higher nutritive content than barley and wheat straws and is more palatable. It should never be used as the sole ration, because of its low protein and mineral content.

Pastures. A mature, healthy horse grazing good pasture is living the natural life for which he was designed, and he needs little supplementation beyond salt (iodized or mineralized salt in deficient areas). Pastures should be lush, free of toxic weeds and chemicals, and low in parasite infestation. The TDN of pasture is higher than hay on a dry-weight basis, but because pastures have a higher moisture content, larger amounts of feed must be consumed. Pasture is higher in protein, vitamin, and mineral content than early-cut hay of the same variety, and it is rich in B vitamins and vitamin E, along with being the best source of vitamin A (carotene). Because grazing animals receive vitamin D from sunlight and synthesize it within their own bodies, the fact that pasture is not a good source is unimportant.

Horses are very selective on pasture; they leave the rank, coarse, and overmature grasses, as well as unpalatable weeds. Mowing the pasture where desirable grasses have overmatured and become tasteless is a good practice, and controlling weeds will make the pasture more productive. Pasture rota-

A catalog of horse-pasture horrors. This old, rusty culvert pipe severely injured a good cow horse, severing a tendon and destroying his usefulness. Rusty, broken barbed wire forms a sickening trap for horses' legs and feet on many Western ranches. An old mowing machine sits abandoned in a pasture, the sickle buried in grass and weeds— sharp, rusty knives await the unwary horse.
(Courtesy Dave Ellsbury)

tion helps control parasite infestation and avoids the continuous grazing that depletes desirable grasses and injures their roots so that they cannot maintain the nutrient value and support of new growth. Dragging or harrowing pasture twice a year will help break the parasite cycle, as does rotating pasture with cattle, since there is no "crossover" with cattle parasites.

The only detriments that a pasture can produce are heavy parasite infestation when overgrazed, toxic weeds, and occasionally toxic minerals (as with high selenium content). Keeping pastures free of mechanical hazards such as wire, nails, and trash is part of good horse management.

The Poisonous Blister Beetle

The blister beetle contains the chemical cantharidin, a powerful and dangerous poison for which there is no antidote. As few as five beetles can kill a mature horse, sometimes within six hours. The poison causes blisters to form in the mouth and on the lining of the digestive tract, and these are ruptured by digestive action. The resulting ulcer-like sores are intensely painful, and the tissue damage is extreme. The horse becomes colicky—the first, and perhaps only, warning sign before it is too late.

Because blister beetles travel in swarms for mating and feeding, many are concentrated in one spot and may turn up in one bale of hay. The beetles are as toxic dead as alive to all livestock, although toxicity varies with the species, and there are three hundred varieties. Many birds feed on the blister beetles, though, and are not affected by the poison.

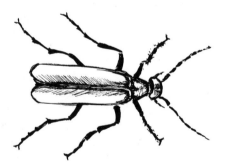

BLISTER BEETLE.
One of about three hundred varieties.

Prevention. Blister beetles are found wherever there is alfalfa, as well as other crops such as potatoes and tomatoes (the potato bug is one). They are less likely to occur in early-cut, first-cutting alfalfa, and more likely to be found in hay baled in mid to late summer. Check your hay well when buying and feeding. Buy hay harvested early in the season (May and June); buy first-cutting alfalfa. Destroy affected bales, preferably by burning.

Treatment. • *Time is of the essence.*
> • *Feed activated charcoal* to soak up most material in the digestive system.
> • *Then feed mineral oil* to provide a soothing coating and help flush the poison from the system.

The time lapse before treatment makes the difference whether or not the horse lives. Once the poison is absorbed into his system, there is no hope for survival.

Blister beetles are six-legged, generally a half to three quarters of an inch long, and may be dull gray or three-striped. Check with your county agent for identification of varieties in your area.

Poisonous Plants

Poisonous plants are found throughout the world. Because most of them have an unpleasant taste or texture, horses usually won't eat them unless they are undernourished and starved for green stuff, which can occur in springtime, when these plants appear before the grass greens up. Talk to your county agent to find out what poisonous plants are a hazard in your area. Ask for information on how to identify them, and then check your pastures carefully so that you know what is there.

Some of the most poisonous include water hemlock, Russian thistle, halogeton, locoweeds and vetches, laurel and rhododendron, some gymnosperms (needle-bearing plants with naked seeds, such as juniper and Japanese yew), bracken ferns and horsetails, death camas, arrowgrass, solanaceous plants such as the potato (not the part we eat), tomato, eggplant, nightshade, and tobacco, and under certain conditions, milkweed and sweet clover hay.

Nitrate toxicity (a problem usually found in the northern Plains states) can cause poisoning when drought and reduced light favor the uptake of nitrates by plants. This can also occur in plants sprayed with certain herbicides (such as 2,4-D), most often oat hay, corn, sorghum, and occasionally alfalfa, barley, and wheat. Since only the vegetative tissues contain high levels of nitrate, not the grain, poisoning would not occur unless the horses were turned out in crop fields after the grain is harvested, or fed corn chop as roughage. All cereal grain hays should be tested for high nitrate levels before feeding to livestock. Weeds that have high nitrate levels include pigweed, kochia, and nightshade.

Cyanide toxicity can occur in sorghums, corn, and Johnson grass during drought periods where the soil contains high levels of available nitrogen and low levels of phosphorus (Johnson grass may have high levels of cyanide at any time). Members of the rose family, including apple, cherry, apricot, chokecherry, and peach-tree foliage (especially if wilted), have high concentrations of cyanide. Large quantities of clippings and fruits from these plants should not be available to horses, especially since they are readily eaten. Wild chokecherries are poisonous throughout the plant.

Red maple poisoning can occur when horses eat red maple leaves, especially those that are wilted or dried, or in the fall after the toxin has been building up over the summer. The toxin destroys the red blood cells, causing acute anemia, weakness, depression, and rapid respiration and heart rate. The blood and urine turn brown, while the lining of the eyes and gums are purplish. Until the specific cause of this poisoning is identified, there is no known antidote.

Foxtail, while not toxic, is extremely undesirable for horses. The feathery awns become lodged in the horse's gums, causing ulcer-like sores. If feeding foxtail hay is unavoidable, the horse's mouth should be checked and cleaned daily (run your finger under the lip against the gum, both upper and lower). Cereal grass hays produce the same problem.

Signs of plant poisoning. One or more of these symptoms may occur:

Digestive disorders	Lack of appetite
Unusual bleeding	Unexplained edema (swelling)
Depression	Listlessness

Unexplained changes in pulse, respiration, or temperature
Nervous disorders such as muscle-twitching, shivering,
   incoordination, staggering, or convulsions.

Prevention:
1. Learn to identify the plants in your pasture. Know which ones are poisonous, which could become toxic under certain conditions, and what percentage of the forage they represent.
2. Eradicate poisonous plants by grubbing out, burning, or burying; if using herbicides, get professional help. Or fence your livestock out.
3. Keep your horses well fed with adequate, well-balanced ration—well-fed horses rarely eat poisonous plants.
4. Check your hay for poisonous plants—especially first-cutting bales that have been purchased away from home.
5. Do not bed horses on ferns, straw that contains poisonous weeds, or cereal-grain straw that has not been tested for nitrate levels.

Treatment: Veterinarians can only treat symptoms as they occur: give sedatives to hyperexcited, convulsive horses and intestinal tranquilizers and mineral oil to colicky horses, and maintain water and electrolyte balance artificially for dehydrated horses.
- Keep horses warm.
- Keep them from rolling.
- Identify plant (or hay) poison for your veterinarian.
- *Remove horses immediately from any source of suspected plant poisoning and consult a veterinarian—to delay may result in death.*

Concentrates

Concentrates are grains and supplements having a high concentration of digestible nutrients and a low amount of fiber, compared to roughage. As a horse's energy needs increase due to hard work or other factors, he needs more concentrates in proportion to roughage. In fact, his system cannot handle the amount of roughage that would satisfy these needs.

Oats are accepted by most horsemen to be the best grain for horses, and when it comes to palatability, the horses seem to agree. Oats are the safest concentrate to feed, since the hull provides enough bulk to prevent the digestive problems inherent in some other grains. They may be fed alone or mixed with other grains, and they may be fed whole, crushed, rolled, or crimped. Processing lowers their nutritive value (especially vitamins), but improves digestibility (good for old horses with poor teeth).

Corn, although palatable, high in energy, and low in fiber, is low in protein and minerals. Yellow corn is best because of its vitamin A content. Since corn is high in starch, it can ferment rapidly in some circumstances and can become toxic (check for musty odor). For digestibility, it is better to feed cracked corn (the outside of the kernel is cracked); crushed or ground corn, however, should not be fed, since its rapid fermentation in the digestive tract can cause colic. Corn is a hot feed in the sense that it is high-energy; however, it does not cause a horse to overheat or sweat. Overfeeding can cause weight

This type of bunk feeder is useful for feeding concentrates to range horses. (Courtesy Dave Ellsbury)

gain and digestive upset. Corn and oats fed together make a good grain ration.

Barley can be used as a substitute for oats; however, since it is low in fiber and very compact, it is thought of as a "heavy" feed that can upset the digestive system and easily cause colic. It is best to use rolled, crushed, crimped, or ground barley that has been steamed, mixing it with other, bulkier concentrates, such as 25 percent rolled oats or 15 percent wheat bran. Barley is less palatable than oats and should be introduced gradually into the diet. Boiled barley may be added to a bran mash to help keep a horse in flesh. Since barley is heating, it should not exceed 30 percent of the total grain ration.

Wheat is generally too expensive to feed in whole-kernel form, and it is not safe for inexperienced feeders to use. *Wheat by-products* from the making of flour (wheat middlings) are generally more valuable as an all-purpose grain. They are a good source of niacin and vitamins B_1 and B_2 and are higher in protein than whole wheat. They are, however, fine and powdery, with a tendency to pack and cause digestive disturbances; if used, mix them with coarse, bulky feed. It is easier to get the same nutrients from other grains.

Wheat bran is palatable, highly digestible, laxative (high in bulk), high in phosphorus though low in calcium, heating, and high in vitamin E. It is often used in the rations of broodmares and stallions to help in reproduction. It may be fed dry, usually mixed with oats (one part bran to four to eight parts oats), or as a mash. Quality should be a major consideration; bran should be clean, with large, flat flakes—not too floury. Taste it yourself; it should be sweet and tasty, never musty.

Bran mashes are often fed after strenuous exercise and before a day of rest to help regulate the bowels, and they are good also for sick horses or those with poor teeth. Some vitamin loss is caused by heating. *To make a bran mash:* In a metal or plastic bucket, mix one part bran, a pinch of salt, a handful of linseed meal, and two parts oats. The oats may consist of one part rolled and one part sweet feed—or all rolled oats with a small amount of molasses mixed in. Add boiling water to the consistency of breakfast oatmeal or a dry paste, stir, cover, and allow to steam until all water is absorbed and the mash has cooled somewhat. Feed warm.

Rye and *milo* are not generally recommended grains for horses; if used, they must be fed with care. Rye has a tendency to ferment quickly and when hot can cause diarrhea and other digestive problems. Rye ergot can cause abortion.

Less common concentrates include beans, peas, and rice, dried brewer's grain, dried beet pulp, and citrus pulp. Availability, processing, and price comparison would be factors to consider when using these feeds, and their vitamin, mineral, and protein content should be checked.

High-Protein Concentrates and Other Additives

For horses that are growing, pregnant, or lactating, and for horses doing heavy work or in high-stress situations, the addition of a protein supplement is necessary to balance the ration.

Soybean-oil meal has the highest-quality protein of these supplements and is a good source of phosphorus, with a moderate amount of riboflavin and thiamin. Soybean-oil meal should be clean, light-colored, and fine; mix it thoroughly into the ration.

Linseed-oil meal (made from flaxseed) is high in protein, has a laxative effect, and helps the appearance of the hair coat more than the other oil meals. It also puts weight on a skinny horse. It is less tasty than soybean-oil meal.

Cottonseed-oil meal is second to soybean-oil meal in use as a high-protein concentrate, but it is less palatable than the other oil meals. It is high in phosphorus. Because it also contains a toxic compound, gossypol, large amounts should not be fed.

Sunflower-oil meal, 41 percent protein, can be used as a protein supplement, but it is low in the amino acid lysine and therefore should not be used as the sole additive.

Fish meal, dried skim milk, and *meat* and *bone meals* are excellent sources of protein, but they are not as palatable as soybean-oil meal and are more expensive. Feeds high in phosphorus, such as bone meal, are unpalatable; it's hard to get horses to eat them.

Molasses. Because cane or beet molasses is very palatable to the horse, it is often added to feeds as an appetizer and conditioner. It is low in digestible protein (less than 1 percent), but high in TDN. It is also high in calcium, and it is more easily assimilated than the average source of calcium. Molasses also acts as a laxative and reduces dustiness in the grain ration. It is heatening, however, and should be used with care during hot weather. Too much molasses will decrease digestibility; the addition of not more than 5–10 percent is recommended. Molasses can also be used to mask unappealing flavors—to disguise alkali and sulfur in water, or the taste of worming powders in grain.

Corn oil. Pure corn oil is an excellent source of vitamin A, is high in calories, and contains fatty acids that improve the luster and texture of the coat. It is readily digested, palatable, and aids weight gain. A full ration of corn oil is one cup per day; however, work up to it gradually.

Apple cider vinegar (about one-quarter cup per day on the grain) apparently helps to keep a stalled horse from chewing wood, and also seems to act as an insect repellent.

Commercial vitamin and mineral supplements. Vitamin E in the form of *wheat-germ oil* (often fortified with vitamins A and D) helps the fertility of both mares and stallions, helps to improve endurance, and produces healthier skin and a glossier coat. The dose is one-quarter to one ounce per day, generally added to the grain.

As a rule, only need should determine the amount or kind of extra vitamins and minerals fed to any horse. Supplements should not contain amounts that greatly exceed the minimum daily requirements, or toxic excesses could occur. For the same reason, avoid feeding several different supplements at once: choose one good supplement that fits the needs of your horse.

Electrolytes have recently come into much use—and probably some misuse —due to the heavier physical stress placed on performance horses (such as in endurance riding and racing). Electrolytes are salts dissolved in the body fluids. An imbalance of electrolytes can interfere with the thirst mechanism, and the horse may fail to drink or eat enough to replace his water loss. Many endurance veterinarians feel that training a horse to eat and drink adequately on distance rides is as important as conditioning the body. It may be wise to feed supplementary electrolytes during such activities when heat, stress, and fluid loss seem excessive.

Poisonous Feed Additives

Urea. There continues to be controversy over the effects of urea on horses. Urea (nonprotein nitrogen compounds) is often fed to cattle and sheep in cubes or pellets as a growth stimulant. Too much urea can be toxic even to ruminants. Urea cannot be used efficiently by the horse because of the limited bacterial action in his digestive system.

Although it seems probable that a low level of urea (under 5 percent of the total ration) does not harm mature horses, some problems have been reported with foals and pregnant mares. It would pay the horse owner to be careful and avoid feeding urea to horses until more facts are known. It is possible to feed urea without realizing it if using a prepared grain mix with synthetic sweetener; make sure of the ingredients you are feeding.

Organic iodine. Mineral blocks (salt blocks with added trace minerals) usually contain iodine in either organic or inorganic form. There is some question about the effects of organic iodine (ethylenediamine dihydroiodide) on horses. Again, until more is known, it may be wise to check ingredients of mineral blocks and supplements, feeding your horses only inorganic iodine.

Monensin sodium (one brand name is Rumensin), a feed additive that stimulates growth and improves feed efficiency in cattle, is a drug that can be dangerous or lethal to horses. It is not readily detected in feed. Symptoms of poisoning are loss of appetite, rolling due to acute abdominal pain, diarrhea, nervous disorders such as stumbling and spastic movements, paralysis, and death. Young horses seem particularly susceptible; however, in winter, when horses are especially hungry and need more feed for maintenance, all horses are equally susceptible. Damage does not result from a buildup of the additive, but the damage of repeated doses will accumulate. Immediate identification is essential to prevent the death of many horses.

Ranchers running both cattle and horses and feeding them together should be especially careful not to feed horses anything that states "for ruminant use only." Accidental poisoning can result from feed companies manufacturing both cattle and horse pelleted feed without careful monitoring of equipment and containers used.

Commercial Mixed Feeds (Formula Feeds)

The use of commercial mixed feeds has increased steadily, since they are convenient to feed, especially for the small breeder and owner of few horses. Many grain companies have a variety of mixtures; choose the mix that best fits your horse's needs.

NET WT. 80 LBS.

A & C FEED COMPANY, INC.
Cheyenne, Wyoming 82001

ROLL MIX

GUARANTEED ANALYSIS

Crude protein not less than . . . 10.0%
Crude fat not less than 2.0%
Crude fiber not more than. . . . 5.0%

INGREDIENTS

Rolled corn, rolled oats, rolled milo, rolled barley, cane molasses.

DIRECTIONS

To be fed as grain portion of ration (with hay or pasture) for horses, cattle, and sheep.

NET 50 LBS.

STEEN'S FEEDS

S.A.N. – 20%
All Natural Protein

GUARANTEED ANALYSIS

Protein (min.) 20%
Fat (min.) 1%
Fiber (max.) 3.5%
Vitamin A (min.) . . . 20,000 U.S.P./lb.

INGREDIENTS

Wheat, Molasses, Soy, Vitamin A Acetate.

Manufactured by
STEEN'S FEEDS
Belle Fourche, S.D.

Sample tags taken from feed sacks, both showing a closed formula. On the left, a popular mixed grain; on the right, a 20 percent cake. (Courtesy A & C Feed Company and Steen's Feeds)

Manufactured commercial feeds must conform to the guarantee of chemical composition and ingredients. If the fiber content is over 12 percent, the feed probably contains a considerable amount of low-grade ingredients. The reputation of the company is an important factor when purchasing commercial feed mixtures. Whether to mix the feed yourself or to buy a commercial mix (assuming equal quality), depends upon the cost, including your labor, and the keeping qualities.

Closed-formula feeds. The ingredients are stated on the feed tag, but not the specific amount of each ingredient. However, the minimum percentage of protein and fat, and the maximum percentage of fiber are stated, along with maximum or minimum for other ingredients, such as vitamin A. Feeding directions are usually included on the tag.

Open-formula feeds. The number of pounds of each ingredient is listed (usually in a ton of this mixture). This method is used chiefly in co-ops and grain mills and is an advantage to the horseman in that he can compare the cost of the formula with making it at home. TDN is also stated.

Cake. Some formula feeds are pelleted. These are grain-concentrate pellets or cubes—often called cake—which should not be confused with the pelleted hay or "complete feed" pellets mentioned earlier under *Pellets vs. long-stem hay.* Cake has several advantages over loose grains. It is easy to handle and suits mechanized or automated handling. Since dust is eliminated, it can be more palatable and avoids dust-related respiratory problems. It is easy to store and takes less space. Cake is convenient to feed, since it can be spread on the ground, on packed snow, or in a strong wind, with little or no loss.

Cake can be purchased with varying amounts of protein (14 percent and 20 percent are common). A good cake for winter supplement for horses on range or pasture has a high vitamin A content.

FEEDING PRACTICES

Commonsense Feeding Habits

1. Treat each horse as an individual. Know his weight, age, temperament, peculiarities, and special requirements. Observe his feeding habits and notice changes that may indicate illness or other problems (or make sure that your employees can do this if they are doing the feeding). Observation and good judgment are the keys to good feeding; calculation alone will not ensure success.

2. For more efficient digestion and use of feed, give small amounts often, rather than one or two large feedings each day. Since horses are night grazers, the last feeding can be given late in the evening and be a larger meal.

3. Regularity of feeding time is important, since it builds stress if a horse must wait for his feed. Horses have built-in time clocks and expect to be fed at regular hours.

4. All feed should be of sound quality, whether hays, grains, or pasture. Avoid any feed that is dusty, moldy, or frozen. Smaller quantities of good feed nourish a horse better than larger amounts of poor feed.

5. Avoid sudden changes in feeds or rations. Because it takes ten days to two weeks for the bacteria in the large intestine to adapt to and properly digest some new feeds, any changes should be made gradually over that length of time to prevent colic and diarrhea. This is especially important when changing from grass hay to alfalfa.

6. In the daily ration, use a variety of feeds that are palatable, practical, economical, and adapted to your horse's individual needs. Select roughage first—the best-quality hay or pasture you can get—and build the grain/supplement ration around it to compensate for any deficiencies in the roughage.

7. A lack or an extreme excess of any vitamin or mineral may be more harmful than a scanty supply of feed. Be especially aware, when feeding young stock, of the calcium-phosphorus ratio and potential deficiencies, which could greatly affect normal development.

8. Feed grain and hay by weight, rather than by volume. Use scales to determine representative weights; a coffee can full of cake may weigh three times as much as that same can full of rolled plain oats.

9. For each horse, adjust amounts and kinds of feed and supplements to one or more of the following:
   a. climate, season, weather, and area of the country (soil deficiencies, elevation, native flora);
   b. temperament (flighty, spirited, etc.), health, and condition;
   c. work or stress;
   d. age;
   e. conformation (a tall, long horse requires more feed than a shorter, more compact horse);
   f. reproduction and lactation;
   g. pollutants in air or water.

10. Integrate feeding and work schedules. Light or moderate work at least an hour after eating aids in the digestion and absorption of nutrients. Strenuous exercise on a full stomach, or feeding grain to a hot, tired horse, can cause colic. Horses at hard work should have their grain cut back by half or more on rest days, to avoid an attack of azoturia.

11. Provide plenty of salt and clean water. Use iodized or trace-mineralized salt in areas where deficiencies exist. Adequate water in winter is critical; snow is not enough, as the horse must use precious energy and body heat to convert the cold snow to liquid.

12. Worm your horses regularly and check periodically to see that their teeth are sound. Check feces for consistency, odor, and color as indica-

tors of how well the horse is digesting his food; take a regular fecal exam for parasite control.

13. When feeding horses in a group, space portions widely and make more portions than there are horses. This enables the timid horse to get his share. It is sometimes necessary to separate the very timid horses—or the aggressive animals—and feed them separately. If there are many horses to be fed, separate them into like groups based on age, condition, and use.

14. Keep clean feed tubs, hay racks, and water buckets. Disinfect on a regular schedule, more often if there is a disease problem. Clean up uneaten grain, as it can ferment and cause colic; hay left on the ground or in tubs can collect parasites or become moldy or dusty. Check low mangers often, to clean out manure.

15. Keep your pastures in good condition to provide adequate nutrition.

A Base Ration

Let us suppose we have a mature, average-weight gelding of eleven hundred pounds, who at the present time is doing nothing at all but soaking up some autumn sun in his corral. He is at home, completely content, healthy, and in good—not fat—condition. He will serve as our "control" horse, needing a maintenance ration—one that will keep him in his present state of flesh —but requires no extras for energy, reproduction, growth, or any other reason. How much should he be fed?

One rule of thumb is to feed about 1.2–1.5 percent of his weight daily: 1.2 percent of eleven hundred pounds equals a bit over thirteen pounds of feed; 1.5 percent equals sixteen and a half pounds. So long as this feed (probably mostly hay combined with some grain) contains sufficient protein, vitamins, and minerals, and so long as he has adequate water and salt, he'll probably do just fine, neither gaining nor losing weight. Careful observation will tell you whether *this individual* needs a bit more or less for maintenance. (If this horse were on good pasture, he would probably need nothing extra beyond salt and water.)

If our hypothetical gelding is to work, of course, he'll need more food for energy—or if he's thin, he'll need more to build condition. Table A, in the Appendix, under "How to Balance a Ration," indicates approximate nutritional needs as work increases, for growing horses and for reproduction and lactation.

Because the many variables work in conjunction with each other to alter requirements, any recommendation can only be approximate. A horse at medium work, for instance, will need more to eat in below-zero weather than he will on a hot summer day. While an average recommended level is given, it is up to you to use common sense in considering your individual horse's needs, whether to choose the average figure or something higher or lower.

Here's another rule of thumb that may be useful, one used by the U.S. Cavalry for horses getting plenty of exercise and being ridden daily: feed 1 pound of grain and 1.1 pounds of hay for each 100 pounds of body weight. At this rate, our 1,100-pound gelding (he's working now) would get 11 pounds of grain and just over 12 pounds of hay, for a total of 23 pounds of feed daily.

Let's translate that into a simplified feed ration for pleasure horses. The following table shows pounds of feed daily per 100 pounds of weight of the horse (the figure in parentheses gives the approximate pounds of feed for our 1,100-pound gelding):

	ridden 1 to 3 hours daily	ridden 3 to 5 hours daily	racing or ridden over 5 hours daily
HAY	1¼–1½ (15 lbs.)	1–1¼ (13 lbs.)	1–1¼ (12 lbs.)
GRAIN	²/₅–½ (5 lbs.)	¾–1 (10 lbs.)	1¼–1⅓ (14 lbs.)
TOTAL POUNDS FED	(20 lbs.)	(23 lbs.)	(26 lbs.)

With this ration, grass hay would be acceptable, with the grain all oats, or a mix of 70 percent oats with 30 percent corn or barley. Provide plenty of clean water and a good salt or trace mineral supplement free-choice.

Heavy Work and Stress Situations

Heavy work and stress present situations beyond the normal. Because of current interest in endurance riding, racing, and intense show or rodeo performance, more people will encounter and need to understand these special feeding problems.

Giving greatly increased protein to hard-working animals does not help—in fact, it may decrease their endurance and have unwanted side effects. Of more benefit is a high-fat diet. Fat appears to help prevent dehydration and lowers the rate of some mineral losses during heavy exercise; it also provides "staying power," since it is not digested as quickly as protein or carbohydrates.

Events requiring quick bursts of energy may be best prepared for by feeding heavier grain diets, while endurance events may be best prepared for by feeding comparatively less grain and more fat. Feeding high levels of vitamins A and D may result in toxicities; the effects of high levels of other vitamins are little known.

Forcing rapid growth in young horses—mainly those destined for show or racing competition—through energy-rich diets is a questionable practice leading to tissue stress and unsound feet and legs (carrying too much condition before the bone structure is ready). The horseman should be more concerned with density and strength of bone, straightness and soundness of limbs, good muscling, and overall physical fitness.

When stress involves something other than heavy work, these different conditions call for a different approach to the diet. Whenever you move animals, for instance, some psychological stress is involved. Some horses bolt their feed due to nervousness; others may not drink adequately.

When trailering horses to a new environment, we send along two or three bales of hay for each horse so that it can be mixed gradually with hay at their new home. Upon arrival, use a light grain ration (one pound morning, one pound evening) for the first two days, gradually increasing after that until the ration is normal. At shows and while traveling, we cut green grass and give a few mouthfuls several times during the day. This stimulates appetite, and gives a feeling of well-being. Avoid grass that may have been sprayed with chemicals. For more suggestions on traveling, see Chapter 9.

Considerations in Feeding for Age

The suckling foal. How fast should a foal grow? Although in some cases it may be economically important to get young foals to maturity as soon as reasonably possible, to work a large, fast-growing animal before he is ready will make him likely to break down. In any case, the diet must be carefully balanced. A ration that is high in energy, protein, and vitamins would produce rapid growth—but if it is deficient in minerals, the foal would have weak bones. Naturally, proper exercise and shelter are as important as diet to make a young horse healthy. As a rule, supplemental feed for the foal is essential for good growth.

When foals are born, they are extremely susceptible to infection and disease. The mare's first milk, or colostrum, provides the immunity they need, and they should nurse within an hour or two. The yellowish, carotene-rich colostrum is produced for only about thirty-six hours after birth—a pint or two seems adequate to get the foal started. There is no cross-immunity between species; that is, cow colostrum will not serve for prevention of illness in foals. Colostrum also has a laxative quality and helps the foal produce meconium—the pitch-like substance that is his first manure.

For cases in which mares fail to give milk, die upon foaling, have twins, or lose much of their colostrum before foaling, it is wise to have some frozen colostrum on hand (keep and freeze some from a healthy mare, taken within six hours of foaling). Frozen colostrum should thaw at room temperature; heating will denature the protein, and its efficacy to immunize will be lost. Freezing in small quantities—several ice-cube trays will work well—allows quicker thawing. For more on feeding the orphan foal, see the chapter on foaling.

Because mare's milk is deficient in iron and copper, foals should have high-quality grain and roughage from the age of seven to ten days. Their grain ration should be highly digestible, low-fiber, and nutritious. Since the foal is unfamiliar with feed, at a week old start placing some grain into his mouth several times a day—rolled oats mixed with a bit of sweet feed can be used.

Many foals develop a sweet tooth (difficult to overcome), so use more rolled plain oats and just a bit of sweet feed.

The foal kept with his mother in a corral should have a container for feed next to and lower than hers. If fed in a stall, a stout board can be placed across one corner, giving the foal access but keeping the mare out—a sort of creep feeder. If you plan to use a creep in a pasture, put it near a watering place, in the shade, or any other place the mares would congregate to rest. The creep-fed grain ration should contain high levels of protein, calcium, and phosphorus, and may consist of 41 percent cracked corn, 30 percent rolled oats, 23 percent soybean meal, 3 percent molasses, 1 percent dicalcium phosphate, 1 percent limestone (source of calcium), and 1 percent trace-mineralized salt (other possible rations are shown in Table 1). High-quality hay or alfalfa can be fed free-choice.

There are pros and cons to using a creep feeder. It may be advisable if the mare does not have enough milk, if the foal is weaker than normal due to a hard birth or illness such as pneumonia, or if the mare is aggressive toward the foal and hogs the feed. On the other hand, if the foal is growing nicely and exercise is limited, extra feed can produce too much fat and growth for the skeletal system. Also, in later life, horses that were creep-fed tend to be fence crawlers, having no respect for either wire or wooden fences.

Foals should have grain with supplements, however, in some way. Since milk production in the mare peaks fairly early, the foal needs the extra nutrients in grain and good forage to supplement the downward trend of the mare's milk production. Due to this fact, many breeders now wean their foals at four to five months instead of six months, especially if the mare has been rebred (and it costs less as well as being more efficient to feed the foal directly than to feed the mare to produce milk to feed the foal, in many cases). The potential to grow is present early in life and must be capitalized on or lost. Good nutrition helps the horse approach his potential.

Weanlings. One of the most stressful times in a horse's life is weaning time. If a foal is used to eating grain, he will do better at weaning. Be sure the young horse has good-quality water, forage, and free-choice, trace-mineralized salt.

The weaned foal should be fed 1½ to 2 pounds per 100 pounds of body weight per day of a good grain ration; the same rations are recommended prior to weaning. The weanling should also be eating at least 1½ pounds per 100 pounds of body weight per day of roughage. Alfalfa is excellent.

Yearlings and two-year-olds. As a yearling, the horse's growth rate has slowed considerably. This will decrease his energy requirements per pound of body weight from that needed during the faster growth period. Therefore decrease the amount of grain fed to the yearling to ½–1 pound per 100 pounds of body weight per day until he reaches 90 percent of his mature weight—then feed for work or maintenance.

Feeding our senior citizens. A horse may be considered old from the time he

Table 1. FEEDING GUIDELINES FOR GROWING HORSES

AGE (projected mature weights of 900 – 1,400 pounds)	DAILY RATION ALLOWANCE per 100 lbs. body weight HAY (lbs.)	DAILY RATION ALLOWANCE per 100 lbs. body weight GRAIN (lbs.)	TYPES OF HAY	POSSIBLE GRAIN MIXTURES Example 1 %	POSSIBLE GRAIN MIXTURES Example 2 %	POSSIBLE GRAIN MIXTURES Example 3 %
SUCKLING FOALS* 100 – 350 lbs	½ – ¾	½ – ¾	alfalfa	oats 50 / wht bran 40 / soy meal 10	oats 30 / barley 30 / wht bran 30 / soy meal 10	oats 80 / wht bran 20
WEANLINGS 350 – 450 lbs.	1½ – 2	1 – 1½	alfalfa or good-quality alfalfa/grass mix	oats 30 / barley 30 / wht bran 30 / soy meal 10	oats 70 / wht bran 15 / soy meal 15	oats 80 / soy meal 20
YEARLINGS second summer 450 – 700 lbs.	1¼ – 1¾	¾ – 1¼	good-quality alfalfa/grass mix	same as above		
				or GOOD PASTURE with no extra grain		
YEARLINGS or coming two-year-olds during second winter 700 – 1,000 lbs.	1 – 1½	½ – 1	alfalfa/grass mix or ⅓ – ½ alfalfa with balance grass	oats 80 / wht bran 20	oats 35 / barley 35 / wht bran 15 / soy meal 15	oats 100

800   42
1,200   49

ALWAYS PROVIDE PLENTY OF CLEAN WATER AND A GOOD SALT OR SALT/MINERAL SUPPLEMENT FREE-CHOICE.

*Based on the assumption that mares of mature weights 1,000 may produce 44 pounds of milk daily.

Adapted from extension workshop material by J. W. Waggoner, Animal Science Department, University of Wyoming.

is sixteen, but if he is cared for conscientiously, he will probably lead a good, active, and productive life for ten years more. (We will deal only with diet here; see Chapter 8 for more on caring for the older horse.) Long-standing problems, such as those caused by strongyles, may accumulate or become accentuated in the older horse. Thus it is important to take extra precautions to maintain a healthy digestive tract by feeding and watering carefully. Feed smaller portions more frequently (three times a day or more), and give grain and water only when the horse is cool. Feed a bran mash once a week (more frequently when indicated). Alfalfa hay is excellent for older horses, because a slightly laxative state is desirable. Since a horse's teeth have a great influence on correct chewing and digesting, older horses should have their teeth checked and floated yearly.

The feed most beneficial to an elderly horse depends on the condition of his teeth. Preground hay of good quality, plus rolled oats and cracked corn, might be necessary if the teeth are in poor condition. An old horse needs more high-energy food as the aging process becomes obvious. Moderate exercise is very beneficial. Increase the allowance of calcium to about 0.45 percent and phosphorus to about 0.4 percent. Actually, the basic supplement for old horses is about the same as for the growing foal. The elderly horse should be carefully checked for weight loss or obesity.

Quality green grass is wonderful for older horses; it seems to prime their appetite, is easy for them to chew and digest, and does more for their general condition than anything else you can feed. A corralled or stalled older horse should have some grazing each day—if not on pasture, then hand-held for one half to three quarters of an hour daily. The elderly horse needs more attention and less competition for food when in a group, so you may have to reshuffle pasture assignments.

Feeding for Reproduction

Preparing the mare for breeding is very important. Although she should be in good body condition and putting on weight at the beginning of the breeding season to help the conception rate, overly fat mares do not conceive readily. Protein is important; too low a level can keep a mare from estrus and cause fetal death (though too high a level apparently neither helps nor harms). The addition of vitamin E in the form of wheat-germ oil in the grain ration does seem to help conception. Both stallions and mares should have it.

Because the fetus is very small during the first two thirds of the gestation period, the nutrient requirements of the mare are not greatly increased. However, during the last third, the fetus rapidly increases in size and nutrient requirements. More concentrated feeds and grains need to be added to the mare's ration, and she should have a smaller quantity of bulky feeds (Table 2). It is usually recommended that mares be self-fed minerals regardless of the

Table 2. FEEDING FOR REPRODUCTION

STALLIONS OR MARES 900 – 1,400 pounds	DAILY RATION ALLOWANCE per 100 lbs. of body weight HAY (lbs.)	GRAIN (lbs.)	TYPE OF HAY	POSSIBLE GRAIN MIXTURES Example 1 %	Example 2 %	Example 3 %
STALLIONS during breeding season	¾ – 1½	¾ – 1½	grass/alfalfa mix or ⅓ – ½ alfalfa with balance grass	oats 55 wheat 20 wht bran 20 soy meal 5	oats 35 corn 35 wheat 15 wht bran 15	oats 100
PREGNANT MARES first two-thirds of pregnancy	¾ – 1½	¾ – 1½	grass hay or grass/alfalfa mix	oats 80 wht bran 20	oats 45 barley 45 wht bran 10	oats 95 soy meal 5
PREGNANT MARES last third of pregnancy	¾ – 1½	¾ – 1½	grass/alfalfa mix or all alfalfa or ½ – ¾ alfalfa with balance grass	with legume hay oats 45 corn 42 wht bran 10 molasses 3	if only grass hay is available oats 42 corn 34 soy meal 10 wht bran 10 molasses 3 limestone 1	
LACTATING MARES peak of lactation	1 – 1¼	1 – 1½ based on level of production	all alfalfa or ¾ alfalfa with balance grass hay or good pasture	PLAIN ROLLED OATS for two–three days after foaling; gradually add other grains as above. Cut back or omit bran and oil meals if foal tends to scour.		

ALWAYS PROVIDE PLENTY OF CLEAN WATER AND A GOOD SALT OR SALT/MINERAL SUPPLEMENT FREE-CHOICE.

Adapted from extension workshop material by J. W. Waggoner, Animal Science Department, University of Wyoming.

level in the ration. Her water needs will increase 10 percent or more during the last trimester.

The mare should come to foaling in good condition, neither too fat nor too thin. Just before foaling (three to four days), we put our mares on a light grain diet: rolled plain oats, bran, and the usual vitamin-mineral supplement. After foaling, we keep the same diet (without the bran) for two to three days, and gradually add other grains. Although a laxative effect of the feed is good before foaling, it could cause the foal to scour; hence bran is eliminated from the mare's diet after foaling. Also, because some mares have very rich milk that tends to scour the foals, the mare's ration should be cut down for a few days. Leave out oil meals as well, as they are laxative. Do not give newborn foals whole eggs to treat scours, as this has been found to negate the effect of the colostrum.

The lactating mare needs greatly increased nutrients. The high-producing mare may need as much as 1–1½ pounds of grain for every 100 pounds of body weight. Observation is the best guide; if she is too thin, increase the ration—and vice versa.

After weaning the foal, the mare should be dried up. We keep the weanling foals in a large corral together and turn the mares out to pasture without grain after gradually cutting down their ration for four to five days before weaning. By late summer or early fall, the pastures have dried up to some extent, and it helps the mare to dry off quickly—and the extra exercise is extremely beneficial.

Feeding the breeding stallion. Most information on breeding stallions seems to indicate that their nutritional needs do not differ greatly from the requirements of maintenance except during breeding season, when protein and mineral requirements increase. The grain ration can be the same as for a mare in early pregnancy. Vitamin E in the form of wheat-germ oil should be added, and of course all his mineral-vitamin needs should be met. Holding the lead-rope in our hands, we let our stallions graze each day for one half to three quarters of an hour on good green grass. Green grass helps coat and condition, and gives a feeling of well-being.

When pasture-breeding a band of mares, the stallion should be fed daily with enough grain and supplements to maintain good condition. In breeding season, most stallions lose some weight no matter how they are fed; therefore they should go into the breeding season in good—not fat—condition. Obesity reduces fertility.

Hobbling, Picketing, and Hand-Held Grazing

In order for some horses to receive green grass, it may be necessary to hobble, picket, or hand-hold them. A suitable fenced pasture is of course better, but in some cases this is not possible. Both a stable mental state and good training are necessary for the horse picketed and left on his own at the side of the road—and even then it may be dangerous. While hand-holding the horse is time-consuming, it is safer and gives the handler time to establish rapport with his horse.

Feeding for Weather and Climate

Weather can determine the types of food fed and stored. Hot, humid weather tends to make some concentrates rancid, especially corn with molasses. Very cold climates tend to freeze and harden mixed concentrates. Roughage must be protected from rain and wet snow in some areas, hot sun and high winds in others. Learn what feeds store well and how to store them best in your climate.

Horses living in hot, dry areas will drink more, urinate more, and thus need more salt and mineral-vitamin supplement. Oats are referred to as a "cool" feed (producing less heat than some other sources), thus would be good for horses in a hot climate.

In cold weather, a horse's energy requirements increase 15–20 percent for every 10-degree-F drop in temperature below his "critical temperature" (around 30 degrees at the beginning of the season, then perhaps down to 15 degrees or so after the horse adapts to winter). Horses acclimate to cold temperature without difficulty, however, if they have enough to eat. Because "hot feeds" such as corn, barley, molasses, and roughage (which is digested by fiber fermentation in the cecum) produce heat or energy, they are good cold-weather feeds. A horse provided with ample hay in cold weather will eat over the greater part of twenty-four hours, thus providing continual fermentation. Body fat provides both insulation against the cold, thus conserving body heat, and a reserve of energy that can be drawn on during periods of food deprivation.

Water is as necessary in cold weather as in hot; horses that do not drink adequate water during winter feeding will usually not consume adequate amounts of solid feed, and therefore have difficulty maintaining weight. If a horse drinks large quantities of cold water at one time (or eats a lot of snow), he can become chilled; an ideal water temperature is 45–65 degrees F—warming the water will avert digestive upsets and keep horses in better condition.

To help the shedding process in the spring, feed two to four ounces of corn oil daily; this will result in a shiny, beautiful coat.

Treats for Horses

Horsemen may feed treats to their horses as an appetizer, as a source of nutrients and conditioner, as a reward, or as a means of dieting. Treats include vegetables or fruits such as carrots and apples, sugar, honey, cake, and molasses. A horse may become a finicky eater due to stress and nervousness, an unpalatable and monotonous ration, nutritional deficiencies, poor health, or lack of exercise. In feeding the finicky eater, adding a treat will perk up his appetite and help him eat his usual ration. Unlimited treats, however, would defeat the purpose, as well as being financially unfeasible. Horse cake may be used for treats as well as for feed.

In training horses, rewards are important, and the food treat is one kind of reward. It is often more effective than other rewards, and may help the trainer gain the horse's confidence. Overuse of hand-given treats, however, may result in greedy, pushy, and nippy horses, especially stallions. Treats should be given with common sense.

Feeding the Fat Horse

You can still sometimes hear the old saying "Fat is the best color." This means, of course, that fat covers a multitude of conformation faults and therefore *looks* good—especially to the less discerning horseman. And it is generally true that the fatter animal sells better and shows better in halter classes. Unfortunately, he is usually not as healthy as a more moderately fleshed animal.

Obesity leads to lethargy, laziness, colic, founder, and poor breeding performance. The fat older horse can produce long, stalk-like fat accumulations that can wrap around his intestines, killing him. Fat is also hard on young horses, since excessive weight places stress on growing bones, leading to unsoundnesses and abnormalities. Fat does have good insulating properties, however, and many horsemen like to see their pasture horses a bit heavy (but not roly-poly) going into winter, especially in rugged climates and high altitudes.

Easy keepers may become fat on lush pasture and need to be corralled for part of the day. Horses with a close-coupled conformation tend to fatten quickly on less feed, as will the quiet, lazy horse.

How do you know when your horse is too fat? His neck thickens or becomes "cresty," his ribs don't show and they are hard to feel, patchy lumps appear around the tailhead, there is a well-defined crease over his spine, and his withers start to disappear.

A horse gets fat when he is fed more than he needs. Most likely he should have more exercise to burn off the excess calories, but if this is not possible, his diet should be restricted. It is important to maintain an adequate vitamin and mineral level while cutting down his total intake. It would be wise to balance a ration for him, see how your present ration measures up, and then cut down enough so that he loses weight. Be sure to make changes gradually —not all at once.

If you love your horse, feed him with common sense, and balance your feeding program with adequate exercise.

CHAPTER 6

EXERCISE, REST, AND STRESS

Exercise and Conditioning

Exercise is necessary for a horse's mental and physical well-being; it should never be neglected.

How much exercise does a horse need? Factors to consider in answering this question include where he is kept, how much he is restricted, how much daily work (and the kind of work) he has, whether he is a breeding animal (the pregnant mare and breeding stallion have unique needs), the weather, and the altitude where he lives, especially if he is moved from low to high or vice versa.

If your horse is stalled or restricted in a small pen or corral, his daily exercise should consist of an hour or more of formalized work such as riding, longeing, driving, or ponying, along with time to relax in a large paddock or small pasture where he can run, play, and roll—at least an hour. The breeding horse needs exercise, not only for muscle tone, but also for general well-being.

Neglect in daily exercise may result in balky, barn-sour behavior, or in overexuberant antics when the horse does have the opportunity to get out. Often, the weekend rider wonders why his horse is difficult to handle: won't stand still while being groomed, may be nippy and fidgety, or bucks, shies, and kicks while being ridden. Most such vices are the result of neglect in exercise.

Feed and exercise are closely related, especially for the highly fitted show horse and the heavily worked horse. On the days of heavy work, the horse should receive adequate concentrates, but on nonwork days, grains should be restricted and in some cases omitted (when stress is involved). Failure to limit the grains when the horse is at leisure may result in azoturia when he returns to work.

Kind of exercise is important as well. A foal that is allowed to romp in a pasture with his dam will have stronger legs and muscles, better balance, sounder feet, and better mental vigor than one restricted to a small area. The yearling and the two-year-old will do better in pasture among those of his own age or gentle older horses. Care must be taken that the young horse obtains his share of feed, however, when fed with older horses. Although yearlings and two-year-olds should not be longed at a fast trot or canter, for

Foals build strength, wind, and vigor, along with mental stability and well-being, as they romp in a pasture.

fear of possible injury to stifles and hocks, the rudiments of longeing may be taught. Ponying is a good method of exercising the young horse if free pasture is not continuously available.

Any breeding animal that has not been saddle trained will benefit from longeing if free exercise is not available (or if the animal is lazy and doesn't take advantage of available exercise). We longe the mare after breeding to settle her down and prevent her from immediately urinating. We also longe the stallion and let him graze (hand-held) on green grass after breeding; this exerts a calming influence and contributes to his well-being.

The riding horse should be ridden, longed, or driven daily when severely restricted to a stall. Formal ring work is more tiring to a horse mentally and physically than trail riding. Both should be practiced. A good routine is to begin the exercise period with formal ring work and then, as a reward, to go trail riding; or alternate the programs daily. A three-part daily exercise program, incorporating ground work, ring routine, and trail riding, will keep a horse learning, interested, and relaxed and go a long way toward producing a pleasurable mount.

Range-raised horses, especially when in a group, exercise almost constantly in the process of finding food. This constant nomadic wandering in a large

Longeing can be a useful alternative to formal riding or free exercise.

area provides enough exercise for most horses, and the freedom of movement keeps them healthy in mind and body—not necessarily conditioned, but certainly kept in acceptable muscle tone.

When it is time to begin training, the young horse that has been pastured is more used to exercise and usually has a better mental attitude than the stall-kept horse. Generally he will also be less fearful of cars, dogs, bushes, water, wind-blown papers, and the like. Horses that have been pastured in the vicinity of trains, motorcycles, traffic, and other frightening objects are steadier and less inclined to shy when out on their first trail rides.

Conditioning your horse can be referred to as "muscling him up"—helping him become strong in wind and muscle and able to withstand the physical stress required for the job presented to him. This process requires formalized exercise, such as riding uphill at walk and trot, with short bursts of speed. His mental attitude toward exercise will improve as exercise is gradually increased; he will become more alert, eager, and ready to please. Physically, the well-conditioned horse will exhibit endurance, stamina, a good state of flesh, and resistance to disease.

Most experts agree that a minimum of two hours exercise is necessary to maintain condition. The kind and amount of exercise depends upon the work the horse is required to perform. Conditioning should always be regular and gradual and within the limits of the horse's strength.

Peak condition can rarely be maintained. It is better to keep your horse in fit condition so that in a relatively short amount of time, carefully scheduled work will bring him to peak condition for competition or endurance riding.

Rest and Sleep

Sleep relaxes the muscles, decreases the pulse and breathing rates, slows down digestion, lowers body temperature—in effect, slows the horse down. This period of revitalization later helps him to operate at top efficiency.

The horse sleeps very little compared to man, perhaps two and a half to three hours a day. Stabled horses sleep more than pastured horses, and foals sleep longer than mature horses. Horses sleep more in hot weather than in cold, both because it takes longer to find adequate food in the winter when on pasture, and because hot weather induces drowsiness.

Horses can sleep standing up, and in the wild this was the safest way to do it. Getting up and down is awkward for the horse, and he spends little time sleeping "flat out," for safety reasons. He locks his joints (knees and hocks), and muscle tension enables him to sleep in an upright position. He cannot, however, experience the REM (rapid eye movement) phase of sleep while standing up (a deep sleep characterized by total relaxation and almost complete loss of muscle tone). REM sleep is important; if not allowed to obtain it, the horse becomes irritable and eventually neurotic and psychotic. Since box stalls enable a horse to lie down, they are better than tie stalls, which restrict him from this kind of sleep.

Diet, handling, and confinement affect sleep patterns. For instance, a horse fed a steady diet of oats sleeps more than one on hay alone; and he sleeps more if fed nothing for a couple of days. Changes in feeding habits have a relationship to length of sleep periods.

Stress

Stress is defined as any state or condition that places an unusual burden on an organism: it can be painful, infectious, a harmful force, or any abnormal state that disturbs the body's normal physiological equilibrium. Stress is evident in horses during long, arduous trailering, at races and shows, in extreme temperatures or altitudes (especially when maximum performance is required), and when experiencing fear (from fire, noise, or cruel or abusive handling) or anger (for instance, a horse forced to cohabit with a horse he dislikes, such as two stallions in adjacent stalls).

Stress causes changes in the body's operation, increasing the heart and respiratory rates, increasing the blood-sugar level (providing the body with more energy) and inducing a buildup of lactic acid (causing muscle stiffness). These (and other) changes may lead to stroke or other serious problems requiring immediate veterinary attention.

How can we minimize stress? The horse should be kept free of parasites and on a high level of nutrition. Every horse needs adequate rest to revitalize his system; if possible, extra rest should be provided during stressful situations.

When trailering, initial training to eliminate fear, proper support bandaging to minimize injury, and good bedding to decrease road vibration will all help reduce stress. Exposure to weather, noise, and drafts—whether in trailer or stable—should be minimized. Make sure that the trailered horse has the opportunity to urinate and that he is drinking an adequate amount of water.

When a horse sweats, he loses water and mineral salts—electrolytes may need replacing in order to maintain the chemistry of his blood. A horse must be acclimatized over a period of time to extreme climates and altitudes; avoid excessive exercise under adverse temperatures or extreme changes of altitude.

Because the show and race circuits are very unnatural ways for horses to live, adequate rest is especially important, along with care that feeding is commensurate with exercise. Make sure your horse is happy with his stablemates and in his environment. A relaxed horse is a happy horse; a horse in continual stress or under constant mental and physical duress will become physically and mentally ill.

In cases of physical injury and bacterial infection, call your veterinarian promptly. Follow his directions, and keep your horse rested, isolated when illness warrants, warm, fed properly, and generally treated with tender loving care.

CHAPTER 7

HOOF CARE AND FARRIERY

THE FOOT

Nature has designed a unique and ingenious foot for the horse. To give our horses the best possible foot care, it helps to know something about the foot's structure and function. We use the term "foot" to refer to the foot and all its internal structures, and "hoof" to refer only to the horny covering of the foot, including the wall, sole, and frog, which have no blood supply.

The hoof is a highly specialized horny shell that covers the sensitive structures: bones, nerves, tissues, and blood vessels. The front hoofs are more rounded than the hind hoofs (which are oval), in order to carry the extra weight of the forehand (usually 60–65 percent of the weight of the horse). As the horse moves, most of his weight is first received by the frogs—wedge-shaped, elastic cushions—which spread and move the bars outward; this in turn forces the heels and the back parts of the quarters outward. The frog transmits the jar upward to the plantar cushion, which spreads and forces the lateral cartilages outward. Thus the frog and the plantar cushion receive the major portion of the concussion, while the wall and bars receive the weight. This continued expansion and contraction as the horse moves acts as a pump, increasing blood circulation and favoring hoof growth as exercise increases.

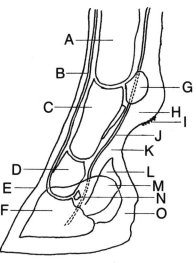

YOUR HORSE'S FOOT
A. Cannon bone. B. Extensor tendon. C. Long pastern. D. Short pastern. E. Perioplic ring (corium). F. Coffin bone. G. Sesamoid bone. H. Fetlock joint. I. Ergot. J. Tendon of digital flexor. K. Pastern joint. L. Plantar cushion. M. Lateral cartilages. N. Navicular bone. O. Bulb.

Lack of exercise, dryness of wall, and poor nutrition hinder hoof growth. The hoof grows continually (three to four inches a year), to compensate for the wear and tear of abrasion.

Another unique function of the hoof is its ability to adjust to climatic conditions. During very wet weather, when the ground is soft, the hoof also becomes soft; conversely, when very dry, the hoof becomes dry and tougher, to reduce wear. Moisture—derived internally from the blood supply and externally from moist soil—is contained in a network of tubules cemented together in the horn. The natural hardness of the horn and periople of the wall tends to prevent the evaporation of moisture. Application of hoof dressing when necessary also helps to retain moisture. A recipe for homemade hoof dressing appears later in this chapter.

Healthy hoofs that stand up for a long life of varied wear and tear depend on good conformation, a balanced diet (supplements such as cod-liver oil promote growth of healthy horn), freedom from injury, proper sanitation and cleaning of the hoofs, and proper use of the horse (shoe him, for instance, if you plan to ride over rough, rocky country).

When the foot has an "ideal" conformation, the axis aligning the front of the foot with the pastern forms an angle of 45–50 degrees with the ground line. The ideal foot is round (front feet especially), dense, uniform, and

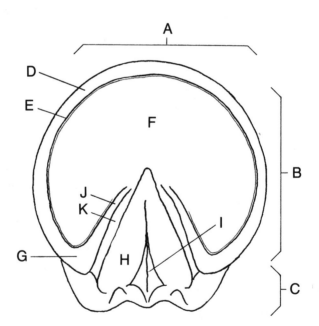

THE FOOT FROM UNDERNEATH
A. Toe. B. Quarter. C. Heel. D. Bearing surface of the wall. E. White line. F. Sole (concave). G. Buttress. H. Frog. I. Cleft of frog. J. Bars. K. Sulcei.

shapely, with smooth, waxy horn, wide heels, strong bars, and a large, elastic sole.

Black Hoofs Versus White Hoofs

One white hoof, buy him.
Two white hooves, try him.
Three white hooves, eye him.
Four white hooves, deny him.

This popular old postulate is not altogether true, since tests for compressive strength and moisture content of white hoofs and black hoofs indicate that one is not inherently weaker or drier than the other. However, the dark pigment in black hoofs does make them more resistant to trimming and abrasion. The light hoof will rasp down—and wear down—more easily. White hoofs are not weaker load bearers than dark hoofs, however.

Hoof Care

The health of a hoof comes from within: good nutrition and adequate exercise on natural footing, supported by good care in trimming and shoeing, with periods of bare-footedness.

Since the old adage "No foot, no horse" will always apply, foot care is a very necessary part of every grooming. The hoof should be cleaned daily when the horse is kept in a stall, and of course the stall must be kept clean and dry; thrush and other filth problems arise from wet, dirty, urine-soaked stalls. Routine farrier work (trimming or shoeing) should also be practiced regularly.

Hoof dressings or conditioners can be applied when necessary to assist the periople in preventing moisture loss. However, they do not heal cracks, prevent thrush, promote hoof growth to any degree, or inject moisture into the wall. For stabled horses, hoof dressings protect the hoof walls from the corrosive effects of urine. Commercial brands of hoof dressing may be purchased, or an inexpensive, very effective dressing can be made using one-third neatsfoot oil, one-third bacon grease, and one-third pine tar. We sometimes use more grease and neatsfoot oil than pine tar, especially in our cold climate (cold tends to make the pine tar hard).

Dressings are applied with a brush; if the horse is shod, apply only around the coronary band (hoof dressing on the nail holes allows the shoe to become loose). Otherwise, apply all over the outside hoof wall, especially if it is dry and has a tendency to crack.

The frog and sole may be dressed if the horse is used little and must stand in a dry corral or stall; however, if he is to be ridden or is pastured on dry, hard pasture, softening up the bearing surface will result in excessive wear, as well as increasing the possibility of bruising or corns.

How to know a needy hoof.

- Dry hoofs have a dull surface instead of the translucent gleam that indicates a healthy periople.
- Superficial vertical cracks and striations may cover the wall.
- The vertical tubular lines are more pronounced on a dry hoof than on a healthy one.
- Brittleness and hardness make a dry hoof difficult to rasp and trim.
- When tapped with a hammer, the dry hoof sounds hollow.
- A dry hoof wall will not leave a condensation ring on a cold, hard surface, such as concrete or asphalt.
- The hoofs walls become increasingly steep and the heels may contract as the condition progresses over a period of months.

If these signs occur and are not corrected or improved by your efforts, consult your farrier or veterinarian to correct the problems before greater ones occur.

When to trim. The feet of most horses should be trimmed or shod every four to six weeks. Colts and growing horses should receive attention more often, to maintain straight legs during periods of rapid leg-bone growth. Feet should be trimmed straight so that they maintain proper shape, length, and angle. Young foals can be trimmed weekly with a minimum of rasp strokes, since their feet are quite soft. Owners can do this themselves; the practice provides good training for young horses. Before trimming, carefully examine stance, conformation, and way of moving—most farriers are pleased to show you how.

Seasonal hoof care. In the West, the big summer pastures are usually dry and perhaps rocky and mountainous, while the winter pasture is often stubbled hay meadow with moist soil. With this type of rotation, horses of good leg conformation usually need little trimming in the summer, especially if the soil tends to be a gravel or sandy type, which acts like sandpaper. It may be necessary to use hoof dressing around the coronet to prevent excessive dryness and to promote good hoof health. In some cases, horses may need shoeing, at least on the forefeet. Horses that have proportionally small feet for their comparatively large, heavy bodies will need extra foot care, whether pastured or not. In the hay meadows during the winter, horses' feet will not wear as much and thus should be trimmed more often.

Broodmares are often neglected in foot care. Although most are not involved in performance activities, they do pull their weight financially and will lead a longer and more productive life on healthy, well-cared-for feet.

Snowballs. When being ridden in wet snow, horses' feet may ball up, making progress hazardous for both horse and rider. Because shod feet pick up snowballs more easily, we like to let our horses go barefoot whenever possible. In either case, however, you can reduce balling by rubbing Vaseline, cooking oil, or other grease on the sole. There is also a kind of Easyboot available for use in wet snow, mud, and for protection from sole bruises. Don't forget to remove shoes from idle horses so that they don't injure themselves moving around on snowballs.

Hoof care hints.

1. Begin when the foal is a few weeks old to train him and care for his feet.
2. Exercise foals on dry ground to allow natural wear.
3. Clean the soles and clefts of the frog often. Use a downward stroke (away from you) with the hoof pick.
4. Do not pare out the sole—clean only.
5. Do not trim away healthy frog unless there is an excess and it covers the sulcei, making it difficult to clean.
6. The foot should have the same angle as the pastern—both approximately 45–50 degrees.
7. Rasp more often if the horse is kept in a stall or small corral.
8. Do not rasp the outside wall (except for flare, and the blacksmith should instruct you on this). Rasping should be done so that the heel is included in each stroke.
9. Keep the feet well rounded.
10. Do not leave shoes on too long. Contracted heels, leg wounds, and puncture wounds from stepping on the nails can result.
11. Use hoof dressing when necessary.
12. Maintain a good working relationship with your farrier.

Safety hints when working with the horse's feet.

1. Tie your horse away from other activity—noise, confusion, dogs, other horses, and people moving to and fro.
2. Crosstie the horse or tie him reasonably short to a vertical post and have your grooming tools handy.
3. Rather than tie a difficult horse, have an assistant hold him. Horses are less apt to act up when held in hand. Plan to hold the horse for your farrier if he prefers.
4. When passing around the horse, do so quietly. Either stay right next to him (too close for a kick to be effective), or else far enough away to be out of range.
5. Avoid surprising the horse by grabbing at a foot. Gently stroke down the leg, tap behind the knee, lift under the fetlock, or use some other physical signal, while asking him vocally to lift his foot.
6. Be consistent in the order of feet you work on, and soon your horse will pick his feet up in anticipation of your request.
7. With a timid horse, do not hold the foot for long or raise it high. Speak quietly and reassuringly while you are working. On difficult horses, we sometimes reward with a treat for each foot well done.
8. If your horse is difficult with his hind feet, lift and bring the foot for-

ward before taking it back to work on. Keep the toe pointed up (makes it harder for him to kick).

9. Make sure that halter and ropes are strong and safe.

Foot Problems

All *puncture wounds* are potentially dangerous. Because they are common and a variety of objects can produce such wounds, policing your stalls and lounging areas in pastures and corrals is a good preventive measure.

The most common way horses puncture themselves is by stepping on a nail. In some cases, the nail will remain; in others, it pulls out and you must take hoof testers to find the point of entry. In each case, it may be necessary to pare down the entry site in order to obtain drainage and allow better entry for medication. If the horse is in pain, restraint such as a twitch may be necessary before working on the foot. If the nail is still imbedded, it can be pulled out with pliers (use a quick pull). Deep punctures should be examined by your veterinarian, since they can involve vital structures.

For uncomplicated wounds, wash the whole bottom of the foot, establish drainage for the puncture, and clean the wound with hydrogen peroxide, an enzyme preparation that digests necrotic tissue, or 7 percent iodine. A syringe without the needle attached, or a special long, narrow attachment for the syringe, will push the medicine deep into the puncture. Soak the foot in Epsom salts for 20 minutes each day for 5 days. The opening of the wound should then be packed with cotton soaked with tincture of iodine, and the foot should be bandaged thoroughly. If possible, the horse should be kept stalled or in a small, dry corral. Tetanus antitoxin should always be administered, and antibiotics may be advisable. Daily retreating and rebandaging will be necessary for seven to fourteen days, followed by application of a drying agent and packing the wound with cotton and tar or other suitable material.

Other wounds. When the flesh is cut, torn, or scraped, the wound should be cleaned and any foreign objects or material removed, and a noncaustic antibacterial agent should be used. Your veterinarian will suggest the best medicine. Proper bandaging should be done to keep the wound clean. In the event the wound gapes open, it should be immobilized with a pressure bandage or cast, to assist healing with less buildup of scar tissue. Again, a tetanus antitoxin should be administered.

Contracted heels. Because of improper foot care (usually shoes left on too long), the frog is no longer able to contact the ground, and the foot becomes narrower than normal. This condition is extremely painful to the horse.

Corns and bruises. Corns are caused by small, repeated pressures to a part of the foot (the horse might be poorly shod or the shoes may have been left on too long). A bruise is caused by a single blow to some part of the foot, usually the sole. The horse will favor the affected foot; however, since lameness can point to such a variety of problems, it is best to call your veterinarian. He will prescribe the proper treatment, which may involve bandaging, special shoeing, or use of Easyboots.

Thrush, a degenerative condition of the frog characterized by a putrid, offensive odor and a black discharge, is an infection that may penetrate the horny tissues and involve the sensitive structures. It is caused by keeping a horse in unhygienic conditions (such as a filthy, wet stall), by dirty, uncleaned feet, and by lack of frog pressure due to poor shoeing or trimming.

To treat for thrush, stable the horse in a clean, dry place, clean and disinfect the affected feet, pare out the affected parts of the frog, and treat with either a commercial medication, chlorine bleach, or the following make-it-yourself treatment (easy, economical, effective, and long-lasting): Using a clean one-gallon plastic container, pour in one pint of formaldehyde; add one teaspoon of methylene blue, and then add enough water to fill the container. Wrap a wad of cotton around a hoof pick, or hold the cotton with tweezers or forceps, and wipe the mixture through the cracks and fissures to their full depth. Continue wiping, using fresh cotton, until no greenish discoloration appears on the cotton. Pouring medication on the area will not give results; only wiping will be effective. Three days of intensive treatment should be sufficient for most cases, except when extensive damage to the sensitive structures is involved. A bar shoe is sometimes applied to exert pressure on the frog until it returns to normal size.

Sand cracks, heel cracks, quarter cracks. "Sand crack" is the general name for a split in the hoof wall. The cracks can originate at the coronary band (caused by an injury) or at the bearing surface (caused by excessive hoof growth, excessive drying, or thin walls). Your horse may not be lame, but if the crack extends into the sensitive tissues, infection can occur. If the crack bleeds after the horse is exercised, it shows that the sensitive tissues are involved.

The treatment varies depending on the site and severity of the crack. Cutting or burning a pattern above the crack (when starting from the bearing surface) may help to contain it. Corrective trimming and shoeing prevent widening of the crack. Severe cracks going down into the sensitive laminae (with accompanying infection) require extensive treatment and corrective shoeing (sometimes with clips on either side of a toe crack). A new procedure is to fill the crack (after stripping or enlarging) with a type of plastic material or fiberglass; lacing with stainless steel wire holds the crack together and serves as reinforcement for the plastic material. Keeping close watch on the crack and using hoof dressing is important to a good recovery.

Laminitis (founder) is an inflammation of the laminae of the foot which results in severe pain. The inflammatory region severely restricts the blood supply to the laminar structures, which may eventually result in "founder ring."

Founder may be either acute or chronic. Although the acute form may result in death, this is not common. Chronic founder is the resultant tissue damage and associated complication following one or a series of acute attacks. A horse has a chronic tendency toward founder if his feet show founder rings (a series of ridges and grooves encircling the hoof), as each ring is the result of an acute attack. When permanent damage is done to the laminae, causing loss of normal attachment of coffin bone to hoof wall, the weight of the horse pushes down on the coffin bone, which after severe attacks may even be pushed right through the sole to the ground.

There are several types of laminitis: grain founder (caused by eating more grain than can be tolerated), water founder (caused when an overheated horse drinks large amounts of cold water), road founder (found in unconditioned horses that are subjected to hard and fast work on hard surfaces), grass founder (affecting horses grazed on lush pastures, especially clover and alfalfa, and most often affecting fat, heavy-crested horses), and postparturient laminitis (caused by the partial retention of the placenta after foaling).

The symptoms of founder are heat and tenderness over the sole, the wall, and the coronary band; faster digital pulse (over the fetlock joint); and anxiety, sweating, and trembling due to extreme pain, increased respiration, and variable elevation of temperature. The horse must be forced to walk and will stumble or shuffle; when standing, he will use the characteristic "founder stance" to help alleviate the pain. Since the front feet are usually involved, the horse stands with his hind legs well under him to bear most of his weight.

To treat founder, your veterinarian will use measures to reduce the inflammation, reestablish the blood supply to the foot, and relieve pain. He will also prescribe management of feed for the convalescent horse. This will probably include being off feed for one to two days, followed by a gradual offering of a small amount of grass hay and observing the horse carefully. In chronic cases, the horse will need corrective trimming, shaping, and shoeing at frequent intervals, since the affected feet will grow more quickly, especially in the toe area. The heels must be gradually lowered, removing excess toe and protecting the sole. Pads, steel plates, and acrylic plastics, as well as rubber (such as Easyboots) can be used for protection.

The disease must be treated immediately, so that the laminar structures will not be permanently damaged and so that the blood supply can be restored.

Navicular disease involves a number of degenerative changes involving the navicular bone, the navicular bursa, and the deep flexor tendon. The bursa becomes inflamed and, as the disease continues, the navicular bone erodes on the rear surface (facing the tendon). The small fibers of the tendon can become torn by the roughened end of the bone, causing progressive destruction of the tendon's surface.

The exact cause is not known, but there are several factors thought to contribute to it. Poor conformation (straight shoulders and pasterns, small feet) increases concussion on the navicular bone. Improper trimming and shoeing and strenuous work on a hard surface make a horse more subject to navicular disease. There may also be nutritional and hormonal influences. The forefeet are usually affected due to receiving more concussion than the hind feet; hind feet are rarely involved.

Lameness becomes progressively worse and can be intermittent. Because pressure on the frog is painful, the horse tries to land toe first, producing a stumbling, choppy gait—the characteristic "navicular gait." At rest, the horse "points" (extends the front feet, trying to reduce pressure on the deep flexor tendon on the navicular bone).

Navicular disease cannot be cured, as the bone has been eroded; however, if the pain is relieved, the usefulness of the horse can be prolonged. This is done by relieving inflammation, by corrective shoeing, and by anti-inflammatory drugs such as phenylbutazone. Sometimes a neurectomy (removing a nerve) can aid in prolonging the horse's usefulness (although the nerve may regrow in six months to two years).

Other important foot and hoof problems are mentioned in the Appendix.

GAITS AND ACTION

The natural gaits of the horse are the walk, trot, and four-beat gallop. The canter is a collected, three-beat version of the gallop. Other gaits—which are often termed artificial even though they may be performed naturally—are the pace, slow gaits (running walk, fox trot, amble), and rack or single-foot (broken amble). A horse maintaining normal, desirable gaits should have his feet balanced and aligned with his body at the moment they leave the ground. When his gait deviates from normal, he wastes energy and places stress on his legs and feet.

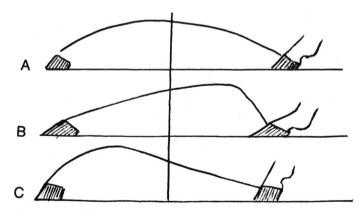

Path of the foot (from side). A. Normal. B. Low heel—long toe. C. Short toe—long heel.

The normal angle of the front foot is 45–50 degrees; the hind foot is nearer 50–55 degrees. The normal path of this foot in flight, as viewed from the side, should make an even arc (see A in the illustration); when viewed from above, the path moves forward in a straight line. There are many ways this path can deviate from normal, however, as seen when watching the movement from the side, from front or back, and from above.

A deviation in the arc can result from a low heel (B), which causes delay in setting the foot down, thereby increasing the length of the second half of the stride. The same effect is produced by a long toe, which delays the breakover, causing the foot to be lifted hastily and shortening the first half of the stride. A short toe (C) causes an early breakover, lengthening the first half of the stride.

Base-wide horses carry their feet forward in a series of inward arcs; splay-footed horses carry their feet forward in even larger arcs. The base-narrow horse moves his feet in a series of outward arcs, or "winds the rope," and the pigeon-toed horse will carry his feet in even wider outward arcs. Other gait defects, such as interfering and forging, are results of abnormal changes in the path of flight.

Not all faults in gait can be attributed to conformation, although poor conformation predisposes the horse to certain defects. Gaits can also be influenced by improperly adjusted equipment or an unskilled rider; a green horse, in the early stages of learning to balance weight on his back, may have unstable gaits.

The flight of the foot is also affected by weight, and farriers make use of this fact in corrective shoeing. The added weight of shoes will always decrease agility and reduce speed; thus a good farrier will use the lightest shoe practical for the work to be done. Uniformly distributing weight in a shoe will increase the length of stride. Weighting one side will cause the suspended foot to swing toward the unweighted side.

Because many gait problems can be corrected in the young horse by knowledgeable farriery, corrective trimming should start early; horses with conformation defects should receive extra attention, so that stress breakdowns in the legs and feet will not occur. While it is usually not possible to correct faulty gaits in mature horses, they can be modified and improved.

Gait Defects and Deviations

Interference refers to one leg hitting or interfering with another when the horse is in motion. Base-wide, and base-narrow with toe-wide, conformation, as well as cow hocks and narrow chest predispose the horse to interference. Temporary causes are fatigue and faults in trimming and shoeing.

There are two basic types of interference: striding-leg and supporting-leg. Striding-leg interference includes:

Forging. The hind feet (toes) stride forward and hit the sole or shoe of the forefoot on the same side when the horse is trotting. A horse with a very short back and long legs is predisposed to this fault. Leg weariness, improper shoeing, poor horsemanship, and poor tack adjustment have a bearing on forging. The farrier must evaluate the cause and determine the cure. There is a characteristic sound of "click, click, click." *Cross-firing* amounts to forging in the pacer. The hind foot of one side hits the diagonal forefoot of the other pair. The flight of the feet deviates from a straight line. *Scalping.* The hind leg at the coronet is hit by the toe of the forefoot. *Speedy cutting.* The hind leg at the pastern or fetlock is struck by the toe of the forefoot. *Shin hitting* is hitting the cannon (shin) of the hind leg with the toe of the front foot.

Supporting-leg interference at the trot and pace is the result of hitting one front leg with the other or one hind leg with the other as it moves past the supporting leg. Most usually, the fetlock is involved, but any part of the lower leg may be involved, up to the knee (knee-knocking). Terms used to describe this kind of interference are *brushing,* when the part is touched but no injury inflicted, and *striking,* used to denote the infliction of an actual wound.

Deviations in the flight of the foot include: *Paddling*—the horse throws his heels outward just as he lifts them from the ground (easily noticed when the horse trots away from you). Toe-in (pigeon-toed) conformation predisposes the horse to paddling, a relatively minor fault, though it is unsightly and does waste energy. Tight longeing encourages paddling in young horses not settled in their gaits. A further flight deviation is *winging out*—an exaggerated paddling found in high-stepping saddle horses and harness horses.

Dishing and *winging* are associated with toe-out or splayfooted conformation. The horse with this serious gait defect throws his front feet inward, which can eventually lead to knee-knocking or other interference. *Rolling* occurs in very wide-chested horses. They roll from side to side as they move, producing a labored, inefficient gait. *Winding,* or *rope walking,* occurs in very narrow, "weedy" conformations. The horse that winds brings his striding leg around in front of his supporting leg, giving the impression of walking a tightrope. This is an unstable and unbalanced way of going. *Trappy* describes a choppy, quick, short-gaited stride. A trappy horse is uncomfortable to ride and rapidly wears himself out with inefficient action. The *pounding* horse produces excess concussion when contacting the ground. Horses with straight shoulders and upright, short pasterns have the conformation that predisposes to this defect.

Detecting Lameness

Lameness is an irregularity in gait that results from moving with pain or difficulty. When a horse is at rest and the lameness severe enough, he will point or lift his foot, putting as little weight on that leg as possible. Symptoms of lameness are accentuated at the trot, although they also may be detected at the walk. The lame horse will nod his head downward as he puts his good foreleg to the ground, and raise and jerk his unsound leg.

When lameness hits both front legs, there will be no nodding to the head, which will be held higher than normal. The gait is characterized by short, stiff, and stilted action. The hind feet are lifted high, while the front feet barely leave the ground. At rest, the hind feet stand forward under the body to take most of the weight (also characteristic of navicular disease).

Detecting lameness in the hind legs may be difficult unless pain is severe, in which case the horse will raise his head when weight is on the sound leg, drop his head when on the unsound leg.

Lameness in both hind legs is characterized by short, awkward movement and lowered head. The front feet will rise higher than normal, and it will be impossible to back the horse.

In shoulder lameness, which does not occur as frequently as is often supposed, the horse drags the toe of the affected leg; pain is produced as the leg is brought forward, resulting in a shorter stride with that leg.

It is often very difficult to find the exact site of the lameness. Observation by comparing the general outline of the legs is a valuable aid, as swellings or bony growths can be detected. Also, inflamed areas can be found by pressing the region firmly with the fingers and feeling for heat.

FARRIERY

Horseshoeing tools are designed for a special purpose; it is possible to start shoeing horses with a relatively small number of tools and financial outlay. However, the best is none too good, so when buying rasps and nippers, for example, buy the best high-quality material, good craftsmanship, and scientific design.

Then give them the best of care, and use each tool only for its intended purpose. Keep knives and rasps sharp—don't allow them to touch other metal, such as hay wire, as they dull easily. Dry them quickly if they get wet, to prevent rust. Keep two rasps and two nippers, saving the best one for use on hoof only—never on nails or any other material.

Trimming

Since there are many good books on farriery, we'll mention here only a few things that the layman can and should understand in order to judge a shoeing job or help in the care of his horse's feet.

For the normal hoof, the farrier will lower the sole only enough that the

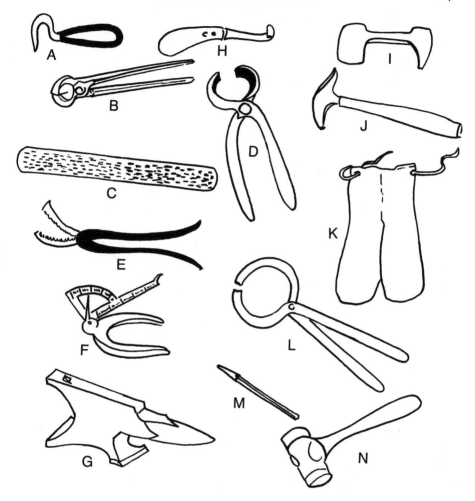

HORSESHOEING TOOLS

A. Color-handled hoof pick. B. Cutting nippers. C. Rasp (16-inch). D. Pincers. E. Clincher, or "duckbill." F. Hoof leveler. G. Anvil. H. Hoof knife. I. Clinch cutter or buffer. J. Driving hammer. K. Blacksmith's apron. L. Hoof tester. M. Pritchel. N. Rounding hammer.

shoe does not put pressure on it; cutting the sole lets the foot dry out and leaves the sensitive tissues more subject to injury. The frog should be let alone. If the frog is trimmed below the normal level, the hoof does not expand, and contracted heels may result; old flakes may be trimmed off, however, if they are building up around the frog. When cutting the excess wall, the farrier uses the nippers; then he levels with the rasp.

If the horse is to go barefoot, your farrier will leave one-quarter inch more horn than normal for shoeing, and will bevel the outer edge of the wall about half of its width so that the wall will not break out. A horse that has had shoes on for a long time will have a wall that is less elastic and will break out more easily.

One rule that farriers use is "Lower the side that points"; that is, if the toe points out, lower the outside wall. The heels should be the same height, with no high or low areas along the bottom of the wall. The wall must be leveled so that a flat shoe will be solid and not rock (an uneven bearing surface will cause the shoe to rock and work loose). The angle must be correct.

Shoeing

The shoe supports the entire wall with no excess—in other words, the shoe should be large enough, but no larger than needed. The hind feet usually take a size smaller than the forefeet. The branches should be long enough to support the bearing surface but should not extend too far beyond the heel (for fast work such as cutting, the branches should not extend at all beyond the heels; a horse with long, sloping pasterns, however, can have longer branches to help support the rear tendons and protect the heels).

A horse's foot changes size as moisture content varies; it becomes larger in the moist spring, smaller in a dry fall. The shoe should always be selected to fit the hoof; the hoof should not be trimmed to fit the shoe. Because the wall

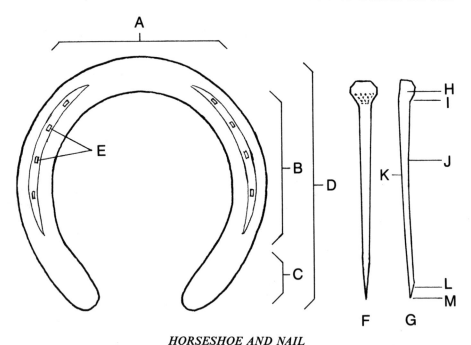

HORSESHOE AND NAIL
A. Toe. B. Quarter. C. Heel. D. Branch. E. Nail holes. F. Front view of nail. G. Side view. H. Head. I. Neck. J. Inner face of shank. K. Outer face. L. Bevel. M. Point.

is thicker at the toe and tapers back toward the heel, nail holes can be set in more at the toe than toward the heel.

Both the hot and the cold methods of shoeing have their advantages and disadvantages. Most good farriers can do both. A horse with a normal foot can do well with a cold shoe put on correctly. In cold shoeing, a ready-made shoe is selected from the assorted sizes available and then fitted to the hoof without heating. The size is measured by the weight of the horse: 800 pounds, size 0; 1,000 pounds, size 1; 1,500 pounds, size 3. Draft horses may take up to size 8.

In hot shoeing, a shoe is made from a piece of iron or an unfinished blank, which is then cut and shaped to size. The Budweiser Champion Clydesdales have handmade hot shoes, not only because they have such huge feet, but also because of their specialized work.

Ease, speed, and low cost are the advantages to cold shoeing, whereas a forge, welder, and accessory tools are necessary for hot shoeing. Hot shoes, on the other hand, can be made to fit any special situation.

A good blacksmith will stand behind his job, and replace a shoe that is lost. If the shoe is not put on correctly, it will not stay on. However, leaving shoes on too long (nail holes wear out before shoes), working a tired horse, and longeing a horse in mud, snow, or sand, can cause him to lose his shoes. It is up to the owner to check his horse's feet and shoes daily.

Removing Worn Shoes

When pulling a shoe, the farrier must first cut or straighten the clinches, using a heavy hammer and a clinch cutter (buffer). When the clinches are cut, the pull-off tongs are inserted under one branch of the shoe and pried up. Each side is pried until the shoe is loose, and then twisted, pulling the toe nails and removing the shoe. Care must be taken not to put too much pressure on the sole, as the sensitive tissues could be damaged. Nails or stubs must be removed from the wall.

Examining each shoe will show whether the horse is wearing his shoes evenly and whether he has excessive wear at the toe or heel—perhaps as a result of pain (short stride wears toes; long stride wears heels). Off-balance wear would show that the walls were too high or too low; your farrier will counteract the increased wear when reshoeing. He will wish to see your horse standing square on the level, and trotting away and toward him in a straight line, to determine whether corrective trimming or shoeing is necessary.

Preparing for the First Set of Shoes

Hoof care begins when your horse is a young foal. Not only can any defects be corrected early, but consistent handling of the feet precludes a fight when your farrier arrives to trim or shoe. See *Basic Training for Horses: English and Western* for information on training foals, young horses, and mature older horses to allow their feet to be handled.

Because it is important for the colt to receive a happy experience the first time he is shod, you should prepare him by consistent handling, cleaning, and trimming. If the colt is frightened, he will be that much more afraid the second time around.

Sometime before his first shoes are to be applied, tap him lightly with a hammer on the bearing surface of the wall. This will prepare him for the pounding of the nails, which seems to be the most uncomfortable and frightening part of the shoeing process. We find that if someone holds the colt and calms him by speaking quietly to him, he reacts far better than when tied alone. Use a little psychology: work the colt (either longeing or under saddle) before shoeing so that he is a bit tired and more willing to stand still.

Choose a farrier that will take his time on the young horse and use humane but firm methods while putting on the first shoes. If the colt has bad habits or any idiosyncracies, tell your farrier—it will make his job easier, with less stress on both horse and man.

How to Select a Farrier

Your horseshoer must deal not only with horses but also with horse owners. To build up his business and gain a good reputation, he must not only do a first-class job but also be courteous and willing to talk with people about their horses, giving advice and adequate explanations. Another important quality is dependability. There is nothing as frustrating as bringing in horses from pasture at a specified time and then waiting for a blacksmith who neither comes nor phones.

Your competent farrier should also have good equipment and keep it in shape, as well as have an adequate supply of shoes available for every foreseeable situation. Many horseshoers keep heavy halters and ropes in case of trouble or if the owner does not have the correct equipment. He should keep a record of horses shod, the date, and pertinent notes on each horse—in other words, carry on his business in a businesslike way. Most good farriers guarantee their work for several weeks, but of course it is up to the owner to keep the horse's feet in good condition (dry, broken feet cannot hold a shoe well, and a horse that paws at fences has trouble keeping his shoes). We appreciate the horseshoer who picks up his dropped nail stubs and other trash.

Another important factor in selecting your farrier is his manner of handling your horses. Your farrier should be patient; he should handle horses sensitively, firmly, and with compassion; and he should expect to take more time with inexperienced horses. On the other hand, if you have not trained your horse properly to accept this handling, don't expect your farrier to put up with a lot of trouble and bad manners. If you are not prepared to be firm, he will have to be in order to get the job done.

Most horseshoers are referred to new customers by well-satisfied regular clients. When coming into a new area, most horsemen choose their farrier by his reputation, passed along from client to client.

Your Obligation to the Farrier

Your farrier travels long distances and meets many people and horses. He has a big investment in equipment, special vehicle, and gas. Have your horse ready when he arrives, and provide an area for him to work in that is safe, level, clean, dry, quiet, and well lighted. If you cannot be there when he comes, arrange for a competent person (one the horses are used to) to be at the barn with the horses ready and any special information available. Someone should either hold the horses for the farrier if he wishes, or at least be around as a safety factor. No horseshoer should have to chase a horse in a pasture and work alone.

Your horse's legs should be clean and his feet in good condition (moist enough—not broken beyond repair). If the farrier has an early-morning ap-

A special grooming and horseshoeing area in your stable or arena will make it easier for you to keep up with trimming and shoeing, and your farrier will appreciate a good place to work. Redwater Hereford Ranch, Beulah, Wyoming. (Courtesy Dave Ellsbury)

pointment, be sure your horses are fed, and exercised if possible; a hungry, thirsty horse full of life can make for a fidgety, obnoxious animal to work on. If a young horse is being trimmed or shod for the first time, someone should be stationed at his head talking calmly, petting him, and perhaps giving a bit of grain or pelleted treat to inspire him with the idea that having his feet handled is a good thing.

If he still gives you trouble even after several trims, you can crosstie him, put a body rope around the girth area (from between the legs, up through the bottom of the noseband of the halter), tying it high but not tight, and have someone with a lead rope at the head (though not standing in front). Another way to provide extra control is to stand the horse parallel to a wall, hold the lead rope snugly around a post (not tied), talk quietly, and hold your hand like a blinker over the eye. If still more control is necessary, cooperate with your farrier in the use of restraints.

Most farriers are proud of their skill and appreciate your interest and praise for a job well done. In cold weather, offer a hot drink and in warm weather a cold drink. The blacksmith has a hard job, with some risk involved; your courtesy and interest will be appreciated. He will also appreciate prompt payment—he can't afford large credit accounts.

CHAPTER 8

HEALTH, AILMENTS, AND

RESTRAINTS

PRACTICAL HEALTH CARE—WHAT YOU CAN DO

Observation is the key to good horse management. You should know your horse well enough to be aware of his normal habits and actions. It is when your horse deviates from *his* normal manner that you can suspect problems, and closer observation at that point should give you further clues.

Physically, your horse should be sound and in good condition, with healthy coat and skin, good vision, and good teeth. The systems of his body should be working properly and should be free of disease. Mentally, your horse should be alert and energetic, yet manageable. He should be interested and observant, without nervousness, panic, or overreaction to stimuli. Good manners and freedom from vices are an important aspect of mental health. A happy horse is one that gets along well with other equines and humans.

General appearance and body language—how he holds his head or ears, the position of his legs, his general movement at all gaits, and the lucidity of his eyes—tell us a great deal about how a horse feels. A horse that camps (stretches forelegs forward and hind legs back) may have a kidney problem, or, more often, colic. A dejected horse—head and neck drooping, hindquarters well under, croup depressed—can have a number of problems, such as azoturia, distemper, or the beginning of colic or pneumonia. You may not know what his problem is, but at least you know by observation that he has one and that it's necessary to obtain veterinary help before more serious signs occur.

Suspect a health problem if your horse goes off his feed, does not keep together with his friends, suddenly becomes overexcitable or lethargic, coughs, has a runny nose or runny eyes, or seems oversensitive to your touch. Rapid, noisy, shallow, or strained breathing is also easy to notice. Other signs of illness or severe deficiency include diarrhea, weight loss, depraved appetite, skin rashes and itching, loss of hair, incoordination, weakness, and rough, dull coat.

Are You the Cause of Your Horse's Illness or Wounds?

Unfortunately, humans are the cause of most health problems in horses. Ignorance or neglect, separately or in combination, can destroy a horse. Neglect in parasite control can cause colic—or even death. Neglect in checking teeth can cause bleeding cheeks and gums, poor digestion of food, and accompanying poor condition. Neglect of feet causes a crooked stance and unbalanced gaits, as well as quarter cracks, quittor, and graveling.

Improper feeding can result in poor nutrition and all its attendant ailments. Keeping horses under artificial conditions, and demanding unnatural performance under conditions that they were not bred to meet, complicate the feeding routine. Prevention of digestive problems can be found in the chapter on feeding.

Neglect in preparing, checking, and repairing the horse's living quarters, whether stall, corral, or pasture, can result in injury and sometimes even death.

The horse owner is also responsible for the helpers he employs. Make sure that your requests are carried out and that your helpers know what to do in an emergency.

An ounce of prevention is worth far more than a pound of cure—and saves money, time, and heartbreak. Practice sound management, know your horse, observe him daily, and anticipate problems before they arise.

Predisposing Conditions That Lower Vitality and Natural Resistance to Disease

Even in well-run establishments, things can go wrong on occasion. When a horse's vitality is lowered, he is more susceptible to illness and infection. If any of the following conditions occur, be especially watchful for the onset of problems. By reducing or eliminating these conditions, health will be more easily maintained.

Exposure. Sudden, out-of-season storms can cause hardship, especially if horses have not yet been moved to protected pastures or shelter. In some areas, radio and TV weather reports give "stockman's warnings" when dangerous storms are imminent; the horse owner can take the necessary steps to protect his animals. Also, a hot horse (one not cooled out sufficiently) put out in a cold wind can get chills or pneumonia. It is especially important to check old horses and very young horses, and to provide adequate protection during inclement weather.

Lack of sufficient feed. Inadequate feed will debilitate your horse. Especially in cold weather, he will not be able to generate enough heat to keep warm. Give more feed in cold weather.

Overwork. Working your horse to exhaustion weakens him. Avoid overwork by gradually conditioning him to his own level of peak performance.

Change of environment. Changing pastures, moving to a new farm or ranch —even changing his stablemates—puts a horse under stress. When it is necessary to change the environment, make sure that the horse is healthy in every way. When changing pastures, lead or ride your horse around his new pasture to acquaint him with the boundaries, especially if it is enclosed with barbed wire. Sometimes it is possible to make a change gradually. For instance, putting a horse alone in an enclosed area where his new stablemates can make friends over the fence will alleviate the "running around" that new horses must put up with.

Prolonged shipment. Horses shipped for long distances must stand for many hours, endure unnatural temperatures, noise, and vibration, be handled by strangers, and may be fed a different diet, all of which contribute to stress, which in turn can lower vitality.

Improper grooming. Lack of or incomplete grooming also includes lack of observation. Such problems as "scratches" occur when fetlocks are clipped and horses are turned out in wet, cold weather. Neglecting to look at or treat the pasterns can result in an aggravated condition. Other health problems such as saddle sores and ringworm could have been found and prevented or quickly cured with constant observation.

Lack of preventive measures. Combatting and controlling communicable diseases should include daily inspection, cleanliness, disinfection, isolation, quarantine, good general care (including parasite control), and vaccination.

Other stress situations, such as a severe wound, fear of a trainer, or incompatible pasture mates, lower vitality and leave the way open for other infection.

Preventing Problems in the Old Horse

Our senior citizens in the horse world should be valued friends and companions. Some of the qualities of the older horse are experience, stability, and trust in his owner/handler/rider. His experience and sense often make up for the stamina, speed, endurance, and strength of the young horse. Your older horse should not be forgotten and retired to the back forty. He should be loved and cared for.

A few simple considerations will keep him feeling fit and help his usefulness to last many years. As his body ages, his joints will stiffen, muscles tighten, and tendons harden; it's important to give him a longer warm-up to loosen his joints before hard work is asked. After work, vigorously rub his lower legs with a good liniment to restore the elasticity of hardened tendons. Older horses have a more difficult time lifting their legs (especially hind legs) to have their feet cleaned. Don't try to lift his feet as high—bend down more yourself.

Because the old horse no longer has a supporting pad of fat along his spine, use extra padding under your saddle. Also, be sure that the fork of your Western saddle is high enough to clear his withers.

Your older horse is a slower and more finicky eater. Watch him closely, and check his teeth at least twice a year. Dentistry cannot be overemphasized in the care of the senior citizen, since immediate correction of any developing problems will keep him eating well—the first step in staying healthy.

To best care for your older horse:

1. Put him on a special feeding program with good-quality hay and grains. Give green grass daily in season—it does more for an old horse than anything else. Feeding more often in smaller amounts will help digestion and will help to alleviate or delay digestive problems due to intestinal damage caused by bloodworms. Increase calcium and phosphorus.
2. Practice regular parasite control. Parasite damage can result in aneurisms, pain, colic, or death.
3. Give adequate protection from the elements. Bring him in during inclement weather to avoid chills, and protect him from cold and dampness. Give warm water in winter to prevent heat loss.
4. Groom the old horse daily, and watch for weight loss, loss of condition, or obesity. Provide regular hoof care; use hoof dressing.
5. Use anti-inflammatory drugs for arthritis and ringbone.
6. Observe and float teeth regularly.
7. Check his eyes often. Since he may not be able to see as well as he used to, be careful of where you ride him.
8. Provide adequate exercise without stress. Give adequate warm-up and gradual cooling out. In workouts, be sure to give him frequent breathers, especially on hills, and be careful working him on hard-surfaced roads or rocky trails. Use liniment. Moderate exercise will aid digestion and general condition.
9. Make sure that children are supervised and instructed. Insist that he be ridden humanely, his tack is adjusted correctly, and loving care is taken of his old bones.

Obesity in Horses

As in humans, obesity in horses is detrimental to good health. Obesity is unsightly, and horses that are fat are not as agile; strain is put on the musculoskeletal system of growing horses (bones, joints, tendons, and ligaments are more susceptible to injury). Founder and azoturia are two of the more common problems occurring in fat horses. See "Feeding the fat horse," in the chapter on feeding.

How to Choose Your Veterinarian

Since most cities and rural areas generally have several veterinarians, there is usually a choice. Referral from your previous veterinarian or from area horsemen is best; however, if you are new in an area, you may have to find out for yourself. Visiting the clinic can perhaps give you some idea of the services rendered—it should be clean and efficient, with adequate horse-care facilities and good-quality feed for stay-over patients. Are the veterinarian and his staff helpful, quiet, and skillful in handling and treating animals? A good horse veterinarian will like horses and have an obvious rapport with them. This is important, as your horse's reaction to the veterinarian will influence the amount of stress he undergoes.

When you have decided on a veterinarian and make dates to treat your animal at home, does he arrive most times as scheduled? Does he return your phone calls? It may be wise to get to know several veterinarians in your area in case one is busy when you have an emergency—don't wait for an emergency to arise before you become acquainted with them.

When Should You Call Your Veterinarian?

In some areas today, it's as hard to get your veterinarian to make house calls as it is your physician. Many veterinarians prefer that you trailer your horse into the clinic, if at all possible—and in any case, they must charge for mileage when they do travel. Veterinary care is one of the expenses of horse ownership and should be planned for. On the other hand, a wise and knowledgeable horse owner will be able to avoid unnecessary expense. As he becomes more experienced, he will recognize many problems and be able to treat them himself. Always call your veterinarian, however,

- in cases of colic or when the horse shows he is in severe pain—any colic case should be treated as an emergency;
- when your horse has a temperature over 103 degrees F;
- for deep wounds or wounds near joints;
- if your horse does not respond quickly to your treatment;
- when there is a thick, yellowish discharge from the nostrils;
- when there are foaling problems;
- whenever there is doubt as to the trouble or health problem.

What to Do Before Calling Your Veterinarian

Your veterinarian will appreciate knowing whether or not your call is an emergency. Be ready to give him as much information on your equine patient as possible. If you live on a ranch or farm many miles from town, your accurate description of the problem may save your horse's life if time is of the essence, or it may be a problem that you can treat with veterinary consultation alone. When the veterinarian comes, be there yourself (with assistants if necessary), so that there is ample help; if you have no helper, let your veterinarian know, so that he can bring assistance. Answering the following questions before calling your veterinarian will help him to determine the diagnosis, treatment, and severity of the problem:

1. Is your horse eating and drinking? How long has he been off feed? Is he sweating, lying down, rolling, stamping his feet, pawing, switching his tail, moving around a great deal, or staying in one place (if in a pasture or corral)? Is there any loss of hair in any spot? Are the feces normal in color and consistency? What is the color and volume of the urine?

2. What is the body temperature (see instructions in this chapter on how to take body temperature, pulse, and respiration)? Is it over 102 degrees F? If so, your horse may have an infectious disease.

3. What is your horse's pulse rate? The normal falls between twenty-eight and forty-two beats per minute; when your horse has an increased rate of pulse, it indicates a circulatory disturbance.

4. What is your horse's breathing rate? The normal rate for a mature horse is eight to sixteen breaths per minute at rest. It is slightly higher in younger animals. When your horse has a painful chest condition causing strong abdominal breathing, he probably has pneumonia.

5. Is there anything abnormal about the head and neck? Are there swellings about the head? Is there a discharge from one or both eyes—and are the eyes dull or bright? Are there color changes in the whites of the eyes (blue can denote founder, and yellow could be jaundice)? Is the lining of the nostrils reddened, and is there a nasal discharge?

6. Is there an odor to the breath? A bad odor could signify disease or teeth that have sharp or broken edges and are causing sores, or perhaps an abscessed tooth.

7. Is there anything abnormal about the body? Are there swellings, cuts, sores? What overall stance does your horse have? If he stands with an extended neck, he may have something lodged in his esophagus. Is he willing to move, or reluctant? Is he stiff?

Intelligently study your ailing horse. If there is not an obvious emergency, take his temperature and check his respiration before you phone your veterinarian. The information may make the difference between a routine call and an emergency call. Look carefully at your horse from head to tail and remember what you see.

What to Do While Waiting for Your Veterinarian to Arrive

Your veterinarian will give you instructions if there is an emergency.

1. Your equipment and animals should be ready. Bring your horse from

pasture into the stable, where electricity and water are handy (unless your veterinarian says the horse should not be moved). Stable blankets should be available, and your first-aid kit should be well stocked and kept up-to-date.

2. Restraining devices should be available (twitch, ropes, and so on) in case your veterinarian should need them. Know how to use them.
3. Provide a clean place to work—a clean, antiseptic stall to put your horse in after treatment, or a clean, nearby paddock or pasture, depending on the problem.
4. Know the normal foaling procedures and call your veterinarian immediately if there is a deviation from normal. Try to keep the mare and foal quiet and warm and in a well-bedded stall, free from drafts.
5. Know the symptoms of common diseases such as encephalomyelitis, equine infectious anemia, and distemper, and isolate the affected horse.
6. Learn to recognize shock and be able to treat for it until your veterinarian arrives.
7. If there is severe bleeding, apply pressure to halt the flow: hold a clean, folded towel or cloth against the wound if necessary. Keep the horse warm and treat for shock.
8. Abide by your veterinarian's instructions.

Stable Pharmacy

The contents of your stable pharmacy will depend on how much you intend to do yourself for your horse. Some owners feel confident to handle wound cleaning, bandaging, and injections, while others prefer to have their veterinarian handle these problems. The number of horses you own will also have a bearing on the medicines you keep on hand. A one-horse owner would find it financially unfeasible to keep a fully stocked pharmacy—emergency supplies would be adequate.

A well-stocked medicine chest should contain:

1. bandages and scissors (gauze and Telfa pads, Ace bandages);
2. leg wraps, roll of cotton;
3. Elastikon (elastic adhesive bandage), regular adhesive tape in 1- and 2-inch widths;
4. scrub brush;
5. bulb syringe;
6. liquid soap and sponges;
7. boric acid;
8. Vaseline and alcohol;
9. hydrogen peroxide, 7 percent iodine, or Clorox—good for cleaning puncture wounds;
10. witch hazel (for bruises, insect bites that swell, or tendinitis, use equal parts witch hazel and alcohol);

11. plastic bottles of sterile water;
12. gentian violet for small-wound dressings, gentle iodine;
13. salt to make saline solution (1 teaspoon salt to 1 pint boiled water);
14. Epsom salts (1 cup in ½ pail of water) for soaking wounds and sprains;
15. Furacin powder and Furacin dressing, or other antibiotic powder and salve;
16. chloromycetin ointment;
17. Absorbine;
18. livestock thermometer;
19. stick-type, rub-on fly repellent;
20. Promazine (oral tranquilizer used in grain).

In refrigerator (or keep refrigerated with cold packs for riding trips):
1. pen-strep;
2. long-acting penicillin;
3. 12cc and 20cc syringes and needles (size 18 and 1½ inches long)—keep with medication and discard after use (or sterilize);
4. 7 percent iodine and alcohol in plastic containers;
5. epinephrine (antidote for penicillin and other allergic reactions);
6. other medications on advice of your veterinarian.

For pack trips and extended trail rides, a compact, complete emergency kit for both horse and rider will keep you prepared and will help avoid unnecessary discomfort. Pack your first-aid supplies in clear plastic bags, which will enable you to see the contents and keep your supplies grouped, as well as keeping them from getting wet or soiled. Prepare a lightweight personal first-aid kit for yourself. For your horse, prepare a kit containing the items listed above, and make sure you also have along hoof picks, a knife, hoof dressing, pliers, needle-nosed pliers, wire cutters, rope, and a twitch. Tape a list of the items to the lid of your first-aid box.

Rules for Drug Safety

1. Seek prompt veterinary attention.
2. Be sure of diagnosis.
3. There are no safe drugs—even vitamins.
4. Never use medicines not prescribed; what may be good for one may not be good for another.
5. Write down all instructions and double-check.
6. Handle all drugs properly; read the label. Keep from freezing, heat, and sunlight.
7. Buy your drugs from a veterinarian or some other reliable source.
8. Note and adhere to expiration date.
9. Adhere to dosage details, schedules, administration times (before or after feeding, etc.).

10. Do not give more than one drug at a time except at veterinarian's direction.
11. Give drugs their full course of treatment (stopping treatment before the full course can give bacteria a chance).
12. Practice cleanliness; assure sterility, especially of syringes and needles.
13. Know the withdrawal time for a drug (how long it takes for the drug to wear off)—some drugs are banned at horse shows and race meets.
14. Keep records on controlled substances; when shots are given for vaccinations and immunizations, they should be recorded for further reference.
15. Lock drugs away from children.

Some Veterinary Skills with Horses

Although some procedures should be undertaken only by your veterinarian (such as suturing or using a stomach tube), there are others that you should know how to do.

How to use a veterinary thermometer. Using a clinical thermometer can give you a great deal of information about your horse. A sustained abnormal temperature is an indication of trouble and certainly warns you to call your veterinarian.

Because the normal body temperature of animals has more latitude than that of humans, it is wise to find *your* horse's average temperature under normal conditions before an emergency occurs; this will be an important guide to the veterinarian when he diagnoses and treats the problem.

Taking daily temperatures, preferably at the same time each day (or even twice a day), is also helpful in observing the course of a disease. Take his temperature when your horse:
• is not eating or drinking;
• has dull eyes, dull coat, or excessive diarrhea;
• has a running nose or a cough;
• is losing a lot of weight in a short period of time;
• has a deep wound.

The temperature is taken rectally. In some cases, restraint may be necessary, but, as a rule, normally quiet horses give no trouble. To take your horse's temperature:
1. Take the thermometer from its protective case; thread a cord through the eye to form a loop.
2. Hold the upper end (opposite the bulb) between thumb and forefinger, and use a sharp, snapping motion to shake the mercury down.
3. When the mercury is below 95 degrees, dip the thermometer bulb in Vaseline.
4. Insert the thermometer gently full length; hold the cord, or use a clip-clothespin to attach the cord loop to the tail.

5. Leave the thermometer in the rectum three minutes; remove it and wipe it clean.
6. Roll the thermometer until you can read the band of mercury (usually the even degrees are numbered—94, 96, etc.).
7. After use, wash it and immerse it in disinfectant; rinse it in cool water, and replace it in its case.

Hot days, pain, excitement, excessive exercise, and infectious diseases raise temperatures. Shock or impending shock give subnormal readings.

How to take your horse's pulse. A horse's pulse rate varies due to a wide variety of conditions and circumstances. Age is one factor:

	birth	80–120	
normal resting	six months	60–80	beats per
pulse	yearling	40–60	minute
	mature	28–40	

Mares have a slightly faster pulse rate than geldings or stallions. A horse's pulse rate increases in hot weather, and during exercise, excitement, fright, or other stimuli. It also increases due to infection. The rate is decreased by poor health, old age, cold weather, and exhaustion. An even pulse rate is normal; an uneven rate is abnormal.

The pulse, or heartbeat, can be measured with a stethoscope, or it can be felt with the fingertips the way a human pulse can be felt at the wrist (do not use your thumb, as your own pulse can too easily interfere). The pulse can be taken at the following points:

1. back edge of the lower jaw (cheek), 4 inches below the eye (facial artery);
2. inner surface of the groove under the lower jaw (external maxillary artery);
3. inside of the foreleg (median artery);
4. inside the left elbow (up and forward against the chest wall) (heart);
5. behind the knee (digital artery);
6. under the tail close to the body (medial coccygeal artery).

The easiest places to feel the pulse are at number 2 (feel along the bottom of the jawbone for a small cord, the maxillary artery) and at number 4 (feel inside the left elbow with the back of your hand flat against the rib cage).

Count the beats per minute; you may count for thirty seconds and multiply by two, or if the horse won't stand still, count for fifteen seconds and multiply by four.

As is the case in taking temperatures, normal pulse and respiration readings both may vary considerably. It is important to find your horse's normal pulse and breathing rates under a variety of conditions in order to read and evaluate stress readings accurately. See pages 369 to 373 in *Basic Training for Horses: English and Western* for a discussion on understanding and using TPR's (temperature, pulse, and respiration readings).

How to take your horse's respiration. Watch your horse's nostrils or flanks; one rise *and* fall of the abdomen equals one respiration count; count either inspirations (when the stomach comes up) or expirations—not both. Avoid touching the horse's flank, as it may distract him and alter his breathing. Count the movements for thirty seconds and multiply by two.

Normal respiration rate is around eight to sixteen per minute, but may go considerably higher. An increased rate is related to exercise, hot weather, fever, pain, stomach distension, pregnancy, age variations, or excitement of any kind. Respiration rate should never exceed pulse rate.

How to give a shot. Injections are often preferred over other types of medication, because the drug is unaltered by destructive properties of the digestive juices and because it is more rapidly absorbed than by other methods.

There are several kinds of injections:

Intravenous (IV). The drug goes directly into the vein. This is the fastest way for the drug to enter the system, but some drugs can injure the veins. This should not be attempted by the inexperienced person.

Intramuscular (IM). This is the second-fastest way for the drug to enter the system and the easiest for the novice to administer. It can have a sustained effect, since it goes from the lymphatic system to the bloodstream and thence to the cells, medicating the entire horse.

Subcutaneous (beneath the skin layers). The drug is slow to absorb, but faster than orally.

Intradermal (into or between the skin layers). This is used for testing and vaccinations.

Before actually giving your first shot, practice by giving injections of colored water to an orange or a grapefruit. This practice does wonders to help the novice gain confidence, accuracy, and skill. If possible, obtain practical instruction from your veterinarian or from an experienced horseman—there can be serious consequences if mistakes are made.

Preparing for the injection:

DO: Obtain correct gauge and length of needle—it should be sharp and straight. Use 18-gauge needle for IM injections; 16-gauge for thick, oil-based medicine. Length should be one and a half inches.

DO: For a small shot, use a small syringe.

DO: Split large shots and inject at two sites; for instance, a dose of 30 cc's should be split into two 15-cc shots.

DO: Clean an area on the horse for the shot: clip, scrub with soap, swab with alcohol.

DO: Use the whole bottle of vaccine; throw away fractional leftovers.

DO: Use sterile equipment at all times. Handle the needle only by the hub; sterilize the rubber cover on the medicine or vaccine bottle with alcohol before inserting the needle.

DON'T: Use the same needle for several horses (can spread disease and can become dull, bent, or broken).

DON'T: Keep a bent needle—dispose of it immediately.

DON'T: Hit a bone, a nerve, or an artery.

DON'T: Inject air into a bottle you plan to keep and use again (can result in contamination).

DON'T: Let air into the syringe before injection. Hold the syringe straight up and press gently on the plunger until the air is out, or push air into the bottle if the whole bottle will be used. Never inject an air bubble into a horse.

DON'T: Use a needle that has dropped, brushed against clothes, or touched an unsterile object, without resterilizing.

To fill the syringe: Fit the needle hub onto the syringe, and fill the syringe with air to same number of cc's as the amount of medicine you plan to withdraw. Tilt the bottle so that the air is at top, align syringe and bottle to form a straight line, and push the needle into the air space—not into the medicine. Tilt the bottle upward so that the tip of the needle enters the medicine, push the plunger to expel the air, then pull back and draw the fluid into the syringe. Tap the barrel of the syringe, expelling any air bubbles from the syringe into the bottle. Then tilt the bottle down; holding syringe and bottle steady, withdraw the needle from the bottle. Replace the plastic cover over the needle until the shot is used.

Your horse must be adequately restrained while the shot is given. Generally it is better not to tie him—have an assistant hold him and distract his attention, perhaps by offering treats. Use a twitch if other distractions do not work. If the horse is allowed to jump around, the needle could break off

Best injection sites for intramuscular shots.

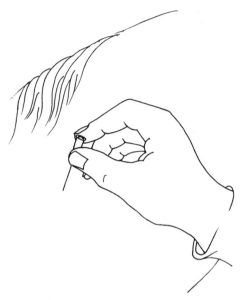

Insert the detached needle with a quick thrust.

under the skin (an added problem you can certainly do without!), the horse may not receive the full dosage, or injury could occur to him or to you.

Decide on the injection site you will use (see the illustration). Intramuscular shots may also be given in the muscled area of the croup. Although shots are sometimes given in the pectoral muscles (chest), this is not recommended, because of the excess swelling that results.

To give the injection:

1. Remove the needle from the syringe (be careful to handle only the hub —do not allow the shaft or the point to touch anything).
2. Hold the hub of the needle between thumb and forefinger, with the point parallel to the horse's neck.
3. Thump the site a few times with the heel of your hand, turn your hand, and firmly, smoothly drive the needle full-length into the site.
4. If blood comes up through the needle, pull it out and try another site.
5. Attach the syringe (make sure there is no air space at the point of the syringe).
6. Firmly and steadily inject the medicine with your thumb on the plunger.
7. Use your free hand to press the horse's neck on either side of the needle as you withdraw the needle and syringe in a smooth motion.

Administering electuaries. Anthelmintics (dewormers), tranquilizers, and electrolytes can be administered in a palatable form called an electuary. To do this, mix the drug with corn syrup, honey, or molasses, or with sugar if the medication is a liquid. This resultant electuary can be rubbed on the horse's teeth and tongue, and will be quickly dissolved and swallowed with the saliva.

Massage is another veterinary skill that you can learn. To "massage" is to rub or knead parts of the body for therapeutic purposes: to alleviate sprains, splints, swellings, bruises, and general muscle soreness. Massage helps lymph circulation and stimulates blood vessels, increasing the flow of blood and nutrients to the affected area. It also frees scar-tissue adhesions between skin and underlying tissue.

Massaging should be done more than once a day, for five minutes each time. To massage:

- Move your hands lightly and flexibly over the horse's body in the direction the hair grows.
- When massaging large, muscular areas of the body, use the palms of your hands. Use your fingers when massaging small, bony areas.
- Use lanolin or Vaseline as a protective and soothing agent if massaging often and the skin becomes irritated.

Hydrotherapy. Spraying with water under pressure (hose) is beneficial in treating leg injuries. The pressurized flow will wash debris out of a wound and has some toning effect, as well as stimulating the healing process by helping the growth of granulation tissues to fill in large gaping wounds. However, water should not be used excessively on wounds where the granulation process has reached skin level; proud flesh may result.

Cleaning the sheath. Good horse management includes cleaning the gelding's sheath periodically, although this is not as necessary as once thought. Debris can accumulate and eventually cause irritation, which can lead to ulceration of the sheath or the penis, swelling, and interference with the passage of urine; it can develop into cancer.

Most of the putty-like debris secreted by the horse is called "smegma." Other debris that accumulates can be mud, dust, bedding, and the precipitation of minerals within the urine. Geldings vary in how often they should be

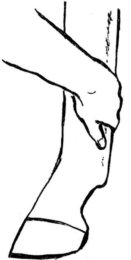

Massaging between the tendons. Cup your hand around the back of the leg and move slowly and smoothly down. Use your thumb to massage in a rotating movement between the tendons. Put the greatest pressure on the upward stroke (toward the heart).

cleaned—from once a month to once a year, if that. You may consider having the sheath cleaned by your veterinarian when he calls on some other routine matter.

You may also clean your gelding's sheath yourself. You will need a soft castile or hexachlorophene soap, with which you will give the sheath a thorough soaping. To do this, use a garden hose (without a nozzle), connected to warm water and with the pressure very low. It is important to use warm water—cold can damage your horse. Insert the hose into the sheath a short way, and hold the sheath closed. It will distend with water, and when you let go, the water will rinse out. When wet, lather your hands with soap, and lather everything within the sheath thoroughly. Smegma accumulates within this pouch, often forming a stone, or "bean." Removing this bean is an important part of cleaning the sheath, since it causes urinary obstruction. It is generally soft enough to be broken apart with the fingers and removed. Be sure to include all parts and folds when cleaning. Repeat the rinsing until all the soap is gone, and let the sheath dry. To finish, smear all surfaces with baby oil or some light antiseptic mineral oil.

When a garden hose with warm water is not available, we use plastic tubing with a funnel at one end. An assistant holds the funnel end (higher than the sheath) and slowly dips or pours in warm water from a bucket.

Tranquilizers such as promazine can be used to relax the penis of your gelding. Be sure to wash your hands thoroughly, both after removing the debris (before oiling) and when the job is finished. Since the debris being removed is teeming with bacteria, any lesion in your skin can result in a severe infection. No, it isn't a pleasant job, but it may sometimes be a necessary one.

Bandaging

Bandaging for other than medical reasons was discussed in the chapter on stable management. Basic bandaging supplies for wounds include gauze squares, a cotton roll, a stretch-gauze roll (primary wrap), cotton quilting for support and padding, adhesive elastic wrap, track bandage, adhesive tape, tincture of benzoin, and ointment.

Pressure bandages are used to reduce swellings, stop bleeding, and cover wounds. Wire cuts on Western horses often produce the type of open injury and attendant swelling that make a pressure bandage necessary to control the swelling, to keep medication applied to the wound, and to prevent the formation of proud flesh. It is sometimes difficult for the amateur to wrap a bandage on the foot or leg that will apply the proper amount of pressure but not interfere with circulation, and stay on for twenty-four hours as well.

For lower-leg injuries, we find that adhesive elastic tape, smoothly wrapped, has a good chance of staying put and is an effective pressure bandage. Track and Ace bandages can be kept in place also, however, with

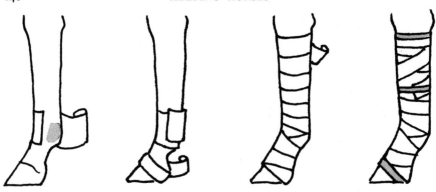

BANDAGING FETLOCK AND PASTERN

practice in applying them. Keeping the horse quiet in a small area is helpful.

Medicate the wound and complete the primary gauze wrap (1). Begin the final wrap at the coronary band (2), extending an inch or two down over the hoof. Wrap tightly, bringing the bandage around under the bulbs of the heel, and follow with another wrap under the heel. If this does not come low enough, the bandage will ride up. Continue to wrap the pastern and fetlock up, keeping a firm, even pressure. You may take an extra wrap or two around the fetlock. Wrap the cannon to below the knee, wind back down with slightly less pressure (3), and fasten on the outside or wrap with adhesive tape (no tighter than the bandage). Secure the bottom of the bandage with several wraps of adhesive tape, letting it come over onto the hoof and around the bulbs of the heel (4). The tape will also protect the bandage where the horse walks on it.

When using a pressure bandage to stop blood flow in the lower leg, place sterile gauze against the wound and wrap the leg with sheet cotton or cotton quilting, then cover with a track bandage or an elastic bandage. The gauze may be wadded to apply extra pressure to stop the bleeding—this must not be left on too long, or circulation will be impaired. Some blood seepage is normal through the wrap. Arterial bleeding, however—which can be recognized by a bright red, pulsating flow—should be stopped by means of pressure until the veterinarian arrives. A cast bandage may also be used as a pressure bandage.

In the case of wounds that require continued bandaging, change the bandage at least once a day—twice if necessary. Your veterinarian will tell you if a bandage should be left without changing for a longer period. Wash the wound, pat it dry, and let it air before remedicating. Rub the leg (except the wound itelf) briskly before rebandaging.

Bandaging the hock. Apply medication on a nonstick gauze pad, then wrap the hock lightly with gauze (1). Use a figure-eight spiral wrap to avoid the point of the hock, and secure the primary wrap (2). Spray the gaskin area above the primary wrap with tincture of benzoin to increase stickiness and reduce skin irritation. Place slim bandage rolls above the hock to protect the

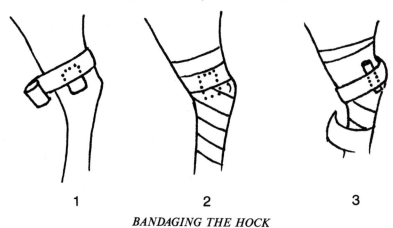

1   **2**   **3**

BANDAGING THE HOCK

Achilles tendon from pressure (3). Wrap with elastic bandage from the coronary band upward, securing the rolls. Avoid the bony projection on the inside of the hock.

Bandaging the forearm. Apply two or three strips of 2-inch adhesive tape vertically on the forearm. Apply the medication on a gauze pad. As you apply the primary wrap, incorporate the ends of the adhesive tape into the wrap; this will keep the wrap from slipping. Finish with an outer wrap.

Foot bandage. The foot may be bound with a track bandage or an elastic adhesive bandage, beginning at the coronary band and wrapping toward the toe. Hold the foot as though for shoeing. To hold a poultice to the sole or infected part of the foot, cover with a plastic bag, then cover all with a bandage cut from a burlap sack to make a boot (leave strips or tails that can be tied). Cross the tails behind the pastern, then bring them to the front and tie them.

A *poultice* draws out puncture wounds, hastens the breaking of abscesses, and soothes angry tissues. To apply, scrub the area thoroughly and clip excess long hair. Add hot water to commercial poultice powder (or antiphlogistine, Epsom salts) to make a thick paste. With your hands wet, mold and smooth the paste directly onto the area a half inch thick; cover with plastic wrap or other sealant (1). Follow with cotton wrap (2). Repeat several times at intervals of twenty-four hours. Do not let the poultice become dry, and do not leave it on too long.

A *spider bandage* is useful in some situations. It can be made of sheet or toweling. Cut each edge into eight or more strips of fringe, leaving the solid part wide enough to go around the leg. Apply medication and primary wrap, then the spider bandage. Tie the top two strips, and then braid down the side of the leg with even pressure. Apply a normal stable bandage over the top for support.

A fracture can be stabilized immediately with an emergency *pillow splint.* For supplies, you will need a large bed pillow, elastic or adhesive bandages,

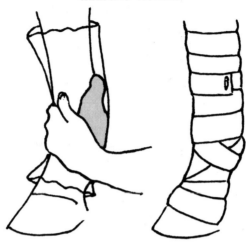

APPLYING A POULTICE

strong sticks, and bandaging materials for an open wound, if there is one. First bandage the wound with gauze, cotton, and elastic bandage. Then wrap the pillow lengthwise around the leg and hold it by tight wrapping of elastic or adhesive bandage, first upward to above the knee, then back down the pillow, and up again. Place boards or sticks on either side of the leg, and secure them with additional bandage.

Dirt and insects can be kept from wounds that you wish to have air by using fine screen or socks (with toe cut off) attached with adhesive tape. This is especially useful on wire-cut wounds on pasterns and cannon bones.

Avoid incorrect bandaging. A poorly wrapped bandage can do far more damage than no wrap at all. Poor bandaging may result in pins coming undone and piercing the leg, or a loose wrapping that unwinds and gets tangled and caught. Too tight a bandage can cause impairment of circulation and loss of hair. Some incorrect bandaging can be serious enough to ruin your horse. Wraps should always start at or near the hair line (coronary band) and extend *up* the leg at least as far as the lower portion of the knee in front or the hock in back.

Here are some warning signs to look for:

- Apparent discomfort that gets worse (for instance, a horse may limp after a bandage is first applied to a wounded leg but, after a few hours, may avoid touching the leg to the ground at all).
- The area above the wrap swells and gets worse (some swelling may be normal, but it should diminish, rather than increase)—there will be no area below the bandage to swell if you have bandaged correctly from the hoof up.
- The thinner the bandage, the more pliable it should be; if it is thin and hard, it is probably too tight.

- If the bandage is too loose, it will bind in some places and produce pressure points. Watch for the wraps slipping or separating before they actually come loose and get caught or tangled.

To remove a bandage:

1. Unwrap it quickly, passing the bandage from hand to hand. Primary wraps may have to be cut and peeled away in one piece; use surgical scissors.
2. Never try to roll up a bandage while removing it.
3. Rub the tendons briskly with the palms of your hands.
4. Wash the bandage if necessary; in any case, hang it up to dry and air.
5. For safety, do not sit or kneel by the horse's legs—bend down or crouch so that you can move quickly if necessary.

Tips on bandaging:

- Run through practice sessions—don't practice on a wounded horse.
- Wrap from the hoof up, to avoid circulation problems.
- Wrap in a steady, continuous motion around the leg, using one hand to hold the roll, the other to smooth the bandage. Keep the pressure even. Wrap by pulling against the shinbone, rather than against the tendon, when applying pressure.
- To help keep a head or neck bandage in place, cover it with tubular elastic-net stocking. Special sizes are also available for hocks, legs, and tails.
- Change the dressings and wraps regularly—pressure bandages over wounds every twelve to twenty-four hours (except for spot pressure to stop bleeding, which must be loosened as soon as bleeding stops), others every eight to twelve hours, unless your veterinarian instructs you otherwise.
- Legs must be aired and rubbed down between bandage changes.
- Thick bandages may be wrapped tighter; thin bandages must be wrapped more loosely and must be flexible.
- Know how to restrain a horse—how to use a twitch, Scotch hobble, or other method. Use of a tranquilizer may be helpful.
- Train your horse to accept handling and fussing before there is a critical need.

Care of the Teeth

Every horse, especially over the age of eight, should have his teeth examined at least once a year. And whenever your horse shows an unexplained weight loss, pain related to eating or drinking, an increased amount of whole grain in the feces, bits of partially chewed food dropped from the mouth, or tipping the head to one side while eating, chances are that his teeth need to be examined.

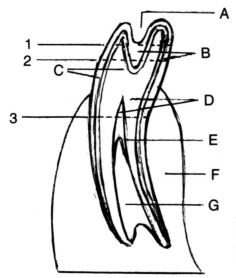

CROSS SECTION OF AN INCISOR
A. Cup (infundibulum). B. Cement. C.
Enamel. D. Dentin. E. Dental star. F.
Bone. G. Pulp cavity (nerves and blood
vessels). 1. Six years. 2. Eight years. 3.
Twelve years.

Horses' teeth are different from almost all other animals' in that they are extremely long but only a small portion protrudes into the mouth. They grow continually and, since they wear down and change as they grow, we can tell the age of the horse by their shape, angle, and markings (see "Age," in the first chapter). Horses have 36 to 44 teeth: 24 molars, 12 incisors, 0–4 canines, 0–4 wolf teeth.

To check the teeth and mouth, grasp the lower jaw with the left hand, and reach into the mouth and pull out and hold the tongue with the right hand. With this method, you can look into your horse's mouth as long as you like, as he will not bite his tongue.

Checklist when examining teeth:
• Do teeth match, one side with the other?
• Do teeth meet with other teeth in correct position?
• Are there a normal number of teeth for the age of the horse?
• Are there teeth missing?
• Are there cuts, abrasions, or abscesses present?
• Check for parrot mouth and monkey mouth.
• At about fifteen months old, check the teeth for sharp edges.
• At two and a half to four years, check for wolf teeth and retained caps.
• When a horse is mature, check for hooks on incisors and sharp edges on molars that interfere with chewing (shear mouth), and wave mouth (should be treated twice yearly).
• Other than the teeth, inspect the mouth for imbedded foreign bodies (splinters, thorns, etc.) and for foxtail lodged in the gums; check the tongue for laceration, and the mucous membranes for color, hemorrhage, and ulceration.

If the teeth do not wear evenly, they will have to be floated (filed) to restore a good grinding surface. This is not a painful process, but it is annoying to the horse, and your veterinarian will sometimes give him a mild tranquilizer.

Anesthesia must be used when he treats less common dental problems such as removal of diseased or decayed teeth (watch your horse for signs of pain especially when drinking cold water, for an odorous discharge from the nostrils, or for a facial fistula). Your veterinarian will usually use a speculum, which holds the horse's mouth open to any degree necessary.

Proper mouth conformation is important to the effective grasping and chewing of food, especially for the Western horse kept exclusively on pasture. Horses with even a mild case of malocclusion should not be used for breeding, because these problems are considered inheritable.

Nothing can be done to help the old horse's smooth mouth—the grinding surfaces of the teeth have been worn smooth. (Don't confuse this with the twelve-year-old horse that has lost the cups in his incisor teeth and is said to be "smooth-mouthed.") It may be necessary to compensate by providing special feed.

When a tooth has been removed or is missing for any reason, its biting partner in the opposite jaw meets no resistance and therefore keeps on growing into the empty space. It must be cut off to prevent damage to the jaw. Occasionally, problems occur as new teeth grow in. A retained cap is a crown of temporary baby tooth that covers or caps the erupting permanent tooth. If the baby teeth are firmly lodged, permanent impaction may occur to the permanent teeth, which are not able to emerge.

Canine teeth (tushes) occur in stallions and geldings almost exclusively. These teeth emerge on the bars of the mouth. A bit hung too low can cause irritation. Wolf teeth—small, rudimentary, or undeveloped teeth—may sometimes appear on the bars in front of the molars and can interfere (cut or pinch) with use of the bit, as well as cause poor use of feed, followed by loss of condition. Wolf teeth should be removed intact as soon as they are discovered.

AILMENTS

A horse owner should work with his veterinarian to keep his horses in the best of health. He should not attempt to take over the veterinarian's job, especially when it comes to diagnosing ailments. As a horse owner becomes more experienced in handling horses, he is able to recognize and treat some problems himself. But he is also more aware of what he does *not* know, and more aware of slight deviations in the symptoms that might require professional diagnosis. The experienced horseman appreciates his veterinarian's knowledge and skills, and doesn't hesitate to seek his advice.

The information in this section is incomplete and is given with the intent of helping you to understand and work with your veterinarian. We would caution you against attempting your own diagnoses and treatments solely on the basis of this limited information. However, while it is up to the veterinarian to diagnose the problem and prescribe treatment, it is up to the horse owner to carry out the treatment and do all he can to prevent recurrence of the problem.

Disease Processes

Shock occurs after most major injuries. It can be described as an acute and progressive failure of blood circulation to the outer body, such as legs and head. When a horse is in shock, effective blood pressure cannot be maintained; the heart weakens, and damage occurs in the kidneys and liver. When it goes far enough, the damage cannot be repaired; beyond a certain point, death results.

A veterinarian must treat for shock, since treatment involves massive replacement of fluids to restore blood pressure and volume. Also, bleeding must be controlled and pain eliminated, since these conditions aggravate shock. The horse owner should call his veterinarian immediately and keep the animal quiet and warm (although if the temperature becomes *too* high, the peripheral vessels can dilate and lower the blood pressure still more).

Closely supervise the horse being treated for shock, as he can quickly relapse and again become critical. You may be able to avoid shock following an injury by immediately giving water (with the chill off) if the horse will drink it, stopping any bleeding, and keeping the horse warm, while waiting for the veterinarian.

Inflammation and healing. Inflammation is a defense process by which the body attempts to destroy, dilute, or wall off an irritating agent—eventually effecting repair of the damaged tissue. Thus, healing is the direct result of the process of inflammation.

There are five primary signs of inflammation: 1) redness, 2) swelling, 3) heat, 4) pain, and 5) loss of function in the area. Controlling inflammation should be done only on the advice and under the supervision of a veterinarian. Wounds cannot heal properly if inflammation does not take place, or if it is excessive (caused by added irritation to strong antiseptics).

Fever usually means an abnormal rise in body temperature due to toxins that accompany an infection. It can also result when the destruction of tissues causes toxins in the blood.

Your horse shows signs of fever by constricting the vessels near the surface of the skin, bringing on "chills," which make the skin feel cold. The pulse will be faster than normal. Shivering results in a further increase in temperature, and then sweating begins. Actually, fever is experienced by horses the same as by humans. It is accompanied by general weakness, sensitivity to touch, and irritability. Loss of fluids can result in dehydration and damage to tissue. Beyond a ten-degree rise in temperature, the body is no longer capable of sustaining life.

Edema is the failure of the body to maintain a balance of fluid between the circulation and tissues; an excess of fluid occurs between the cells within the body tissues, and appears as swelling.

Causes of edema (noninflammatory) are parasite infections, heart and kidney disorders, and poor nutrition. Many pregnant mares near term that have insufficient exercise will form "ventral" or "midline" edema along the lower side of the abdomen and sternum. Giving adequate exercise to heavy mares is important.

Horses kept in stall or horse trailer for long periods of time will "stock up." This can be reduced by supportive bandages. Edema caused by lack of exercise (often showing in the hind legs) will disappear as soon as the horse is given adequate exercise.

Because edema is a secondary disorder, your veterinarian will treat the cause.

Arthritis. There are many types of arthritis, which is an inflammation of the tissues associated with a joint. The signs of arthritis are similar to those experienced by humans: pain in the affected joint, heat and swelling in the joint area, and if chronic movement of the joint will be reduced and prolonged, solidification of the joint due to new bone growth.

Treatment for arthritis depends on the type—it may be prolonged, and usually includes the use of pain relievers. Rest—often six months or more—and relief of pain are very important. Very light exercise—no riding or work—will prevent restriction of movement when the worst inflammation is reduced.

Arthritis can be prevented to some extent by proper shoeing of horses with poor conformation, and disinfecting the navel cords of newborn foals to prevent navel ill, or joint evil. It is important to obtain veterinary advice and treatment early.

Necrosis and gangrene. Necrosis is cell and body-tissue death while the body is still alive; it is usually involved with inflammation. Some causes are poisons (chemicals, plants, tissue toxins), insecticides, mechanical injuries, and burns. When cells are deprived of blood or nerves, they usually die. Prolonged or severe pressure can also cause necrosis.

Gangrene is the invasion of dead tissue by bacteria that can live only on dead tissue. Gangrene produces a foul smell, and the affected tissue is black, moist, and swollen. Dry gangrene appears light-colored, shriveled, dry, and leather-like, since there is a limited supply of blood to the affected tissues. A veterinarian must surgically remove gangrenous tissue, since the bacteria can spread throughout the body.

Septicemia (blood poisoning) exists when large numbers of disease-causing bacteria (or their toxins) in the blood cause fever, a rapid pulse rate, and prostration, usually resulting in death. The toxins interfere with carbohydrate metabolism. Shock can occur, which further magnifies the imbalance. The horse then weakens, showing dullness, depression, and coma, with death resulting unless reversed promptly by antibacterial drugs and antitoxins.

Again, prevention is the best course: use hygienic measures for foaling, give prompt treatment of the navel stump, and see that the foal receives colostrum as a source of antibodies. Older horses can develop septicemia from neglected wounds and infections. Reasonable care and nursing will usually prevent a mild infection from becoming a septicemia.

Dehydration is a condition resulting from excessive loss of body fluid (water). It can be caused by fever, diarrhea from disease, severe hemorrhage, increased sweating or urinating, or simply not taking in enough water. The outward signs of dehydration are a slight rise in body temperature, an increased respiratory rate, and a weak pulse. Skin loses its flexibility and appears dry and wrinkled. The eyeballs seem to sink into the skull, and the horse loses weight rapidly. Muscular weakness, lack of appetite, and increased thirst are signs that death is imminent.

If the cause of dehydration is through insufficient intake of water, the horse may be treated by giving small amounts of water at frequent intervals. If due to excessive fluid losses, he should be treated by a veterinarian.

Hemorrhage is uncontrolled loss of blood from a vessel; the blood can escape outside the body, into a body cavity, or into surrounding tissue space. Causes can be a break or cut in the wall of a blood vessel, destruction of a vessel by ulcer or tumor, rupture of a vessel wall due to parasites or larvae, injuries to the vessel wall from toxins or other poisons, disorder in the clotting mechanisms, or rupture of vessels due to stress.

A horse with visible signs of hemorrhage will show a pallor of the mucous membranes, weakness, staggering, lying down, rapid heart rate, and subnormal temperature, and he will be thirsty. Whem hemorrhaging is acute, rapid blood loss can result in shock. When chemical imbalances result from slower blood loss (withdrawal of fluid from blood stored in the liver and spleen), edema, dehydration, and anemia can result.

The control of hemorrhaging is of first concern. When an artery is severed, it is characterized by spurting bright red blood. It should be treated with a pressure bandage until your veterinarian arrives. Warm, moist tea bags help to stop bleeding. In an emergency, cold water, ice, or snow may be used to decrease minor bleeding but can introduce contaminants. Whole blood is the best replacement if blood-matched donors are available. A typical thousand-pound horse contains over eleven gallons of blood. At least one fourth to one third of the total blood volume must be lost to cause death. It takes four to six weeks to replace red blood cells.

Anemia is a condition of the blood involving a deficiency in the quality or quantity of the circulation, the red blood cells, or the hemoglobin (oxygen-carrying element of the red blood cells). Good nutrition and physical health help the normal production and replacement of red blood cells. Heavy parasite infestation by strongyles and poor feed are the principal causes of anemia. The general symptoms are poor hair coat, paleness of the mucous membranes, muscular weakness, depression, lack of appetite, and increased heart rate. Edema, jaundice, and hemoglobin in the urine may accompany anemia.

The cause for the anemia must be treated first, whether nutrition, parasitic infestation, viral or bacterial infection, or severe hemorrhage. Iron is usually given, along with vitamin B_{12}. Prevention is best—good sanitary management, parasite control, a good-quality feeding program, and mineral supplements where needed.

Tumors (neoplasms). There are many kinds of tumors, and their cause is still not well understood. All have several characteristics in common: they grow and multiply continuously, the cells are not arranged in an orderly manner, and the cells serve no useful purpose. Benign tumors are not dangerous unless they interfere with the functions of the body. However, malignant tumors grow rapidly and infiltrate adjacent tissue; the simple pressure of the runaway growth can stop a vital function, thus bringing death.

Tumors are usually treated by surgical removal, and the prognosis is fair if a removed growth does not grow back. Cryotherapy (extreme cold) and treatment with heat have also been used successfully.

Horse Diseases You Can Catch

There are infectious agents that are capable of producing disease in both humans and animals, and they seem to be increasing in significance—probably because there are so many opportunities existing in our environment for direct and indirect contact between humans and their animals. Horsemen should try to determine if the horse's ailment is a threat to their own health. If there is any question, seek professional advice. An infection or disease transmissible from animals to humans is called a "zoonosis." There are about twenty-five zoonoses that affect horses and their handlers. Beware of the following health problems:

Rabies. With many horses now moving into areas inhabited by wildlife such as skunks and foxes, the incidence of rabies is higher and more significant to the horse than ever before. It can be especially dangerous to humans, since it may be so unexpected if a wound is not obvious—a horseman may treat his horse for a number of other problems before he realizes he is dealing with rabies.

Salmonellosis is another contagious disease considered one of the most important zoonoses. Because the infectious agent is passed into the feces, make an extra effort to clean and disinfect stalls and to replace bedding often. All feed and water containers should be washed and sanitized. Also, anyone working with horses infected with salmonella should thoroughly wash his hands with an antiseptic and change clothes, including footwear. Young children should be kept away from infected horses.

Brucellosis, also called Bang's disease, occasionally infects horses, where it is associated with fistula of the withers and poll evil. Abortion in mares has been reported as a result of brucella infections. If the diseased areas are draining, horsemen should be especially careful.

Anthrax is a zoonosis that affects virtually all animals. Humans can develop local lesions, such as carbuncles and pustules, from contact with infected blood or tissue and can acquire pneumonia from inhaling the infectious agent.

Other zoonoses of horses caused by bacteria are *glanders, tetanus, tularemia, tuberculosis,* and *leptospirosis.* Even though they are not often seen in horses, they are a threat to human health. A zoonosis of horses caused by fungi is *ringworm* (dermatomycosis). Because this infection is easily transmitted to humans, effective sanitary measures should be employed and all debris from fungus-infected lesions should be treated chemically or burned.

Whenever a zoonosis is suspected, contact your veterinarian; remember that it is easier to use precautionary measures and prevent diseases than to fight them.

Prevalent Problems

A number of ailments are listed in the Appendix. Because of their prevalence and importance, however, you should be especially aware of the following problems:

Coughing. A cough is a protective reflex to remove foreign substances from the air passages, to allow easier breathing, and to protect the lungs. Once started, the coughing itself may create irritation and become self-perpetuating.

Casual coughs are relatively harmless, even though they may be loud and explosive. Coughing may be caused by dust, bad habits such as cribbing, environmental conditions such as ammonia from urine and manure in poorly ventilated stables, taking a horse out of a warm, closed stable on a frosty morning, or other reasons.

Coughs originating in the upper respiratory tract seldom produce mucus or other matter; they usually occur as a single cough or occasional spasm of several coughs. Coughs originating in the lower trachea, bronchi, bronchioles, and alveoli of the lungs will sound more muted, be more frequent, and produce more matter; they are less apt to be caused by food particles or irritants. Influenza is a common cause of coughs from the lower air passages.

Coughing may be considered serious when the following signs occur:
- The coughing spell occurs either at work or at rest, or increases when at work.

• The cough gradually worsens.

• The cough seems painful or shallow.

• The cough is a deep wheeze or is accompanied by flatulence.

Serious coughs may or may not have pus or fluid. Get the attention of a veterinarian immediately.

Preventive care to minimize coughing:

1. Be knowledgeable and observe the daily habits of your horses to know immediately when a horse is not feeling well.
2. Keep your horses in well-ventilated, draft-free stabling, especially when several horses are confined together.
3. Keep dust, ammonia, cough-provoking irritants, or abrupt changes in temperature at a minimum.
4. Vaccinate for serious and common infectious diseases, such as influenza and rhinopneumonitis, especially before moving an animal.
5. Maintain a feeding program that keeps a horse in top physical shape.
6. Maintain an exercise program that prevents overexertion of an unconditioned horse.
7. Allow convalescent horses to get plenty of rest; do not work them too soon after an illness.
8. Quarantine incoming horses for ten days before stabling near or with resident animals, and minimize exposure to sick animals whether or not the horse in question is sick.
9. When trailering horses, use good judgment on where to stay overnight, and use your own pails and grain buckets.

Heaves (pulmonary emphysema, broken wind) is a chronic respiratory disease (usually seen in horses five years old and older) characterized by difficult breathing, a wheezing sound, a chronic cough, and poor condition. These symptoms are aggravated by exercise, dust, and hay of poor quality. Heaves can follow a respiratory infection or can occur when horses are suddenly transported from very high altitudes to sea level; it is commonly thought to be an allergic reaction to mold spores or other inhaled matter.

The lungs are unable to properly expel air. The horse breathes in normally, but must use his abdominal muscles to force air out; thus, he breathes out with two distinct movements. A potbelly can develop from the stretched abdominal muscles, and a furrow ("heave line") develops at the muscle attachments along the ribs extending toward the hip. The heart gradually weakens, and the horse is short-winded, with little stamina. There may be a nasal discharge. Food will be poorly digested, because of the labored breathing and because the horse swallows a lot of air; flatulence occurs.

Heaves can be controlled if caught in the early stages. The lungs should not be strained by running, pulling heavy loads, roping, jumping, and the like. Avoid legume hay (which is more likely to have mold), and feed small amounts of the best-quality native meadow grass hay or prairie hay. You can also sprinkle the hay with water. Green pasture is best of all. Pelleted feed, beet pulp, and special rations are also beneficial for horses with heaves. Water the horse before feeding, and never work a horse with heaves on a full stomach. There are also drugs that can help.

Pneumonia is an inflammation of the lungs in which the alveoli are filled with fluid, usually accompanied by inflammation of the bronchioles and pleura (membrane that encloses the lungs in the chest cavity). In young horses and foals, pneumonia is generally acute; in older horses, it may be chronic and progressive. Horses with pneumonia will have rapid, shallow breathing with abnormal respiratory sounds, fever, occasional nasal discharge, breath odor, loss of appetite, accelerated pulse, depression, and a dry or moist cough. When large areas of the lungs are affected, there is a bluish discoloration of the skin and mucous membranes.

To treat the disease, your veterinarian will prescribe antibacterial drugs for at least a week—often two to four weeks. Care includes placing the horse in a warm, draft-free, well-ventilated stall. Blankets during fever periods may be desirable, along with light but nourishing food and plenty of fresh water. Administering intravenous electrolytes may be necessary to prevent dehydration. Normal body temperature and respiration rate, improved appetite, and alertness signal the return to health. Allow adequate rest for at least three weeks for full recovery.

Foal pneumonia is thought to be most frequently caused by bacteria, although viruses, fungi, and parasites may also cause the disease or bring on the bacterial infection by weakening the foal's defenses. Man contributes indirectly to the disease by providing the conditions that induce it: stress, disease concentration (large numbers of horses kept in relatively small areas), and constant contamination of pastures, feed, water, and bedding. Foals show symptoms of fever, rapid pulse, rapid respiration, and a cough, often with nasal discharge, watery eyes, and diarrhea.

Horsemen should not attempt to treat a foal without a veterinarian's help, since infections involving more than one organism are not uncommon, and treatment aimed at one may not have any effect on the others. Improper treatment can be fatal. The veterinarian will evaluate the foal's immune system and prescribe treatment, which should continue at least one week after the symptoms have disappeared.

Early diagnosis is vital, since foal pneumonia has a high mortality rate; even when diagnosed in the early stages, it may be difficult to save the foal. Conscientious nursing is very important. There is no available immunization.

Equine influenza is perhaps the most common and widespread respiratory infection of horses. It is caused by one of two viruses that produce similar symptoms, although severity may vary considerably. Influenza spreads rapidly, since it has a short incubation period (one to three days) and because of the frequent and explosive cough that spreads the virus over a wide area.

Some symptoms are fever (101–106 degrees) lasting about three days, a characteristic cough lasting for several weeks, and depending on the severity, a watery nasal discharge, weakness, stiffness, loss of appetite, depression, and difficulty in breathing. The actual infection lasts from two to seven days. Complications can arise from influenza, even though by itself it is considered a relatively mild disease. However, it leaves the horse in a weakened state and ripe for the onset of bacterial pneumonia (which may be fatal, especially for young horses) and other complications.

To treat equine influenza, complete rest in a clean, well-ventilated area for a full three weeks is critical—longer if it is a severe case. A horse may never regain his former level of performance if he is exercised too soon. There is an equine influenza vaccine that protects against both viral types. When horses are stressed, kept in large numbers, and moved often, they will be more prone to catch influenza, and vaccination makes good sense.

Equine viral rhinopneumonitis is an acute, highly contagious upper respiratory infection, most likely to affect young horses, especially after weaning, and causing abortion in pregnant mares. It is caused by an equine herpes virus and spreads rapidly. Symptoms are similar to those of influenza but usually less severe: it can be distinguished from flu by the presence of a moderate to heavy nasal discharge. Complete rest is necessary; in uncomplicated cases, recovery can occur in seven to fourteen days.

Symptoms of rhinopneumonitis include fever that lasts two to five days, nasal discharge, swelling of the eyelids, congestion, coughing, and loss of appetite. Reinfection can occur at four- to five-month intervals, but in such mild form that symptoms are not visible.

During the high-fever period, the herpes virus is present in mucous droplets, blood, and possibly feces. Even aborted fetal membranes, placental fluids, and the fetus will contain the virus; it can live several weeks when dried on horse hair. Abortions caused by rhino are a major threat to the equine breeding industry.

Vaccination is available. Any new horses should be vaccinated and quarantined for two weeks. In the case of an abortion, the fetus should be sent to a lab for examination, the foaling area should be disinfected, and the mare should be isolated.

Equine infectious anemia (EIA or swamp fever) is a circulatory problem. The most serious aspect of EIA is that antibodies are unable to eliminate the virus from the horse. If it is unable to kill the horse, it persists in the blood as long as the horse lives. The only way to determine the presence of EIA virus in horses is the highly reliable Coggins test, which is run from a blood sample. If a positive reaction occurs, the test should be repeated to be sure of the result.

The first sign of acute EIA is a sudden fever of 105 degrees or higher. Rapid weight loss, anemia, and hemorrhages of the mucous membranes accompany the fever for ten to thirty days, when death usually occurs.

Control, rather than eradication, is the goal of all existing programs. The Coggins test and quarantine are important and fairly successful measures. Since the disease is transmitted by any mechanism that transfers blood from one horse to another, horsemen should control biting flies and mosquitoes around stable areas, and carefully sterilize surgical instruments and hypodermic needles (or use disposable needles). Isolation of new animals until a negative Coggins test is obtained should be a rule of the stable—or do not allow any horse on the premises without a current negative Coggins.

Tetanus (lockjaw) is an infectious disease of the nervous system caused by the germ *Clostridium tetani,* which can be found in the feces of horses, in their intestinal tract, and in the soil. Horses are more susceptible to tetanus than any animal other than humans, but of all bacterial diseases, it can be the most effectively controlled by preventive measures.

The tetanus bacillus enters the tissues through a wound. Because this germ requires the absence of oxygen for germination, puncture wounds are common areas for growth of the bacteria. When the tetanus toxin eventually attacks the nerves, the victim suffers horrible paralytic spasms of the jaw muscles (lockjaw) and other muscles of the body, and after prolonged suffering, dies from asphyxiation. The incubation period can be from three days to a month or longer.

To immunize against tetanus, use tetanus toxoid, a harmless and deactivated tetanus toxin given in two doses, thirty to sixty days apart. A once-a-year booster keeps the immunity at a high level. Tetanus toxoid is given *before* an injury occurs. If your horse has never been immunized and suffers a wound, tetanus antitoxin is given (protects against tetanus, but for only about two weeks). Eliminating the bacteria can be accomplished through the use of penicillin or tetracycline. Supportive therapy may include intravenous or stomach-tube feeding; use of well-bedded, dark quarters; careful treatment of any skin lesions; and the use of enemas and catheterization in case of constipation and urine retention. Sedation is almost always used as well.

Mares given toxoid in the last two months of pregnancy will pass the immunity on to the foal through the colostrum in the mare's milk. At six months of age, the foal should be immunized. If the mare was not immunized, the foal should be immunized with antitoxin at birth. In newborn foals, infection can result from contamination of the umbilical stump. Since tetanus toxoid is so effective and easily administered, it behooves every horseman to protect his horses from the tragedy of death by tetanus.

Encephalomyelitis is a viral infectious disease that causes degeneration of the central nervous system. There are three distinct viruses active in the United States: Eastern (EEE), Western (WEE), and Venezuelan equine encephalomyelitis (VEE). All three can be spread from animal to man, mainly by mosquitoes, while rodents, birds, and wild animals are reservoirs of the disease. The various strains can be diagnosed only by laboratory examination.

The symptoms of all three strains are similar, following an incubation period from one to three weeks: marked depression, high fever (104–106 degrees) persisting for twenty-four to forty-eight hours, hypersensitivity to sound and touch, periods of excitement, apparent blindness and incoordination, involuntary muscle movements (yawning, tremors, grinding of teeth), and drowsiness, followed by inability to swallow, urinate, or defecate, and paralysis.

There is no known cure at the present time. WEE progresses more slowly and has a 50 percent mortality rate, whereas VEE and EEE have 90 percent. Immunization, however, is available. Horse owners should have a veterinarian give an annual vaccination for the appropriate strains. Fly and mosquito control is effective as well.

Rabies. A viral infection of the central nervous system that can affect any warm-blooded animal is rabies. The virus is carried in the salivary glands of infected animals and spread by their bites. In horses, the incubation period is from three weeks to three months. The earliest symptoms are excitability and mania; rolling; uncontrollable actions such as biting, vicious striking, blind charges, and sudden falling, as well as biting and tearing at the site of the original bite from the rabid animal. Muscular spasms accompany this violent behavior, and in the last stages of the disease, paralysis of the hind legs, difficulty in swallowing, and convulsions occur, with increased pulse and respiration rates.

Rabies occurs rarely in horses. Isolation of the affected horse is necessary, as well as keeping the horse alive so as to confirm the diagnosis of rabies. If the horse must be killed, the brain should be kept intact for laboratory examination. There is no treatment for the disease, but cleansing the wound immediately may prevent the infection. Immunization against rabies is the best preventative, especially if the area is known to have cases of rabid skunks, foxes, dogs, cats, or bats.

Colic. Because colic, or abdominal pain, is a symptom of most diseases of the digestive system, it is important to obtain your veterinarian's diagnosis as soon as possible—with some problems, early treatment is critical. *Every case of colic should be treated as an emergency.* Walk your horse slowly (to keep him from rolling), and let him graze green grass if he will, until your veterinarian arrives. Symptoms are refusal to eat, sweating, looking around at flanks, pawing, rolling, and getting up and down.

Ringworm (girth itch) is a contagious skin fungus; some forms are communicable to dogs, cats, and humans. Since there are many kinds of ringworm, the appearance will vary from one or more scaly, hairless spots anywhere on the body to lesions that are thick and crusty. A lab test is usually necessary to determine if the skin disease is a fungus or if it may be another kind of dermatitis.

Treat by applying iodine, glycerine, or thiabendazole ointment directly on the affected area for one to two weeks. Washing the entire body with a fungicidal shampoo or fungicidal dip also has good results and should be done to prevent spread of the disease.

After diagnosing and treating an affected horse, do not groom him until cured, and do not use the affected horse's tack or equipment on other horses.

Disinfect grooming tools and other equipment by soaking in ordinary chlorine bleach diluted with water.

Azoturia (tying-up syndrome, blackwater disease, Monday morning sickness) was a common disease in workhorses before the automobile age. Although less common today, it occurs often enough in our light horses for the average horse owner to need to know what causes azoturia and how to prevent it. It is a metabolic disease in which certain muscles cramp and break down due to an accumulation of acid within the muscle cells. The condition is associated with forced exercise after a period of rest during which feed has not been reduced. When exercise is resumed, the horse "ties up": it is painful for him to move.

Symptoms come on suddenly, with the muscles of the legs (usually both hind legs) and loins becoming cramped and painful if pressed. The muscles tremble and the horse sweats due to pain; if forced to move, he may even sit down like a dog or fall down and be unable to rise. With the breakdown of muscle tissue, muscle pigments are released into the blood and thence into the urine, causing it to be dark in color (hence "blackwater" disease).

The usual history of azoturia calls for the horse to be in fit condition on a high-grain ration and working hard every day. When he is laid off for a day or two and still fed his high-grain ration, and then resumes work, azoturia sets in. However, azoturia may occur in any horse at any time and on any diet. Horses can be affected after long hauls in trailers or exhausting work. It seems more common in the winter months, with most of the victims young and fat.

When azoturia is suspected, the horse should not be moved (even to his stall), but blanketed (due to sweating) and made as comfortable as possible where he is, and the veterinarian should be called immediately. Feed no grain. To prevent azoturia, follow these suggestions:

1. Carefully regulate the diet.
2. Reduce feed during periods of inactivity. Bran mashes the first day will flush the digestive tract.
3. Warm up your horse gradually.
4. Carefully cool him out after work.
5. Before shipping fat horses long distances, it may be well to tranquilize them.

It is thought that there may be two separate conditions of azoturia, or tying-up: 1) true azoturia and 2) muscle cramping and spasms due to overwork (no kidney damage).

Hyperthermia. Horses suffer from heat exhaustion and heatstroke, as humans do. Hyperthermia is a malfunction of the body's heat-regulating mechanism. A horse suffers from heat exhaustion when there is, for a long period, high environmental temperature, high humidity, and poor ventilation. The symptoms are weakness, rapid breathing, muscular tremors, and collapse. The pulse and body temperature may gradually increase, and the horse will sweat heavily. He may have a staring expression, and eventually the body temperature may rise up to 115 degrees. Death often results before effective treatment can be given. Heatstroke, which is just as serious, is different in that the horse does not sweat.

The most important part of treating heat exhaustion and heatstroke is to bring the body temperature down. This can be accomplished by spraying the horse with cold water, or standing him in ice water to constrict the blood vessels in the feet, thus helping the circulatory system maintain adequate pressure for body functions and prevent collapse. Your veterinarian will probably administer fluids to replace those lost in sweating. Your horse should be placed where there is adequate ventilation (even using fans) and given plenty of fresh water.

To prevent hyperthermia, the horse owner should take great care in conditioning his horse, especially when working in the summer months. Salt should always be available.

Internal Parasites

Internal parasites are the greatest single cause of death in horses, as well as being a factor in many respiratory, digestive, and performance problems. Of over fifty kinds of parasites that infest horses in the United States, strongyles, ascarids, and bots are the most damaging.

Control through sanitation and management.
1. When possible, rotate pastures, rotate grazing stock within a pasture, or graze more than one species of animal—this helps destroy parasite eggs and larvae. Avoid putting young horses on a pasture immediately after older horses have grazed there, since they can be infested with parasites by grazing over the manure of the older group; let the pasture rest a year or be grazed by cattle or sheep.
2. Avoid overstocking pastures. The proper number of horses on a pasture allows nature to take care of egg and larva destruction.
3. Pastures that are high and dry are better than ones that have wet, marshy land, as stagnant water provides breeding grounds for many parasites.
4. Keeping pastures clipped destroys the shade that some parasites need and exposes them to the elements. Chain-harrowing the pasture to spread manure will expose it to heat, light, and dryness, thereby killing eggs.
5. During botfly egg-laying season, horses should have a dark shelter where they can get away from open ground and fly attacks. Or keep horses off pasture except at night.
6. Grooming and clipping removes some bot eggs before they hatch. Also, washing with warm water and soap, or using 2 percent carbolic

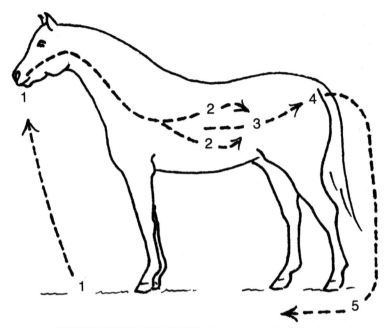

STRONGYLUS VULGARIS (large strongyles, bloodworms)
1. Horse ingests larvae on vegetation. 2. Larvae migrate through the intestinal arteries. 3. Larvae migrate and return to mucous membranes of digestive tract, mature, and reproduce. 4. Eggs leave horse in manure. 5. Eggs develop to first, second, and third (infective) stage in feces or soil. Symptoms: colic, diarrhea, sunken eyes, unthriftiness, tucked-up, anemic—can cause rupture of arteries. Treatment: phenothiazine compounds, Thiabendazole, Pyrantletartrate, Cambendazole.

acid dip, hatches the eggs before they can hatch in the digestive tract; rubbing with a mixture of one part paraffin oil to two parts sweet oil will remove the eggs and deter the flies from laying more.

7. Pick up manure in stalls and paddocks daily. Always ferment manure for at least two weeks before spreading on fields where horses will graze. The heat of fermentation kills most eggs and larvae.

8. Provide clean water (uncontaminated with manure) and quality feed—healthy horses are less likely to be affected seriously by parasites. Clean feed and water containers often. Protect feed by using hayracks and feedboxes that are up off the ground in stables and corrals.

9. Periodic fecal examinations determine the amount of parasite infestation, the kind of parasites present, and whether your chosen method of control is working. You can learn how to take microscopic fecal examinations to save dollars and provide better health care.

10. Take necessary precautions when deworming foals, pregnant mares, and heavily parasitized or debilitated animals. Use safe anthelmintics and deworm with the advice of a veterinarian.

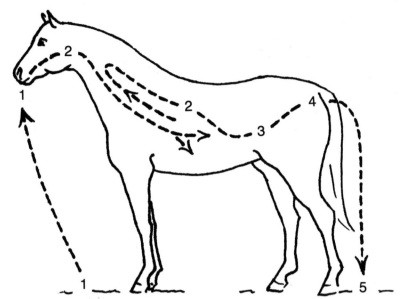

PARASCARIS EQUORUM (ascarids, roundworms)
1. Horse ingests eggs from feces, soil, vegetation, or environs. 2. Larvae migrate from digestive tract through liver and lungs—coughed up and reswallowed. 3. Larvae mature and reproduce in small intestine. 4. Eggs leave in feces, and larvae develop within three-layer protective coating. 5. Eggs can remain viable for years. Symptoms: potbelly, colic, diarrhea, unthriftiness—roundworms do most damage to young horses. Treatment: piperazine compounds, Mebendazole, Dichlorvos; treat at eight weeks and every six to eight weeks until two years; then several times a year, depending on individual and examination of feces.

Control through use of anthelmintics. Using as wide a variety of controls as possible gives the best result; even with the best sanitation and management, the use of anthelmintics is necessary.

1. Have your veterinarian diagnose your parasite problem and recommend proper treatment. Follow his directions, as deviations can cause injury or death.
2. Treat every horse on the ranch or farm. All transient or new stock should be quarantined and treated before turning out with regular inhabitants.
3. Don't rely on one drug or mixture of drugs, since parasites can become resistant. Instead, rotate the drugs upon advice of your veterinarian.
4. When worming for bots, worm after the first or second hard freeze in the fall, since botflies cease to bother in cold weather. At that time, they will be eliminated from the system and not be able to do damage during the winter. Since the bot cycle ends in the spring (eggs pass out in the feces), it is not necessary to worm for bots in the spring. Bot medicine is

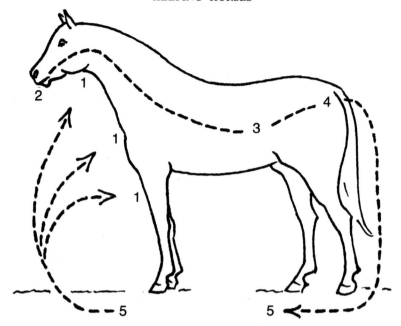

GASTROPHILIDAE (botflies)

1. Eggs laid by botfly on hairs of throat, nose, shoulder, or forelegs. 2. When eggs are licked, hatching larvae enter mouth, finish hatching, and burrow into mouth tissues. 3. In one month, larvae migrate to stomach, attach to white lining, and feed on blood over the winter. 4. In the spring, throat and common bots pass with manure; nose bots reattach to rectum and anus before passing out of the horse. 5. Larvae pupate in ground and emerge as adult flies. Symptoms: colic, unthriftiness—botfly larvae cause anemia and stomach ulcers. Treatment: thirty days after first killing frost, administer carbon disulfide dewormers—keep horses groomed, botflies removed. Trichlorfon, Dichlorvos, carbon disulfide.

strong, and if the horse does not need it, it is not wise to put an unnecessary strain on the system. Because the powerful dewormers could cause abortion, contact your veterinarian before deworming the pregnant mare, especially for bots.

5. Use a low-level deworming program for young horses so that high concentrations of parasites will not be killed all at once and cause impaction in the intestine. This method prevents contamination of pasture with infective larvae: the action of phenothiazine results in the cessation of egg production by adult female strongyles and inhibits the development of infective larvae in the feces and digestive tract. Using the low-level system is thought to slowly bring about the removal of adult worms from the digestive tract as well.

Give two grams of phenothiazine in the feed for the first twenty-one days of the month. No toxic effects from this system have been noted.

If low-level therapy is not used, treatment every two months with drugs recommended by your veterinarian is usually adequate to control strongyles. Another combination we find effective is the low-level system for ten days, wait ten days, and then give a paste wormer orally. This eliminates the possibility of high concentration of parasites, causing impaction, colic, or even death.

6. Don't forget that drugs that control parasites are poisons and should be treated as such. Store anthelmintics according to directions, to preserve efficacy.

Ways of administering anthelmintics. Tubing (passing a tube through the nose to the stomach) is thought by many veterinarians to be the most effective, since there is no loss of medication. Other veterinarians feel that besides the problem of damaging the nasal septum and causing profuse bleeding, tubing may also induce inflammation of the pharynx or esophagus. And it may be excessively frightening to young or nervous horses.

Packaged wormers (granules, pellets, and powder) used in the feed can be effective (as well as convenient and economical) if eaten within three to four hours. Refrigerating (not freezing) packages and paste wormers decreases the odor and taste, increasing palatability. Also, adding wheat-germ oil, molasses, or glycerin will improve taste as well as cause the particles to adhere to the feed, rather than sift to the bottom and be left.

Paste wormers (dose syringe) are convenient, economical, and efficient, since you can "dial" the correct dose after calculating body weight and since they are difficult for the horse to spit out. To administer, first be sure the horse has no feed in his mouth. Then:

- Having determined the weight of the horse, select the proper dosage.
- Remove the cap from the syringe.
- Insert the barrel of the syringe into the side of the mouth in the interdental space, and quickly deposit the dosage on the back of the tongue.
- With your hand on the lower jaw, raise the head and stroke the cleft of the jaw until he swallows. It helps to position his head over a grain pan so that if any medication slips out, it will be caught in the grain and eaten.

External Parasites and Insect Pests

External parasites such as *fleas, ticks, lice,* and *flies* cause blood loss, severe irritation, rough coat, unthriftiness, and poor growth, and may reduce milk production. Constant itching causes horses to rub, and hair loss results—often in large patches.

Control includes application of specific insecticides (consult your veterinarian) and prevention through quarantine, sanitation, and maintaining a nourishing, well-balanced feeding program. The heaviest infestation of external parasites occurs on poorly nourished, unhealthy, and young animals.

Mange (scab, scabies) is caused by several species of mite. Females burrow beneath the skin, causing discomfort, itching, and encrusted patches, leading to formation of thick, wrinkled skin. It is contagious.

Flying insect pests spread disease and account for many horse problems. Horses trying to escape irritation can lose weight and injure themselves running into fences and projections. Control:

- Let horses stay in a darkened shed or stable during the day.
- Put a "fly-knocker" on the halter of horses corralled nearby (or on safety halter): suspend fourteen-inch strips of light material (such as cotton sheet) from the browband attached to the halter. When riding, keep nose flies from bothering by attaching strips or netting to the noseband of the bridle.
- Use fly tapes (flypapers), flytraps, electronic bug killers, or an automatic fly killer system (dispenses vapor every fifteen minutes—most are for six thousand cubic feet).
- Spray or wipe horses with safe fly and mosquito repellent. Use fly blankets.
- Dispose of manure; use good stable hygiene; cure any drainage problem.
- Take care and ask advice when using insecticides—be aware of residual toxic substances, food and water contamination.
- Some people contend that free-roaming barnyard chickens cut down on flies—especially botflies—by scratching out manure and eating larvae.

RESTRAINTS

Restraints are often used to physically control a horse for treatment of an injury, during breeding, and when giving some dewormers. Since a horse is usually frightened and in pain after an injury, using a physical restraint will keep him from further injuring himself or you. However, you must consider your horse's temperament and size, the kind of work to be done, and the location and duration of the restraint, in order to make a knowledgeable choice of the mildest, most humane restraint that will provide effective control. Some horses may panic when restraints are applied; in this case, perhaps a chemical restraint should be used, either alone or along with physical control. When handling excitable horses, be calm, firm, careful, and confident, and use an area such as a large stall or shed where the horse can do little damage.

Mechanical Restraints

How to tie a horse. The last thing you want to have happen when restraining a distressed horse is to have the equipment break. Because of the

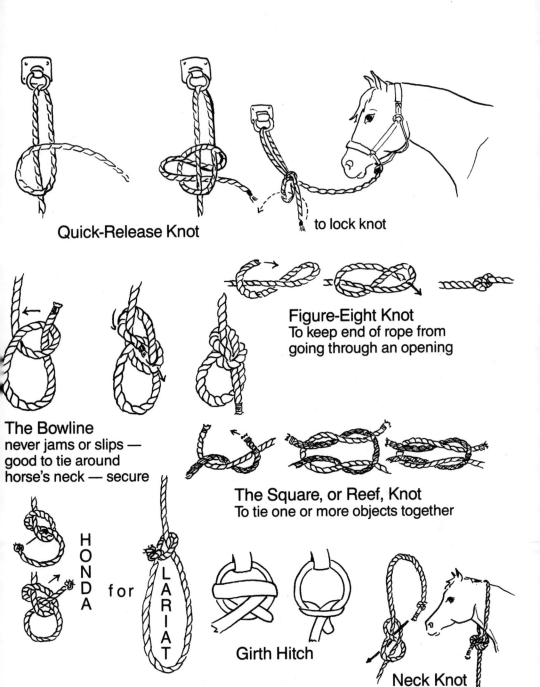

Quick-Release Knot

to lock knot

Figure-Eight Knot
To keep end of rope from
going through an opening

The Bowline
never jams or slips —
good to tie around
horse's neck — secure

The Square, or Reef, Knot
To tie one or more objects together

H
O
N
D
A

for

L
A
R
I
A
T

Girth Hitch

Neck Knot

USEFUL KNOTS

extra stress applied at these times, make sure your equipment is strong and in good condition. Your halter should be made of quality reinforced nylon or strong rope. Your lead rope should be cotton (three-quarters of an inch in diameter), ten to fifteen feet long, with a heavy-duty, quick-release snap. Nylon rope is stronger than cotton, but can cause rope burns to horse or handler.

In any case, tie your horse to a solid, stationary, vertical object such as a fence post set well into the ground. Your horse should be tied at least as high as his head, to reduce neck injury and the chance that a leg can catch over the lead rope.

A quick-release knot and other useful knots are shown in the diagram.

The twitch (Yorkshire twitch) is one of the most common physical restraints. It consists of a thirty-six- to forty-eight-inch handle with a rope or chain loop on one end. It can be made by cutting off an old fork or shovel handle; the rope is usually of clothesline type. Use of the twitch is based on the principle that a horse thinks of only one thing at a time; when pressure is applied on the sensitive nerves of the lips, the resultant discomfort diverts his attention from the procedure or treatment going on. Care must be taken that the twitch is not used for long duration, as it can cut off circulation, and when numbness sets in, it no longer will have a diversionary effect. Alternate the pressure so that sensitivity will not be lost. Excessive pressure will result in a cut lip.

To apply a twitch, follow these directions (although you can apply a twitch from either side, the left side seems the more usual):

1. Grasp the twitch handle firmly at the center with the right hand.
2. Loop the rope or chain around the middle three fingers of the left hand.
3. Grasp the horse's upper lip with the left hand and slide the rope or chain around the lip while folding the inside in to protect the mucous membrane.
4. While holding the folded lip with the left hand, rotate the handle clockwise so that the rope seems to climb, rather than go down off the lip. If your horse makes it difficult to put the twitch on, sometimes taking a roll of skin over the shoulder or grabbing an ear will give momentary distraction until you get the twitch on. Do not put the twitch on an ear, as it can break the cartilage that supports the ear, and a blemished horse will result.
5. With both hands, hold the lead shank and the twitch handle near the end of the handle.
6. Occasionally rotate the twitch back and forth to keep your horse distracted. Even tapping on the handle will help if you must keep the twitch on for a long time.
7. Take care that you hold the handle firmly; if the horse should toss his head and pull it free, it can swing around dangerously.

Chain lead restraints and war bridle. In almost all cases, passing the chain under the jaw or over the muzzle will give all the restraint that is necessary.

Humane twitch. A one-man twitch that is easy to use and seldom slips.

Screw-end twitch. (English twitch). A one-man twitch used to exert constant pressure.

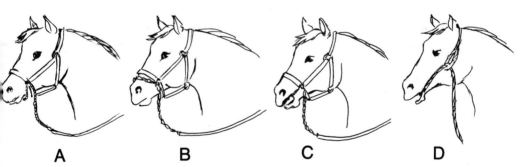

A   B   C   D

CHAIN LEAD RESTRAINTS AND WAR BRIDLE

A. Mildest. Chain passed under jaw (snap attached to right ring of halter). B. Mild. Chain passed over muzzle. C. Severe. Chain passed over gingiva (gum)—use with care, as this can damage gum. D. War bridle. Most severe. Can be used on horses that fight twitch or are vicious. Chain lead restraints can be used as a training aid, to lead an unruly horse, or while treating or working on feet. Never tie a horse with any of these chain lead restraints or the war bridle.

Cradling is a safe, humane way to hold a young foal, before he has learned any other method of restraint. Tie the mare in a familiar stall or corral. Standing on her near side, push the foal close to her with your body, one arm around the foal's chest, the other around his rump. (Courtesy Freda Dickie Weaver)

The other methods should not be used by inexperienced people, as they are very severe and can do a great deal of damage to the horse. *Never* tie a horse with one of these restraints.

Cradling is an excellent way to restrain a young foal, as shown in the illustration.

Tailing is another way to hold a very young foal for treatment. Cradle his chest with one arm, and grasp his tail firmly *at the base* (right up against his body). He can be easily held in this manner. Be careful not to twist the tail or bend it up—you could injure the spine. Start within a few days after the foal is born to get him used to your handling and to accept restraint without panic.

Foreleg restraint. On the same side that you wish to treat the horse, have an assistant hold up the foreleg (as though for picking out the hoof). You can also use a knee strap buckled around the cannon and the forearm of the flexed leg—but use this only on an unexcitable horse, as it could injure the horse or the handler if the horse were to panic.

The *Scotch hobble,* a traditional restraining method, has several advantages. A hind leg can be held up for a much longer time than a foreleg without causing discomfort. It needn't be pulled high, just forward enough so

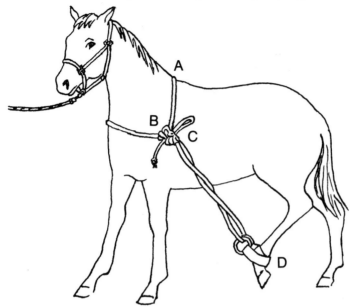

The Scotch hobble. A. Use one-inch, thirty-five-foot, soft cotton rope. B. Tie a bowline around the neck. C. Use half hitches to hold the leg to the neck rope. D. Use a Western cinch or take a double wrap with the rope.

that the horse can't kick and his mobility is limited. If he can be handled, you may use a Western cinch, as shown, or a leather hobble and D-ring around the pastern.

If the horse is difficult or dangerous to handle, snub him while you tie the neck loop (use a bowline); there will be a lot of rope left over. Throw this long end of the rope between the hind legs (or lay it out on the ground and haze his hindquarters over until the rope is between his feet). Then bring the end of the rope around one pastern, run it through the neck loop, and pull the leg forward. To avoid rope burns, use soft cotton rope.

There are several types of *casting harness* for throwing a horse; one of these flexes the hind legs and pulls them forward, sitting the horse down, from which position he is rolled over onto his side.

Stocks. Doctoring stocks will completely control and immobilize the horse for breeding, applying medicine, or cleaning. These are designed to protect the handler and are made from pipe or stout lumber. The sides or parts of the side may be removed. Most large-animal veterinarians have stocks in their clinics.

Body restraints. When you must restrain a horse for a very short time and have strength in your hands, a variety of body restraints can be used:

1. Shoulder twitch: grasp the skin over the scapula and twist down and forward.

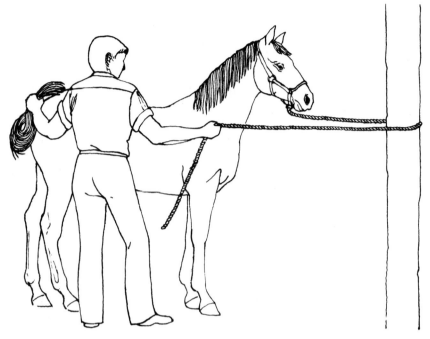

One way to restrain the older foal, small horse, or pony. Run the lead rope around a post or other upright, crowd the colt next to the wall with your body, and pull his tail firmly toward you and up. Use caution, as you can cause bone distortion or coccygeal fracture. When the colt resists, take up the slack in the lead rope and tighten your hold on the tail. When he quiets, quickly relax your holds. This method can be good for training as well as for restraining. (Courtesy Freda Dickie Weaver)

2. Hold an ear down by the base; pull down, but do not twist too hard.
3. Grasp the upper lip as in a twitch.

Restraints to prevent bandage chewing. When wounds begin to heal, they sometimes itch, causing the horse to chew his bandages and even mutilate a wound. Before using the following restraints, try applying Tabasco sauce to the outside bandage. Some commercial preparations can cause burns to the skin, so use with care.

The *muzzle, neck cradle,* and *leather bib* are illustrated in the chapter on stable management. The bib can be attached directly to the halter and can be used in conjunction with the neck cradle.

If a hind leg has been bandaged, you can use a *side stick* to keep the horse's neck from turning. This is just a sturdy, straight stick running from halter to surcingle. If there are clips at both ends, it is easier to attach.

If your horse needs even more restraint, you can try an *overcheck* from halter to surcingle, making your horse unable to flex his neck far enough to disturb his bandage. He will still be able to move about his stall. An over-check from a harness will work as well.

The overhead *swivel tie* consists of a rope dropped from an overhead beam and attached to the noseband of the halter with a swivel snap. Your horse will be unable to lie down but will be able to walk around his stall. It is quite safe, since he cannot catch a leg over it.

The *crosstie*. We have a gelding that managed to get out of all restraints to chew not only his bandages but also the deep wound on his upper forearm. The crosstie was the answer, and because of the restriction and boredom, we moved him at least three times a day (he had to be restrained for three months). We crosstied him at a manger in a stall at night; during the day, we crosstied him in a loading chute (his head into the end of the chute, his chest up against it as with a manger); then, part of the day, we loaded him into a horse trailer. We also exercised him twice a day. He was worth all our energy, since the wound healed almost without a scar, and mobility was not harmed. He went on to win second-level dressage tests.

The *body sling* can be used to support a part of a weak horse's weight, although there are few horses that will tolerate a sling. The *blindfold* provides quick protection and restraint for a cast horse and is a means of quieting a balky horse and persuading him to move. There are some horses, especially when injured, that will be stimulated by a blindfold, so be careful and continue to monitor a blindfolded horse.

The body sling.

Chemical Restraining Agents

Tranquilizers and sedatives such as promazine and acepromazine are familiar drugs to most horsemen, and they can be used outside of a veterinary hospital. However, *any* chemical restraint should be used only with the consent and advice of your veterinarian.

Tranquilizers are sometimes used when floating teeth, during simple examinations, when repairing wounds, for pregnancy diagnosis, when hair clipping, when shipping, and so on. They can be either injected or given in the feed, and are often longer-lasting than sedatives, which can sometimes be a disadvantage. If a tranquilizer is given to an excited horse, it is possible for the horse to respond with the opposite effect; tranquilizers must be given while the horse is calm, and he should not be moved or subjected to noise and commotion until after the drug takes effect. Dose each horse according to body weight.

Sedatives quiet a horse. They are used prior to a standing operation and can be used for procedures that may cause momentary pain. "Rompun" (xylazine) works well for minor surgical and dental procedures, although it does drop the animal's head. Our veterinarian used Rompun when our two-month-old filly broke her leg and had to be transported in a trailer thirty miles to the clinic.

CHAPTER 9

TRANSPORTATION AND INSURANCE

TRANSPORTING HORSES

Our society is a mobile one, and unless you have the vehicles to transport your horse—and a horse that is willing to be transported—your horizons are limited. Shows, trail rides, clinics, rodeos, and trips to the veterinarian require that you and your horse travel from home stable to another location. The means of transport can sometimes loom as a major item in the horseman's life.

Commercial Transport

Horses were often shipped by train in the nineteenth and the first half of the twentieth centuries, but rail routes and schedules are now less convenient than hiring a commercial van. There is a twenty-eight-hour law that applies to the interstate shipment of horses by truck and rail: at least every twenty-eight hours, horses must be unloaded for rest, feed, and water.

Air transport is fast, less stressful, and safer than long over-the-road transportation. However, the cost is almost prohibitive, and usually only very valuable horses are shipped by air. Air cargo carriers provide detailed shipping instructions.

One of the safest and most satisfactory ways of transporting horses is by van or semitrailer especially fitted for horses. Special stalls are provided for mare and foal, or for a stallion. Diagonal stall dividers are used in some large vans, and the horses ride well. When making a contract with a commercial horse transport company, consider the following:

1. Obtain a written statement confirming the kind of vehicle to be used, cost, care provided on the trip, the route, and duration of layovers. A full vanload going near a horse's destination will cost less per horse than a trip involving only two or three horses in a six- to eight-horse van. Commercial carriers wish to fill their vans and often must plan a layover or longer route for this purpose. Rates are based on prevailing Interstate Commerce Commission guidelines, but can vary.

2. Provide the commercial transport with Coggins papers, brand inspection where applicable, health certificate, papers of identification, and

any feeding or special-care instructions. Provide a list of articles that
accompany the horse, such as halters or blankets; this list should be
presented to the recipient, along with the horse, at the other end of the
trip.

3. If you have insurance on your horse, give the driver telephone numbers
   and all pertinent information in case of injury.
4. Horses should be immunized against contagious diseases.
5. If your horse must have special feed, provide the feed and feeding instructions.
6. Obtain a reference or two, and insist on a written contract.
7. Ask if first-aid equipment is on board and if vehicle inspection certificates are current.

Most companies require at least a 50 percent deposit before the trip starts.
Arrange for trip insurance if you do not carry insurance on your horse.

Private Trucks

Enclosed stock trucks can be remodeled for horses, adding partitions and
mangers. When hauling loose horses, there should be some partitions so that
the load will be stabilized. Good footing and adequate ventilation are a must
when hauling many horses in an enclosed space. Mares in foal and with foals
at side should be hauled separately from all other horses; stallions also should
be hauled separately. Ship horses of similar size and age together to lessen the
risk of injury. Safe loading ramps should be installed when converting livestock trucks.

For short hauls, horses may do well in a regular, open livestock truck if
tied to a sturdy upright and protected by a high headboard.

When adding a stock rack to a pickup, the choice of pickup is important,
since live weight can cause instability even with a heavy-duty truck. Use a
three-quarter- or a one-ton pickup with heavy-duty shock absorbers, springs,
and suspension, and with a large radiator. Handling a pickup with horses in a
stock rack requires very smooth, careful driving.

If traveling with open racks, provide a barrier over the cab to give protection from the wind, or provide the horses with hoods and goggles. A closed
stock rack is the better choice.

A van-type body with ramp can provide a good rig if it is well constructed.

Trailers

Your hauling rig should be thought of as a unit, as safety depends on how
the particular combination works. Before buying, renting, or relying on someone else, examine and read about all kinds of trailers. Constant care, a good
product, and a reputable dealer are key points when selecting a trailer.

Many Western ranchers own stock trailers, since they are versatile and can be used for hauling cattle, hay, lumber, and machinery, as well as horses. A sixteen- to eighteen-foot covered stock trailer can have a manger installed in the front (most stock trailers do not have them), with a saddle compartment underneath. A good stock trailer is usually less expensive to buy and of more rugged construction than a regular, two-horse trailer. However, because wind, rain, snow, and cold can penetrate through the sides of the trailer, it is a poor choice for carrying horses in inclement weather unless protection is added.

Open stock trailers may have no roof at all or may have overhead frame bars over which a tarpaulin may be fastened. Although not usually recommended for hauling horses, open trailers have one advantage: often a horse that refuses to load in any other kind of trailer is unafraid with the open top and will load easily. The front and sides are usually high enough to offer wind protection.

Gooseneck trailers (some of which incorporate living quarters) have the advantages of maneuverability and security—overall, they pull better than a bumper-hitch trailer. Some tow-truck operators, however, feel that goosenecks are very dangerous in a wreck, since the extension can shoot forward to remove the top of the pickup cab. Another drawback is the lack of space in the pull vehicle.

The most common means of transporting horses is the two-horse trailer. It can be towed by a pickup or a full-sized automobile. These trailers have many options, such as step-up loading (two doors) or ramp loading, tack storage, dressing rooms, and feed mangers. They should have tandem axles for stability and safety. Most two-horse trailers have an escape (walk-through) door toward the front. It is possible to have both step-up type and ramp type in one trailer, and extra-high or extra-wide trailers are also available.

Large gooseneck stock trailer and double-axle horse trailer. (Courtesy Dave Ellsbury)

Dave Ellsbury constructed a sliding, pull-out saddle rack for the tack compartment of his trailer. It holds two saddles. By welding horseshoes on the door, he made a convenient place to hang lead ropes, bridles, and other gear. (Courtesy Dave Ellsbury)

The in-line trailer is longer than the two-horse, tandem-axle type but with little room for storage, and it is difficult to back, turn, and park. However, since the whole rig is narrower than the two-horse trailer, there is better visibility, both for the driver and for vehicles coming up behind. An in-line trailer places far less weight on the tongue and on the tow vehicle, is more economical on gas, and produces less overall wear on the towing vehicle. Also, a detached in-line trailer (with wheels blocked) can be loaded without being attached to a vehicle, whereas a side-by-side should not.

As is the case of the in-line, the single-horse trailer is not very popular, due to limited storage space. Even folks with only one horse prefer the two-horse trailer, so that the other stall can store feed, tack, and so on.

What to Look for in Buying a New or Used Horse Trailer

Pull vehicle:
- Must be strong enough for the trailer you select: adequate-size motor, heavy-duty suspension and springs, adjustable shock absorbers, sway bars, and a large radiator to prevent overheating. For safety as well as economy, it should be heavier than the towed vehicle.
- Both tow vehicle and trailer should be equipped with a usable spare tire, a suitable jack, and an anti-sway attachment.
- The trailer hitch should be welded to the frame—never to the bumper— and should be rated for your maximum load. The ball on the hitch should be the correct size—never too small, as the trailer hitch clamp could pop up and release the trailer.
- The height of the hitches on trailer and tow vehicle should be the same for balance, control, and equal tire wear.
- There should be large rearview mirrors and a convex "blind spot" mirror to see passing traffic.

Frame of trailer:
- The kind of frame supporting a trailer is perhaps your most important consideration, as it is paramount in determining the safety and durability of the vehicle.
- Look for a strong frame constructed with boxed channel iron (not square tubing) (Fig. 1), channel iron (Fig. 2), or I-beam (Fig. 3).
- Next best is heavy angle iron (Fig. 4). Avoid frames constructed with light angle iron, or the no-frame, unibody construction, which can be dangerously weakened by rust or cracking.
- Look at the way in which the springs are attached to the frame: they should be attached to pieces of steel that are bolted, welded, or riveted along the two frame rails—rather than attached directly to the frame rails or to mounting pieces welded to the lower edge of the frame rails.
- Look beneath the flooring. There should be several crossbeams supporting the flooring, rather than one or none.

Exterior of trailer:
- There should be a reliable, sturdy hitch with heavy-duty safety chains.
- The knob or ball should be machined out of one piece of steel, with a 1-inch shank (threaded part). Most horse trailers take a 2-inch ball; get a 2 5/16-inch ball for large trailers with dressing rooms or stock trailers. Purchase replacement knobs at a quality auto parts store.
- Brakes—surge brakes with a breakaway braking system are advisable.

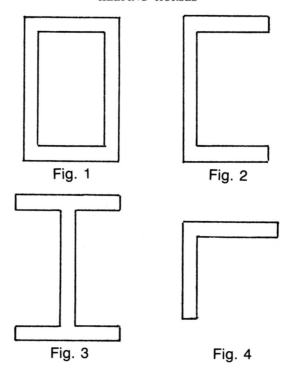

1. Boxed channel iron (not square tubing). 2. Channel iron. 3. I-beam. 4. Heavy angle iron.

- Tandem axles, for stability and safety. Proper wheel alignment to reduce or eliminate swaying and help stability. Safe, fully inflated, heavy-ply tires (same kind as on tow vehicle, to minimize sway).
- Double steel walls with wood liner between. Frightening noises are lessened with good insulation and soundproofing.
- White or off-white roof—light colors reflect summer heat, allow a cooler, more comfortable ride. Fiberglass tops give a light interior.
- Escape doors of adequate size, well-fitting (no rattle), with secure latches.
- All door latches (including tack and escape doors) should be *very* secure —if in doubt, add a bar across the back of the trailer. The pins in the back-door hinges should not be able to come out. Hinges should be rust free (horses have been killed when back-door hinges have broken or come apart). Latches on partitions should be easy to close, and secure when latched—not able to bounce or jiggle free. They must be strong enough to withstand a sudden impact and horses leaning on them.
- Adequate running lights, brake lights, and turn signals should be working.
- There should be solid outside tie rings, well separated and positioned on the side, for tying horses.

- There should be a sturdy spare-tire mount, positioned so as not to interfere with the view from the rearview mirror.

Interior of trailer:

- Sufficient head room, leg room, and knee protection (adequate padding).
- Removable partitions with head (manger) divided. Partition extending to floor is usually preferable. Remove for easy cleaning or for hauling a mare with foal.
- Well-constructed floor in good condition. Check for weak spots, rotting wood. Surface should be nonslip. Use heavy-duty mats.
- Butt chains, straps, or bars (chains should be covered with hose). These are a safety feature in case doors open accidentally or must be opened without the horse backing out. Also they help the horse balance against a sudden jerk or long uphill grades.
- Tie rings—firmly mounted and easily reached. Use panic snaps for security and easy release.
- Should be light-colored and have adequate lighting and ventilation.

An *open trailer* is not advised for hauling horses. If one is used, however, your horse's eyes and head should be protected by a windshield or a hood and goggles.

Trailer Maintenance

Protecting your considerable investment with good care will pay off in convenience and safety. Check and service your trailer thoroughly at least twice a year—before storing it for the winter, and in the spring to ready it for use.

Winter maintenance tips:

1. Store your trailer in a garage, carport, or barn, if possible (never under a tree). If this is not possible, park it in the most protected spot you can find—never where horses can bite or dent the trailer.
2. Sand rust spots smooth, prime, and repaint these spots. Buy a good wax and apply two coats to all painted surfaces inside and out. Be sure to check latches and hinges for rust.

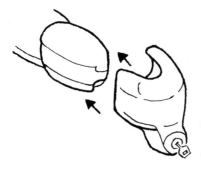

This type of lock prevents an unattached trailer from being hitched to a towing vehicle. The lock blocks access to the coupler cavity by covering it with a protective housing.

3. Park your trailer at an angle so that any water from snow or rain will drain out. Leaving the trailer with good ventilation will keep the inside from sweating into the paint, wood, and upholstery.
4. Clean the upholstered padding and apply a vinyl preservative.
5. Use a screwdriver to check the condition of the floorboards. By picking at the wood, you can tell if they are cracking, brittle, or flaky—if so, replace them. Wood preservative will help keep the boards in good condition.
6. Check the wiring for lights and brakes.
7. Replace tires that are worn or weather-cracked. To eliminate and prevent "checking" (hairline cracks from weather exposure), brush on special tire paint. Use a piece of plywood, or wrap a tarp around the wheels, to protect the tires from exposure. When storing the trailer, take the weight off the tires by jacking the wheels up slightly.
8. Pull the wheels and check the bearings for seals and packing grease.
9. Your hitch wheel should rest on a block of wood, not on the ground.
10. Give all moving parts a dose of lubricant and preservative.
11. Spray the electrical hook-up plug with dry lubricant, and protect it with a waterproof cover.
12. Remove the battery for the breakaway brake system and store it in a warm, dry place; check its power before reinstalling it in the spring.
13. Recheck your lights, brake, wiring, hinges, latches, and locks before using them in the spring.
14. For quick tire changing on a tandem-axle trailer, construct a wheel riser by beveling a 6 × 6-inch beam so that you can drive up onto it with one wheel, leaving the other wheel (on the same side) off the ground. Store it in your tack compartment.

Care of your trailer between trips:
1. After each use, take out all old hay (from manger) and bedding, and scour the trailer. Pull out floor mats—scour them as well as the floor. Sprinkle wooden floors with lime to keep the trailer smelling sweet.
2. Clean butt chains or bars—caked manure can wear off hair and tail to produce an unsightly posterior.
3. Clean windows; close windows and vents or set them for ventilation.
4. Clean mud and dust from all lights; check brakes; give a lube job often; grease if needed (some modern trailers can't be greased).
5. Check the spare tire—be sure it's carrying enough pressure.
6. Check for any needed repairs—loose nuts, nails sticking out, splinters, loose or pulled-apart padding.
7. Grease the fitting on the dolly-wheel crank. If there is no fitting, extend the dolly jack so that grease can be worked into the cogs.
8. Check wheel bearings, axles, and running gear.
9. Remember that your towing vehicle will require more maintenance due to stress—towing burns more spark plugs, uses more oil, and stresses motor, transmission, and brakes.

TRAVELING WITH YOUR HORSE

Preparing Your Horse for a Trip—Paperwork and Immunizations

Several weeks before the time you intend to leave, ask your veterinarian about the health papers that will be required at your destination. Traveling across state lines usually requires a negative Coggins certificate (within six months) and a health certificate (within ten days). Because it may take a week or more to receive results on a Coggins test, be sure to leave enough time. In most Western states, brand inspections are required. Horses traveling out of the United States require even more complicated documents—your veterinarian can advise you. All these documents should be assembled together with ownership and descriptive papers. When traveling, your papers should be readily available with you in the hauling vehicle. If you don't wish to take your horse's original registration papers, make photocopies.

When planning a trip through an unfamiliar area, plan your route well in advance. Interstate highways are easier for you to drive and your horse to ride; map out daily mileage and if possible write ahead for overnight stops. There are guides to overnight stops available, or you can get advice from breeders in the area. Because overnight stabling (fairgrounds, auction yards, and boarding stables) has such a high turnover of horses, reduce the possibility of your horse's catching a communicable disease by having the full scope of immunizations, using your own water and feed buckets, and not allowing your horse to drink at public water troughs. You should know—or find out—whether your horse is allergic to penicillin, so that this knowledge does not come as a surprise on the trip.

Preparing Your Trailer or Van

Your truck and trailer should be prepared ahead of time, because as soon as your horse is loaded, it's usually best to take off immediately, rather than run around making noise, packing, and slamming doors.

Installing a citizens-band radio in your truck and taking out a membership in a motorists' club are two ways to be sure of extra help on your trip if you should need it.

Begin with your regular maintenance check (see *Care of Your Trailer Between Trips,* in the previous section of this chapter, and follow with special considerations for this situation: removal of partition to haul mare and foal, perhaps, or adding additional padding for a horse that kicks or rubs his hocks. Make sure that windows are clean, and repair windows and ventilators for the trip. Bed the trailer deeply with straw or sawdust to ease the effects of vibration and road bumps on feet and legs and to encourage the horse to urinate. Place in a clean manger or hay net the highest-quality roughage you can find.

Load truck and trailer with necessary items, including your personal clothing, boots, and so on. Use the following equipment checklist to suggest items for your own checklist; keep the list with you in the cab of the truck:

first-aid kit

hock protection, head bumper, extra leg wraps

tail wraps

surcingle, longeing equipment

tack for riding

map with route outlined

horse's papers

2 flashlights (1 with red-shield end) and extra batteries

loading ropes (including one of cotton, 1-inch diameter, 30 feet long)

padlock and chain to lock stall door or pen at night; keys

fire extinguisher

feed tubs, preferably rubber

water buckets, preferably rubber

hay net

extra lead shank

extra web halter

blanket and/or sheet

broom, shovel

grooming and farrier tools

bran, grain, hay, minerals

additive for water

pliers, wire cutters

tire gauge

jumper cables

extra fuses, light bulbs, for vehicle and trailer

Park trailer for loading—on level ground with emergency brake on (if you must load your trailer while it is unhitched, block the wheels securely and block up underneath the back door or ramp to prevent the trailer from tipping up as the horse steps in). Find a spot where the step up is not too high—sometimes moving forward or back a few feet will make a big difference. If there is any question about the horse's willingness to load easily, wrap any outside projections with burlap sacks, including the licence plate if it projects, so that if your horse becomes frightened, rears, or fights, he won't be injured on the trailer.

If loading at night, put on the trailer's inside light; the horse will enter a lighted area more willingly. During the day, a horse may enter more willingly if the sun shines into the back of the trailer than if it is shining in his eyes. Brace the ramp or doors if necessary, especially if it is windy.

Trailer Loading and Unloading

Preventing injury—to yourself, your assistants, and your horse—is a primary consideration in loading. Some factors that help prevent injury are as follows:

1. Train the horse as a youngster to load into a trailer—and certainly before an actual trip.

2. Train him to lead directly to the trailer and enter without a handler; if you must go in with your horse, either enter on the opposite side or have the escape door open and ready for your free passage. Never place yourself in a small area where a horse can trap you.

Take the time to train your young horses to load. Preparing properly makes the job easier on both you and the horse. Block the wheels, prepare a loading ramp (set a railroad tie or other large block of wood behind the doors of a step-up trailer so that there is no gap to step over, and cover it with dirt), and wrap license plates and other sharp protrusions with burlap. Use enough experienced help to accomplish the job with a minimum of fuss, and praise the youngster calmly when he enters. A few times in and out will convince him it's just part of the day's work. Sodergreen Ranch, Buford, Wyoming.

3. Load and unload in a safe area—a place that is quiet and level, has safe footing, no distractions, and is out of the wind. If possible, position the trailer near a board fence or barrier (not barbed wire!) if the horse is not used to loading easily.
4. Use safe equipment, strong cotton ropes and halter.
5. Load into a well-lighted trailer.
6. Wear gloves and have a jackknife handy.
7. Don't leave the manger door open (unless someone is positioned at the door) when you load your horse, since he may put his head out and get cut as he pulls it back in.
8. After the horse has entered the trailer, fasten the butt chain or bar and close the door before going to the front of the trailer to tie him.
9. When unloading, discourage the horse from rushing out (usually raising his head and hitting the roof as he does so). To help prevent and restrain, tie a rope to an outside tie ring of the trailer so that it goes around the horse's hindquarters, and hold the end in your hand (with your gloves on). Gently keep constant pressure on the horse's hindquarters as he moves backward. If he persists, stronger contact with his hindquarters may help discourage fast unloading.

10. One of the most important things you can do is to give yourself plenty of time. If a horse stands and studies a trailer for several minutes and all is calm around him, he will often decide all is well and walk right in. On the other hand, if the people are rushed, tense, and pushy, this is immediately communicated to the horse, who becomes nervous also, perhaps backing away, which in turn makes the people more hurried and start slapping at him—and the fight is on. *Your* calm and confidence do more to load a horse than you might think.

There is nothing more satisfying than a horse that willingly enters a horse trailer, and nothing more frustrating than an unwilling, balky horse or one that violently objects. For methods of trailer-training horses of all ages, see *Basic Training for Horses: English and Western.*

Tips on Driving and Traveling with Horse and Trailer

1. Before hauling horses, practice driving with an empty trailer to find out how much space it takes to turn, back, park, and get into a line of traffic. Observing, and obtaining instruction from, an experienced, expert driver is a good way to learn how to drive safely with horses.

2. Take time to make a quick but thorough safety check each time you start off—rolling down a crowded highway at fifty miles per hour is a poor time to discover you have a loose wheel, your brakes have failed, or Joe thought *you* had closed the trailer door! Walk completely around your rig, and check lights, tarps, and lashings; check the hitch for cracks and broken spots and that it is tight and secure—check underneath the hitch ball (nut tight, ball solid and tight); make sure the dolly wheel is run up and secured, wires are plugged in firmly, all tires have proper pressure and are free from bulges, cracks, or sharp stones in the tread, and that all doors and latches are secure. Check underneath vehicles for cats, dogs, babies, and blocks left under the wheels.

3. If the wheel hubs are hot during a trip, the bearings need lubrication; if they aren't repaired soon, they may freeze, locking the wheels.

4. Remember that hauling a trailer with live weight is more tiring than just driving an ordinary car. Don't drive when overtired, and stop and rest often—it's good for both you and your horse.

5. Because your rig is much longer and heavier than a car, it takes longer to accelerate, slow, and stop. Allow more time and distance to stop, to pull out into traffic, and to change lanes and pass other vehicles. Trailer wheels travel much closer to the inside of a curve—give plenty of room when turning to the right. Tailgating and "beating the traffic" should never be attempted—keep plenty of space between your vehicles and others.

6. Too high a speed can cause the trailer to vibrate and sway—if it does,

use your trailer brake controller and accelerate slowly to straighten out your rig. Jackknifing occurs when you slam on your brakes.

7. Take turns slowly and smoothly. When slowing down or stopping, shift to a lower gear and touch the brakes gently (do not ride the brakes). Avoid sudden stops and starts. Be especially careful driving downhill and around downhill turns, in crosswinds, and when being passed by semi-trucks and buses.

8. Ride in a horse trailer sometime and you'll appreciate good driving habits.

9. On dirt roads or where dusty, close the trailer door curtains so that dust will not roil up into the back of the trailer. Mud flaps help.

10. Make sure no exhaust fumes are being sucked into the trailer.

11. Before backing a trailer, always check behind for children, pets, or anything hidden from view.

12. Carry chains for your towing vehicle and your trailer for travel in winter—put chains on the braking wheels as well as the driving wheels.

13. Before pulling over onto an unpaved shoulder of the road, get out first and check the ground.

14. To load one horse in a two-horse trailer, use the left side—on a crowned road, you could flip your trailer if the horse shifts to the right and the wheels slip off onto a soft shoulder.

15. Be conscientious about placing horses that like each other next to each other. Horses that do not get along will create hauling problems and can cause injury. Partitions that keep horses' heads apart will keep trouble to a minimum.

16. Make sure all horses are tied properly. Use a quick-release knot or a panic snap. Tying prevents the horse from trying to turn around or getting his head down between his front legs.

17. Carry a twitch, pocketknife, pliers, and other tools.

18. A horse should be unloaded every three to four hours, as some horses will not urinate in a trailer. Leading him around for ten to fifteen minutes helps restore circulation and prevent stiffness and fatigue on a long trip. It's good for you, too. With a difficult loader, leave him in the trailer until you find a safe place to stop.

19. If you unload during the trip, do not let an inexperienced person hold the horse.

20. In very hot weather, check your trailer often; water and unload horses more often than usual.

21. In winter, your horse should be provided with a warm blanket. If vanned with several other horses, he'll be warm enough and should have a blanket only when unloaded. Horses vanned from warm climates to cold areas should be given special consideration.

22. If several horses are traveling together, or if the trip is long, it may be advisable to remove the shoes to help prevent injury.

23. Obtain advice from your veterinarian if you have a difficult traveler. He may advise using a tranquilizer.

24. If lights should fail at night on a trip, wire or attach a flashlight to the back of the trailer (preferably one with a red shield) until repairs can be made. Keep a strong flashlight next to you on the seat in case the headlights fail—it may give you enough light to pull off the road safely. Keep extra batteries on hand.

25. If you arrive in a town and have no idea where to stop with your horse, inquire at a feedstore or a saddle shop. It's better to write ahead to breeders for this information.

When Someone Else Transports Your Horse

Taking the offer of a ride should involve some consideration:

• Is your friend a good, steady driver, or does he stop and start like a jackrabbit? How does he take curves?
• Does your friend's trailer adhere to all safety standards, and is it clean? Is the pulling vehicle adequate and safe?
• Is your friend the sensitive type—a person who would stop and check the horse if unusual motion or noise comes from the trailer?
• Do you have an agreement as to who is liable in case of any destruction to the trailer or equipment or injury to your horse?
• Does your friend have insurance to cover your horse, his trailer, or medical bills?

Whenever someone else transports your horse, write down your instructions for the horse's care, and be sure the person both understands them and will abide by them. Include where you may be reached in case of emergency.

Feeding

Horses have a tendency to become constipated during trips, perhaps from stress or the fact that they do not drink as much and do not have the accustomed exercise to keep bodily functions working as effectively. Several days before the trip, add a small amount of bran and oil to the feed once a day. Alfalfa is also a laxative feed; if you have been feeding grass hay, however, include only small amounts of alfalfa mixed with the grass hay.

Giving hay in small amounts on the trip will help keep your horse occupied and less bored, as well as help keep him from wasting or hurrying his feed. Hay bags or mangers can hold the roughage; however, if you use a hay net, be sure it is hung up high enough so that when the hay is finished, the bag will not be low enough to allow a foot to be caught.

During the trip, we feed only plain rolled oats—a lesser amount than normally and only when the trailer is stopped. Ideally, your horse should be unloaded and allowed to eat while standing on solid ground. If he is the nervous type and inclined to bolt his grain, it may be wise to omit grain altogether, or to feed it only after hay. Your decision should be based on the temperament and welfare of your horse.

To avoid dehydration, constipation, and digestive upsets, your horse must drink enough water. He'll drink more readily if the water doesn't taste strange to him. Begin a week or more ahead of time to offer him water from the bucket you will use on the trip. Flavor the water with a few drops of peppermint, wintergreen, or molasses, and continue doing so during the trip.

Exercise

With a quiet, sensible "easy loader," you can stop every three or four hours and walk your horse around for ten or fifteen minutes. At meal breaks, unload and tie him to the trailer with a hay net, and offer him water. Traveling is stressful to the best of horses, so give him relaxing exercise and plenty of TLC. Ride him, longe him, or just give him a good walk. Make sure the area you choose is safe (no dogs, motorcycles, or animals he isn't used to, such as peacocks or pigs), and watch for barbed wire, glass, snakes, and other hazards hidden in the grass.

One of the greatest boons to traveling horsemen is portable corral panels that fit onto the sides of the larger trailers. Most of the commercial kinds make a 10 × 10-foot pen, and are built of welded pipe. You can make your own. In either case, make sure the welds are smooth, as they can really cut a horse up.

Keep insect repellent and a blanket handy in case of need.

If your horse gets motion sickness, which is rare, always walk him out of it. Never stall him without giving him mild exercise, or he may get severe colic.

Bandaging and Other Considerations

If your horse must endure over two hours of trailering, the support of bandages can help alleviate ligament and tendon fatigue, as well as help prevent injury. When deciding whether to use bandages, consider the hours your horse will be in the trailer, the types of roads you'll be traveling, the way your horse rides in a trailer, and how soon and for what purpose he will be used at the end of the trip. In mountainous country, and on unpaved and curvy roads, the tendon and ligament fatigue will be greater than on a level, straight four-lane highway; you should probably bandage his legs even for a short ride.

If a horse might be stepped on by a traveling companion, or if he is a nervous traveler, bandaging assists in preventing serious injury. Also, horses that tend to "stock up" when standing still for any length of time would benefit from leg bandages. In commercial vans, haulers feel that leg wraps cause more trouble than they're worth; they often use bell boots with Velcro fastenings to protect the coronary band without the nuisance of leg wraps.

Leg braces are drug mixtures that are massaged onto the lower legs to increase circulation and help reduce soreness and swelling. A good brace can be made from one-half rubbing alcohol and one-half Absorbine. Since bandages generate some heat, straight Absorbine under the bandages may blister some sensitive-skinned horses.

In very hot weather and on long hauls, standing your horse in cold water will help reduce swelling. This cold-water therapy should last for about twenty minutes. If there is no cool stream or irrigation ditch nearby, you can fill rubber buckets and let him stand in them, or play a hose on his legs.

It is wise to wrap your horse's tail, especially if he sits on the butt chain or bar and if you anticipate a mountainous route.

A shipping halter should fit comfortably and be fairly loose around the nose—however, not so loose that it can be rubbed off. If you use a chain lead, double the chain around the bottom of the noseband; this will allow you to hold the horse near his head without gripping the chain itself. Sheepskin around the noseband will keep it from chafing. Head protectors are available, but if a head bumper becomes hot, the horse will try to rub it off and will rub his halter off as well. Your horse should be accustomed to any protective or supportive clothing—do not put them on the first time for a trip.

Hauling a Mare and Foal

Healthy mares and foals (at least a week old) can travel successfully in a trailer. Because foals nurse frequently and should have that opportunity, your trailer should either be arranged so that the foal can nurse at any time, or you must stop every two to three hours.

If possible, remove the center partition and make a box stall (deeply bedded with good footing). The mare can be tied and the foal can move around or sleep at will. We have never known a mare to step on her foal if the trailer is hauled carefully. The foal should not be tied. If the center partition is only a bar at shoulder level, the mare may have more stability and the foal will still be able to nurse under the bar (which should be padded).

The trailer should be prepared so that the foal cannot jump out the back. For good ventilation in warm weather, we use V-wire against and above the back door. In inclement weather, the trailer should be closed up though well ventilated. Make sure the escape door is escape-proof for the foal: it may be wise to lock or wire it. On long trips, unload the mare and foal and put them in a box stall or corral with shelter at night.

Make sure your mare has plenty of good, clean water, as she is nursing a foal and needs more than a nonlactating animal does. Minimize stress as much as possible.

Transporting Stallions

It seems that stallions travel more miles than other horses, due to shows or more changes of ownership. A stallion's education in loading, traveling, and unloading should be undertaken with care, patience, and thorough, expert training. When they are traveling with other horses in the same trailer, there should be a solid partition not only between the horses but also between the mangers. No stallion should be allowed room to bite or bother another horse, and vice versa. Also, while loading other horses, be sure that they are safe from interference by the stallion.

Be especially cautious when fastening the butt chain and rear doors—if possible, close one side completely before loading a second horse. Even a usually well-mannered stallion may feel cornered when another horse is coming in so close behind him, and he may kick out with one or both feet. Don't bring the second horse up close until the first is secure and no one is standing behind him.

Use strong equipment and take care to tie the stallion correctly and safely. When being led to the trailer and when being unloaded, a stud chain may be used (over the nose or under the jaw) for better control.

Either the stallion should be unloaded every few hours, or the trailer should be stopped (provided it is large enough for him to stretch out), so that he can urinate.

If your stallion is high-strung, seek advice from your veterinarian, and if he concurs, give a mild tranquilizer. The person handling the stallion should be experienced, alert, and able to anticipate situations that could cause his or another horse to become unmanageable (the proximity of a mare in heat or another aggressive stallion). Never tie a mare in heat in front of a stallion.

Problem Horses

Difficult loaders. Horses that know how to lead, back up, move forward, and stand obediently are undoubtedly good loaders—they have a good basic education. A horse that has not had the above training should be drilled in leading well at your shoulder and in responding to verbal as well as physical commands. Any training you give your horse near and in a trailer should be happy experiences. Conditioning to punishment whenever you work at trailer training will give your horse a negative attitude and increase your problems. Review number 10 under "Trailer Loading and Unloading."

A horse—especially a sensible one—may have very good reasons for not loading. His good sense and reliability are qualities you may well respect on other occasions. Let's look at some of these reasons:

- Your trailer may be dark and look too small for him to enter. Repark to take advantage of the best lighting.
- The trailer may be unstable (it rocks, or the tongue lifts when the horse puts weight on the back end). Brace the trailer, hitch it to a pickup, and block the wheels; if necessary, block under the doors.
- The trailer may rattle and creak ominously as the horse steps, and thus may seem unsafe to him. Maybe he's right: check your trailer floor—horses seem to know when a bridge or trailer floor is unsafe—and use heavy floor mats.
- Some horses do not like to make a high step up into a trailer; they may be afraid of hitting their head. Repark the trailer in a better position, or try a ramp; or you can build a dirt loading ramp for the trailer.
- Other reasons for not loading may have to do with his past experiences riding in a trailer. More about this in a moment.

A horse that will not load is one that none of us can afford. In the event you meet one that will not load, keep calm and try everything you can to prevent violence. When all else fails and a horse must be loaded against his wildest determination to prevent it, get the help of knowledgeable, calm horsemen who can be firm without resorting to anger or brutality and who are experienced enough to keep themselves out of danger. Take advantage of such helps as are available, such as a loading chute. When the horse is finally loaded, take whatever course is most likely to calm him and make the experience less fearful.

Scramblers. The scrambler has undoubtedly had a bad experience while being hauled—perhaps the driver of the rig took corners too fast or drove at excessive speed with a trailer that swayed. The scrambler tries to take more room than he has by trying to "climb the walls." He steps all over himself and scrapes himself up on the walls of the trailer.

It may not be possible to cure him, but you can minimize the problem. The partition can be removed to give him more foot room, or if he only scrambles on one side, position him on the other side of the trailer. A pipe or padded partition that does not go to the floor may be the answer. If he has the room to spread his legs wider and brace himself, he will have more confidence. Also, careful driving will add to his security.

Fighters. The fighter is generally a very aggressive, "top of the totem pole" horse that bites and picks on other horses. You should have a solid head divider, or if the trailer is not so equipped, tie his head to one side, away from the center of the trailer. If he is really savage, it may be wise to haul him alone. You can also block his sense of smell by putting a small amount of Vicks ointment in his nostrils.

Kickers. Kicking is a difficult habit to correct, but as with scrambling, it can be minimized. Kickers lash out with their hind feet because of ill temper, nervousness, or resentment of a noisy, cramping trailer. Hauling up front in a four-horse trailer with no horse behind him will give him plenty of room, and if he kicks out, there will be nothing behind him to fight against.

Stompers. The stomper rarely hurts himself or causes injury, but his pounding on the floor shows nervousness and is an irritating habit. Extra bedding under the horse will minimize the noise and vibration, and perhaps not being able to hear his stomping noise will cause him to stop this habit.

Past experiences. A horse may be unwilling to load in a trailer because of an experience in the past—perhaps a trailer wreck, an injury by another horse in that trailer, or whipping and abuse when being loaded. Uncomfortable and frightening experiences in the trailer due to poor driving habits can also affect a horse's willingness to load—a driver that has a heavy foot on the gas pedal can scare sensitive horses badly. If a trailer travels far with its front end too low, a horse suffers severe strain and may have permanently damaged hocks. Sudden stops and starts and taking curves at excessive speed are frightening to any horse, and he will remember the trailer as his instrument of torture.

Knowing the reason for your horse's aversion to a horse trailer is helpful, since this knowledge can be used to reeducate him. Even if you don't know, however, we suggest going back to basics as mentioned under *Difficult loaders.* Then try loading in a different kind of trailer; change from a two-horse to a four-horse trailer or a van, or from a ramp to a step-up type. Park in a corral or a pasture, so that your horse can be fed in it—start by putting his feed close to the back of the trailer and keep moving it up until he must enter to eat. When he enters willingly, quietly close the back door (do not tie him at first). If you take out the center partition, so that you have a box stall instead of the usual straight stall, it allows him to move around at will; he can face the rear if he wishes and will have a less claustrophobic feeling.

When he seems quiet and content in the trailer, take him on several short rides, perferably on smooth, straight roads at slow speeds. A quiet, dependable horse pal going along is helpful. Although it is illegal in most states to ride on the highway in a pull-type trailer, you could go along in the adjoining stall for a few rides around your premises—your calming influence and the added security of your presence may make the difference. When he is quiet on short trips, take longer ones. Be sure everything to do with the trip is relaxed and unhurried.

INSURANCE AND LIABILITY

Nothing can replace the animals we love. However, since loss by death through an accident or sickness can happen quickly, it helps to at least ease the financial loss through insurance.

Horse insurance is not for everyone, but some horse owners should consider it. If you are a novice show competitor who has saved for years to buy your fifteen-hundred-dollar horse, insurance would be wise. Or if you buy an expensive horse for breeding or put a sizable amount into a syndicated horse, protecting your investment is sensible. Most insurance brokers do not recommend insuring horses valued under a thousand dollars.

There are other reasons for obtaining insurance. If you sell a horse on contract, the buyer should pay for insurance to cover the worth of the horse; then, in case of death, the seller would be compensated, and the buyer would not be paying for a dead horse. Also, two or more partners owning a horse should insure him so that neither partner would suffer a loss.

Transportation and the first months in a new stable involve a certain amount of stress and uncertainty; horses are then more prone to accidents and disease than at any other time. Think seriously about insuring your investment during this unsettling period.

All-risk mortality insurance is similar to human life insurance, covering death, loss through accident, injury, sickness, and disease. Loss because the horse becomes unsuitable for a particular use or purpose would not be covered. Most companies include intentional destruction for humane reasons as a valid claim for death loss. Theft is an extension of mortality coverage; it is paid only when a horse is taken by illegal and forcible entry into an enclosure where the insured animal is located. Another coverage is mortality, listing specific perils such as fire and lightning, collision (transportation), or accidental shooting. Insurance companies also list exclusions (those things that they will not be liable for).

The policyholder also has responsibilities, and most companies require: immediate notice of death, illness, or accident to any insured horse; notification of change of ownership; obtaining permission for gelding or any other surgical operation; notice of increase of insurable value (amount of increase and substantiation for it); notice of decrease in insurable value; and notice of cancellation of coverage. Because the adult horse's value must be justified, the insurance company may ask for a bill of sale, receipt from the trainer, show record, or the opinion of an impartial third person.

The cost of livestock insurance (the premium) is based on a percentage of the horse's value. Policies are generally written for a one-year period and renewed with a veterinarian's certificate and an annual Coggins test. Since policies and rates will vary from company to company, it pays to shop around. The cost can be influenced by breed, use, and age. Most companies will not insure a horse for the first time if he is over twelve years old, and will not insure a foal until over three months of age (or will ask a very high premium). Stable discounts are usually available.

If you are transporting someone else's horse as an act of friendship (no money involved), this is called a gratuitist bailment and you have the duty only of *slight care* (legally). If this transportation is to benefit both of you (for instance, if you are taking someone else's mare to your stallion), then you have the duty of *ordinary care*. However, if you are transporting a horse for your own benefit (money), then you have the duty of *great care*. When there is an accident, the laws of the state where it occurs would be applicable and the duty of care must be determined. Written agreements are always recommended. The fact that the horse owner has full mortality insurance does not necessarily relieve the bailee of liability.

The condition of the horse and of the trailer to travel a given distance is of prime consideration in judging transportation court cases. Because of the complexity of transportation cases, contact your attorney to discover the risks and exposure you incur and his advice on adequate insurance coverage.

The most common claims are those involving death through colic (usually caused by high infestation of parasites). On most policies, you are asked how often your horses are wormed. Actually, accidents causing severe injury and trailer accidents are relatively rare.

Owning a horse for pleasure without a profit motive will not necessitate extra insurance coverage if you have a standard homeowner or tenant policy (including general liability coverage for personal injury and property damage). Horse activities that involve the farming business (coverage on hay, feed, supplies, farm vehicles, your own animal accidents, damage to property of others, etc.) should be covered by farm insurance.

Horsemen caring for and working with other people's horses or giving services to the general public will need a "commercial" policy. This will be broad in scope, covering property as well as people; the premium cost will be high. Training and breeding ranches will also need "care, custody and control" coverage.

Seriously consider an umbrella policy which gives coverage in areas where your exposure may not be adequately covered by a horseman's other policies. Obtain professional help in deciding the amount, type, and risks you are incurring in your horse activities.

An ICC carrier (trucker regulated by the Interstate Commerce Commission) must carry mortality insurance, but the horse owner should also carry either trip insurance or, preferably, full mortality for the worth of his horse. Although trip insurance is good for thirty days, the ICC carrier will undoubtedly not have the full coverage for the full worth of a very valuable horse.

Anyone transporting horses should have appropriate insurance to cover any liability.

Part III

RAISING HORSES

CHAPTER 10

THE BUSINESS OF RAISING HORSES

There is nothing more satisfying than to see a foal come into the world and grow to be a top-quality horse. But whether it is a once-in-a-lifetime experience or a full-scale operation, the business of breeding horses should not be taken lightly. The investment of time and finances alone is formidable. Even so, there are many people who feel that the commitment is well worthwhile and the reward a richer life.

The glossary, in the Appendix, includes terms that relate to breeding, genetics, and foaling.

SELECTION OF BREEDING STOCK

General Considerations in Selecting Breeding Stock

1. Know what you want to produce before you try to produce it.
2. Select for a good disposition.
3. Select stock as close as possible to the breed-standard ideal.
4. Study both foundation and recent bloodlines. The immediate forebears —sire, dam, and grandparents—contribute more to the foal than do distant relatives.
5. Study the genetic makeup of both parents to determine whether the genetic pool for a particular characteristic is strong or weak. A lack of uniformity in the offspring denotes a lack of concentration in the genetic pool. Select sires and dams that have uniformity and have predictably passed on desirable characteristics to their offspring.
6. Study the progeny of the horses under consideration, as well as the collateral relatives: brothers, aunts, uncles, cousins.
7. Choose a stallion that is strong where your mare is weak—if the mare is light in the hindquarters, the stallion should have ideal hindquarters.
8. The mare's value should be at least twice the cost of the stud fee.
9. Select for health and soundness. A complete veterinary health check should be a prerequisite of selection.
10. Select for symmetry and proportion—keys to athletic ability and structural quality.

11. When selecting a horse for a specific purpose, choose one from an appropriate breed. For example, if you wish to breed cutting horses, select a Quarter Horse. Although performance individuals need not be limited by breed (you may find outstanding cutting horses that are Morgans, Arabians, or Thoroughbreds), your greatest chance for overall success in breeding is to follow this rule.

12. Study the types of horses within each breed, and select according to the performance you desire. For instance, Quarter Horses have three distinct types: the "Thoroughbred" type for racing, the heavily muscled "bulldog" type for steer roping and bulldogging, and the versatile middle-of-the-road type for dressage, trail riding, and jumping. Breeders often have two types in their breeding program.

13. Make a thorough study of the competitive records of sire, dam, and offspring.

14. Remember that the horse—of all domestic animals—is the hardest to breed successfully.

Selecting a Stallion

Selection of the right stallion is considered to be the most important factor in producing superior foals. The stallion might sire eighty to a hundred foals in a single year, whereas a mare produces a relatively small number during her entire lifetime.

When selecting a stallion, look at the total picture: does he have the masculinity, conformation, and breed type you are looking for?

Prepotency—the ability to stamp his likeness on his offspring—is an important consider-ation in selecting a stallion.

The stallion you select, whether as a potential herd sire or to breed to your special mare, should be the best example of his breed that you can find and afford. His conformation should be as nearly perfect as possible, with a mas-culine look. Look at the total picture of the stallion, not just his pretty head or level croup. Refer to the first chapter in this book, to the conformation judging sheets in the Appendix, and to the individual breed conformation ideals.

Equally important—and readily inherited—is the stallion's disposition. He should have the "heart" and temperament to do the job he is asked to do; yet he should be tractable and have a reasonably quiet, even disposition.

Study the stallion's ancestry. His pedigree will tell you how you can expect him to perform, and it will give you a hint as to his ability as a sire. Proven, popular bloodlines rarely go out of style. Especially when purchasing a young, unproven sire, the pedigree is important.

Although an outstanding performance or halter record will not ensure outstanding foals, it is a good indication of what you can expect from this stallion's offspring. Look at as many of your potential stallion's progeny as possible. Look for consistency and good characteristics, and select a stallion that will complement your mares.

Prepotency is another important consideration. His ability to stamp his likeness on his offspring makes the results more predictable. If the sire and dam of the stallion are closely related, a greater degree of prepotency can be expected than if the sire and dam are of unrelated lines. Inbreeding strengthens prepotency, but care should be taken that any bad traits are not doubled. Two weak croups, for instance, will produce a foal with a very weak croup.

The question of whether to buy a young, unproven stallion or an older, proven one is usually a matter of economics and personal preference. Since the proven stallion will pay his way immediately, he will cost a great deal more. The young, unproven stallion (three years or younger) will be a challenge, since showing and proving him is a gamble.

In purchasing a stallion service for your mare, the process of selection is the same, but you must consider the stud-fee cost and the distance involved. However, do not choose a stallion on the basis of price and convenience alone. The proven stallion will command a higher stud fee, but again, his foal will be an almost guaranteed superior breeding animal and command a higher price if sold. If you have a well-known superior mare, a stallion owner may give you a reduced or free breeding to persuade you to breed to his stallion—the resulting foal will be good advertising for the sire.

Another alternative is to purchase part of a syndicated stallion, thus ensuring that you will always be able to breed to that particular individual.

Castration and Geldings

Not all stallions are potential sires and not all horse owners should own stallions. A dedicated breeder selects his sires carefully in order to improve the breed; only the best should be considered as future breeding animals.

Even so, there is often the temptation to leave the colt entire, especially if he *does* seem to the owner to be an outstanding individual. If the owner does not have the facilities, experience, or time to handle a stallion (or an additional stallion), the temptation should in most cases be resisted. If the colt is indeed that good, perhaps he could be sold early to someone who can better care for him. Remember that although a mediocre stallion may become an excellent gelding, it takes an outstanding colt to make an outstanding gelding.

Most breeders castrate colts as yearlings or two-year-olds. (Because both testicles must descend into the scrotum before castration can be done, colts cannot be castrated at birth.) Colts castrated early are less likely to hurt themselves in rough play, and many behavioral problems are avoided. Nor do they take on a "studdy" appearance. Further, they are much easier to care for, since they can be turned out with other geldings and fillies. Castrating healthy horses at older (mature) ages is relatively safe; even so, because the spermatic blood vessel enlarges in the older horse, it is better done early.

Traditionally, colts are castrated in the spring, when green grass makes a clean bed and before the flies are out. Now, although clean facilities, preventive immunizations, and controlled exercise make the time of year less important than formerly, castration during very hot and humid weather should be avoided. New methods allow the colt to remain standing during the operation, avoiding the necessity of putting him down. Castration should be performed by a veterinarian, who will be able to handle any complications that should arise.

After the operation, the wound must stay open to drain properly (it cannot be sutured). Some swelling is normal; if sufficient exercise and clean surroundings are provided, it will be kept to a minimum. If there is excess swelling, however, or if the swelling becomes hard, or if the drainage becomes pussy, call your veterinarian immediately.

The entire testicle—with epididymis intact—must be removed, or the gelding will be "proud-cut." The behavior of a proud-cut gelding is usually undesirable, and although he cannot sire foals, he can savage mares or geldings if pastured with them. "Proud-cut" refers more to behavior than it does to physical status; it implies a rank disposition.

If a stallion has only one dropped testicle—the other remains tucked up in the abdomen—he is a "ridgeling," or cryptorchid. The lodged testicle is usually sterile, since heat from the body will kill the sperm. Abdominal surgery must be performed to remove the lodged testicle. Ridgelings vary in personality, as stallions do, and care should be taken that they are not sold as geldings, either unscrupulously or by accident. Uncastrated ridgelings have a higher risk of becoming tumorous than stallions with normal testicles.

Breeding is the one purpose to justify stallion ownership—but geldings may be used for every other purpose you can name.

How to Judge a Foal

Because it is very difficult to evaluate a young, fast-growing horse, the old adage that one should look at the horse at three days, three weeks, and three years is still true. Even though the foal's legs are disproportionately long compared to the rest of his body, the parts of the legs should be in proportion. It is important to know your breed specifications, since proportions are influenced by these standards.

Experience in looking at horses of all ages is necessary to have confidence in your eye to see good symmetry and proportion. There are some parts of a horse that will not change from birth unless interfered with by inappropriate training or accident. The configuration of the cervical spine and the position and angle of the shoulder will not change. Nor will the functional length of the back, the slope and angle of the pelvis, sickle hocks, rotational deformities (toeing in and toeing out), bowlegs, or other such problems, although many asymmetries become more severe with age if not corrected, and proper foot trimming and care can help to alleviate or correct deficiencies. The refinement and proportion of the foal's head will also stay the same.

Look at the overall quality of the foal.

Pedigrees

A pedigree is a record of ancestry. The value of the pedigree (five or six generations) depends upon the merit of the individuals recorded. It is a waste of time to memorize names in pedigrees without becoming familiar with the performance and produce records of individuals in the two or three generations closest to the horse in question. Pedigree selection is important when the horse you are considering does not have an individual performance record.

Notice the number of foals produced (taking into consideration the age of the horse) and their quality. A mare twelve years old with only two foals and offered for sale should be looked at very carefully. Perhaps she was shown extensively at halter and in performance, thus not bred until her show career was over; however, if she had no show career or other use, she may be a problem breeder.

When two horses have equally acceptable pedigrees but differ in regard to performance, always choose the stallion or mare with the performance record, even though the other horse may be favored on the basis of a potential nick.

Pedigree information can be helpful in providing a genetic explanation for the chance-bred horse. An unusually good horse bred from poor or mediocre stock on both sides of the pedigree suggests that this animal is a result of a lucky combination of several genes. Since it is not likely that this chance-bred horse will "breed on"—produce as good as himself—he is not a good breeding prospect.

Popular pedigrees cannot guarantee a successful performer, nor do popular pedigrees, coupled with outstanding performance, always guarantee success in the stud.

GENETICS

Genetics—the basis for breeding—is very complex, but there are a few basic concepts that every serious breeder should understand. Since we can only touch on this subject, please refer to the reading list in the Appendix for more detailed information.

Pedigree of a Morgan mare, Collier's Romany, foaled May 26, 1977, bred and owned by Roy H. Collier.

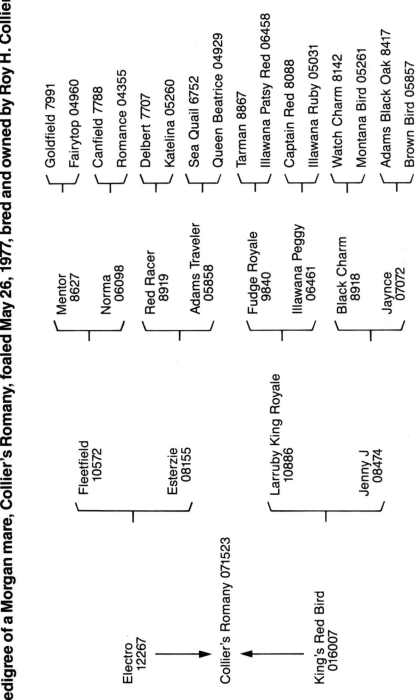

Collier's Romany 071523

Electro 12267

Fleetfield 10572

Mentor 8627
- Goldfield 7991
- Fairytop 04960

Norma 06098
- Canfield 7788
- Romance 04355

Esterzie 08155

Red Racer 8919
- Delbert 7707
- Katelina 05260

Adams Traveler 05858
- Sea Quail 6752
- Queen Beatrice 04929

King's Red Bird 016007

Larruby King Royale 10886

Fudge Royale 9840
- Tarman 8867
- Illawana Patsy Red 06458

Illawana Peggy 06461
- Captain Red 8088
- Illawana Ruby 05031

Jenny J 08474

Black Charm 8918
- Watch Charm 8142
- Montana Bird 05261

Jaynce 07072
- Adams Black Oak 8417
- Brown Bird 05857

Genes determine how a horse will look, his disposition, his size and color, and all the characteristics that are in his makeup. When the sperm of the stallion fertilizes the egg of the mare, it provides a set of genes for all the characteristics. Some genes will be expressed by the mare, others by the stallion; that is, a foal may have the color of the mare and the size of the stallion. The gene not expressed in the foal is still carried in his genetic structure and could show up in the next generation.

Genes may be dominant (will show up in the foal) or recessive (will not show up in the foal unless a similar recessive gene is also inherited from the other parent). For example, since the color black is dominant over the color chestnut, a black stallion bred to a chestnut mare *should* produce a black foal.

However, genetics do not follow through in a straightforward manner. Because the black stallion may have had a chestnut dam, he would be heterozygous black, and his foal could be another color—for instance, bay. However, if both his parents were without recessive chestnut, his color would be dominant and would be considered prepotent and valuable for producing black foals. Of course, the action of the genes that control body processes is not the only thing that affects them—environmental factors, nutrition, training, disease, and accidents affect them also.

You cannot completely avoid confusing environmental and heritable traits. However, there are ways of minimizing such confusion to a certain extent:

1. Keep accurate records. Each animal should be listed with each trait that needs improvement.
2. Compare animals in as nearly the same environment as possible.
3. Select the best individuals—ones that are genetically superior. The homozygous individual is likely to produce the better individual.
4. Select for the traits that are most heritable.

Linebreeding, Inbreeding, and Outbreeding

One of the biggest controversies in raising horses is the practice of linebreeding and inbreeding. They are excellent tools for improving a herd if used properly. Linebreeding is inbreeding, but inbreeding is not necessarily linebreeding. The closer the parents are related, the more the offspring will be inbred. In linebreeding, you concentrate the inheritance of the offspring to one ancestor in the pedigree, or to one line of ancestors.

Because inbreeding uncovers recessive genes (and most genetic defects are recessive) by bringing them together in pairs, it can cause a decline in size, fertility, and overall vigor, as well as increasing the incidence of genetic defects. On the plus side, inbreeding increases breeding purity. Individuals within an inbred line are more alike genetically, which may cause them to look more alike. They usually breed better than they look, but noninbred individuals tend to look better than they breed. Breeding closely related individuals (father to daughter or brother to sister) can be expensive, since some resultant individuals would be culls. Only large, profitable breeding farms would be able to practice this kind of program.

The ultimate in inbreeding is for the breeder to produce two highly inbred lines that are unrelated to each other. When you cross these lines, hybrid vigor results. The lines that cross well can produce offspring called "nicks," which are far above the average.

Outbreeding (outcrossing) can improve horses as well. It refers to the mating of individuals within the same breed that are not closely related within the past three or four generations. It is especially important to consider these factors when breeding, to compensate for weaknesses in both stallion and mare.

Genetic and Nongenetic Defects

Environmental defects at birth may be caused by virus infections (causing malformations such as heart disease or blindness) or drugs like thalidomide in humans. Some defects are not genetically determined—accidents in embryonic development, perhaps duplicate body parts such as two heads. Genetic defects arise because of a mutation in a particular gene. Most are recessive, but if two mated individuals carry the same recessive gene, the probability of any one offspring showing the recessive defect is one out of four.

To eliminate the recessive gene, homozygous recessive individuals must not be bred; it is also necessary to find and discard for breeding all carriers of the recessive gene. However, progeny testing is slow, costly, and almost impossible to do for a mare, since so many progeny must be tested and such a long time is required for the test. The best way to proceed when the detrimental gene appears in a foal is to eliminate the foal, its parents, and close relatives from the breeding program.

BREEDING CONTRACTS AND RECORDS

Contracts are oral or written agreements between two or more persons and are recognized by the courts as binding. However, with an oral contract, misunderstandings or violations of the agreement can easily occur and then be difficult to prove, due to there being no record. It is wise for horse owners and breeders to become familiar with written contracts. Don't depend on the old saying that a man's word is his bond.

There are many kinds of breeding contracts, such as the stallion service contract, the co-owner agreement for stallion and mare, the breeder's lien, the lease agreement for stallion and mare, and syndication agreements. A few sample forms on the following pages may be used as a guide and changed or expanded for your individual need. Be sure to always include proper descriptions, correct age, and clear statement of the terms and conditions. Contracts that involve syndication, and other complicated technical agreements that involve many people and large sums of money, should be prepared by an attorney.

Stallion Service Contract

A good stallion breeding contract is critical to a successful stallion-standing operation, and it is just as important for a mare owner to have proper arrangements made. Here are a few provisions that should be included:

Fees. You must not only state the stud fee, but definite and specific provisions should be made for when payment is due. If part of the fee is nonrefundable (such as boarding and handling fees), this should be stated.

Board, care, and other charges should be clearly stated along with the due date of payment. If interest will be charged on amounts due over thirty days, the rate of interest should be down in writing. When board rates depend upon whether the mare has a foal at side, is kept on pasture or in a paddock or stall, or must have special exercise, this should be considered and stated.

Guarantees. As a mare owner, you will probably choose a stallion that has a "live foal guarantee" (L.F.G.). However, this does increase the risk to the stallion owner, as he has no control over the mare once she leaves the premises; thus usually the breeding fee is higher. Make sure that the definition of "live foal" appears in the contract—for instance, "one that stands and sucks," or "one that lives forty-eight hours," or just "born alive." In most cases, the cause of death of a foal is determined by a veterinarian, and this, too, should be written into the contract. The stallion owner should also consider a handling fee for mares that require rebreeding. If a mare does not conceive for two years, will you require a substitution of another mare, retain the right to refund part or all of the stud fee, or make other provisions?

Liabilities and insurance. Injury or death to the mare or to persons or property should be anticipated. An agreement or an insurance policy can resolve this issue. Also, the stallion owner should be protected with "hold harmless" or "indemnity clause" liability for injury to (or loss of) a customer's mare through no fault of the stallion owner or his employees. It is wise to consult with your local attorney, as state laws vary widely.

Transferability. There should be a simple clause stating that the breeding cannot be transferred, if you do not wish substitutions.

Required examination. Many breeding farms require that a visiting mare have certain tests prior to her arrival at the farm: a negative Coggins test and negative uterine culture, along with immunizations important for that area. Also, other requirements, such as removal of shoes, should be stated. Another

SAMPLE BREEDING CONTRACT

It is hereby agreed to breed the mare _____
Reg. No. _____ in the year _____
to the stallion _____
The fee for such service shall be $_____
One Hundred ($100.00) dollars payable at booking.
Board for mare shall be at the rate of Four ($4.00) dollars
per day; Four and 50/100 ($4.50) dollars with foal.

The stallion owner or agent may have mare checked by veterinarian for normal breeding condition, the cost of which mare owner shall pay. Stallion owner or agent shall assume no liability for mare that will not breed, cannot conceive, or for accident, sickness or death of the mare or colt, but will exercise every reasonable effort to settle mare and good judgment in care and supervision of mare. Mare owner shall not be responsible for injury or accident to stallion. All board and veterinarian charges incurred shall be settled by owner before mare leaves Sodergreen Ranch.

A live foal is guaranteed — meaning a foal that can stand up alone and nurse. Should the foal die at birth, with certification of same provided to stallion owner, the owner will rebreed the mare the following year, without further charge for stallion service. Mare owner will be responsible for board and vet fees only.

Should the mare prove barren, or should the foal die at birth, owner will send notice of same, signed by a licensed veterinarian, within five (5) days of such barren determination or death.

The mare owner agrees that: Upon arrival the mare will be halter-broken, have the hind shoes removed and be accompanied by a health certificate signed by a veterinarian. The stallion owner may request a culture after arrival of the mare. The mare owner must provide a Negative Coggins Test for the mare not more than six (6) months old.

The above stated conditions and terms are agreed to by:

MARE OWNER	STALLION OWNER
Name _____	Name _____
Address _____	Address _____
City _____ State ____ Zip ____	City _____ State ____ Zip ____
Ar. Code	Ar. Code
Phone (____) _____ Date _____	Phone (____) _____ Date _____
Mare Owner Signature _____	Stallion Owner Signature _____

point to make is that if the required examinations are not performed prior to arrival, they will be performed at the mare owner's expense. Some breeding farms request a history of the visiting mare in order to better understand her needs.

Other stipulations. There should be some agreement in case of lawsuit. Attorneys' fees should be paid by the losing party, and the parties should agree on where the suit may be brought and on the state whose laws will apply in the event of a suit.

The contract should also state that the written contract contains the entire agreement, since it is possible that one party may claim that there were some oral promises not included in the agreement.

The stallion owner should also be told the mare's insurance carrier and all particulars of her insurance. Then if the mare owner cannot be contacted when needed, the insurance carrier could be notified.

Syndication

Syndication is merely common ownership of a horse. A syndicate is formed for the specific purpose of purchasing, managing, and disposing of a single economic asset (a horse), whereas a partnership is an ongoing business relationship (of two or more people) that may involve many horses or other assets. A syndicate is characterized by the holding of fractional interests or shares in the ownership of a specific horse. A syndication agreement is drawn up stating the rights and obligations of each owner. Primarily it centers around the right to breed a mare or mares to the syndicated stallion. Historically, a stallion-breeding syndication had approximately thirty-two to forty fractional interests or shares; but, due to the possibilities of artificial insemination, one stallion can service more mares than with natural service. A modern syndicate may have sixty fractional shares—and on occasion even over a hundred.

The fractional interest holder is entitled to one or more breedings to the stallion each year (annual nomination). He must also pay a pro rata portion of certain operating expenses (liability insurance, advertising, showing, and any other expenses agreed to by the terms of the syndication agreement) and a handling fee for each mare bred to the syndicated stallion.

There are advantages for the syndicate member as well as for the original owner of the stallion. The syndicate member may own a part of a prestige stallion that he could not afford by himself. It spreads the risk and cost of owning a top-quality stallion, as well as upgrading the quality of the foals the member owns. The member will have a guaranteed access to the stallion and need not worry about the time and talent it takes to train, show, and otherwise promote the horse. There are also tax advantages for stallions twelve years of age or older.

The stallion seller can also spread his costs and risks, can realize a substantial income from the sale of the syndicate memberships, and can enjoy the same benefits as the other members.

There are also some potential legal problems with syndicates. These agreements must be drafted properly with regard to tax laws, securities laws, and antitrust laws.

It is also possible to syndicate for other purposes, such as show and breeding—usually done by a smaller breeder who does not have the funds to pro-

BREEDING RECORD

Mare _____
Stallion _____ Reg. No. _____ Color _____ Age _____
Owner _____ Reg. No. _____ Stud Fee _____ Board _____
Address _____ Phone No. _____ Status of Mare _____
                                City _____ State _____

	1	2	3	4	5	6	7	8	9	10	11	12	13	14	15	16	17	18	19	20	21	22	23	24	25	26	27	28	29	30	31
Dec.																															
Jan.																															
Feb.																															
Mar.																															
Apr.																															
May																															
June																															
July																															
Aug.																															
Sept.																															
Oct.																															
Nov.																															

+ In   − Out   T Treated   AI Art. Insem.   C Culture   S Speculum   P Palpate   Pr Pregnancy

Diet and feed information _____

Foal at side by _____ Born _____ Due _____ Sex _____ Color _____
Foal by _____ Born _____ Sex _____ Color _____
Notes _____

OWNER INFORMATION SHEET

OWNER'S NAME:_____ DATE:_____

ADDRESS:_____ PHONE:_____

_____

MARE INFORMATION:

1. *Name:*_____ *Reg. No.:*_____

   *Color:*_____ *Age:*_____

2. *Immunizations:*

Tetanus	YES__NO__DATE_____	VEE	YES__NO__DATE_____
Flu-vac	YES__NO__DATE_____	Rhino	YES__NO__DATE_____
WEE and EEE	YES__NO__DATE_____	Strangles	YES__NO__DATE_____

3. *Allergic sensitivities:*_____

4. *Most recent worming (date and name):*_____

5. *Normal feeding procedure:*

   KIND OF HAY_____ AMOUNT_____

   NO. OF DAILY FEEDINGS_____ KIND OF GRAIN_____

   SUPPLEMENTS_____

6. *Date of last foaling*_____

7. *Has mare ever been treated for genital-area infection?*_____

8. *Has she ever produced a dead or nonviable foal?*_____

9. *Has she ever aborted?*_____

10. *Does she have a history of retained afterbirth?*_____

11. *Has she ever received progesterone to maintain a pregnancy?*_____

12. *Does she show good visible signs of heat?*_____

13. *Give previous breeding and foaling history, with dates and details (use back of sheet).*_____

14. *Has mare had history of colic or intestinal problems?*_____

15. *Has mare had any medical problems that should be known?*_____

16. *Has mare any stable manners, habits, idiosyncracies, or teasing or breeding conduct that should be made known?*_____

_____

17. *Has she ever slipped a diagnosed pregnancy?*_____

18. *Must she be rectally examined to detect heat cycle?*_____

19. *Does she foal only every other year even if bred every year?*_____

20. *Please give name and phone number of veterinarian who knows this mare:*

_____

_____

MARE MUST BE ACCOMPANIED BY PROOF OF NEGATIVE COGGINS TEST TAKEN WITHIN ONE YEAR OF ARRIVAL DATE.

HIND SHOES MUST BE REMOVED BEFORE ARRIVAL.

mote a young horse to reach the top. A mare syndication can enable the purchasers to breed top-quality mares they could not otherwise afford and to divide the profits of the resulting foals among the members.

Keeping Records

Ranch or farm records for all horses on the premises are an important tool for good breeding management. Good records tell at a glance such things as a mare's heat cycle, when teased and when bred to which stallion, medical history, veterinary treatment, teeth care, show records, foot care, and parasite control.

Certain records are necessary for any professional horseman, since tax returns are subject to examination. Memory is not enough: when a tax return is examined, the burden of proof is on the taxpayer, and his figures will not be accepted unless he has supportive records. Besides retaining canceled checks, deposit slips, bank statements, invoices, and all paid bills for at least three years (longer in some states), records of all details pertaining to a capital purchase (hot-walker, tractor, breeding horses) should be kept indefinitely, especially dates of acquisition. Records must be substantiated for travel and showing, and payroll records must be kept for four years.

An up-to-date inventory of all horses on the farm should be kept, with name, registry number, birth date, pedigree to four generations, date acquired, value (and depreciation rate), production record, show record, and health record. Also include stallion contracts, certificates, and lease agreements.

In the case of a visiting mare, a receiving form should be filled out. Prepare a teasing chart for her and record daily teasing, any problems or injuries, and all veterinary attention. With such a chart, a manager can answer a client's questions precisely, giving the day, time, and treatment. Other forms include the foaling report and breeding card—cards should be sent to mare owners with this information, and copies of all records should accompany the mare when she leaves the breeding farm. When dealing with broodmares and their owners, a good record-keeping system and open, honest lines of communication keep the client satisfied and returning to do business.

PROMOTION AND MARKETING

Since competition is fierce in the horse business, advertising is important and puts your name before the industry. If you are a large, successful breeder with unlimited funds, you can hire an advertising agency. Most of us on a limited budget must invest time, thought, and money on our own advertising.

Answering these questions will help you to focus and prepare your ads:

Who are your potential customers?

> New or potential owners
> Specific breeders or breed owners
> General horse-loving public
> Local horse people

} or a combination of these

How do you reach them?

> Published advertising
> Personal contact
> Correspondence
> Direct-mail fliers

You can buy mailing lists from all-breed publications, clubs, or breed associations, or you can develop your own. Make sure these lists have been updated. After determining your audience, place your advertisement where it will be seen. For instance, an ad for an Arabian Egyptian-bred stallion for sale should be placed in an Arabian publication, specifically an issue that features Egyptian bloodlines.

Know the closing dates for monthly magazines, and submit an ad well before that date. A "camera-ready" advertisement insures against error and can often save you the 15 percent advertising agency commission charged by publications. You can also save by signing an advertising contract. Asking for special positioning of your ad (such as front page or cover) is usually costly. The best place for an ad is on a right-hand page, close to the front, and on the outside of the page (avoid the inside, or gutter, if possible). When you use more than one advertisement, keep records and judge your results from each publication (key each ad so that you can tell where a response comes from). We have also found that classified ads bring good response.

To write your ad effectively, see suggestions in the chapter on "Buying and Selling Horses."

Brochures, fliers, and business cards, as well as stationery with your logo, help take your message to prospective customers. A good reputation is built not only with effective, honest advertising, but also through personal exposure such as horse shows, clinics, or any place where you and your horses are visible to potential customers. Enhance your image and professionalism by arriving in a clean, polished truck and trailer with matching stable blankets, buckets, trunks, and towels with your logo attached (iron-on lettering is inexpensive and effective). Refreshments help relax and encourage "horse talk." Any folks interested in stopping by should be put on your mailing list (ask them to sign an attractive guest book), and follow up with a telephone call or letter where appropriate. You and your employees should be courteous, kind, and helpful, and never "bad-mouth" other owners, horses, judges, or officials.

When people wish to visit your farm to view and possibly to buy or breed to your stock, give them explicit directions; an attractive sign at your entrance will give a good first impression. Again, project your professionalism by preparing your horses (well groomed and trained) and your barns (neat, clean, and well organized)—this reflects the kind of care a visitor's mare will receive and the efficiency of the entire operation. Your professionalism should also be reflected when taking telephone calls. You and your employees should be pleasant, speak audibly and concisely, and offer assistance. Equip both your barn and house phones with pencil and paper for names, addresses, phone numbers, and messages. Your employees should not discuss your clients or business with anyone and should be aware of how important each telephone call is. Be sure to return any call and look into the feasibility of an answering service or telephone answering machine.

EXAMPLE OF A DIRECT-MAIL ADVERTISING LETTER
Sodergreen Ranch and Horsemanship School

January 31, 1983

Dear Friends,

Standing at stud at Sodergreen is the beautiful stallion Kamars Sharif. This 1974 stallion was bred by the Babson Farm, known worldwide for the finest in Egyptian breeding. Kamars Sharif consistently produces foals with the great disposition which he possesses, a trait of all Babson horses. We are delighted with the quality, refinement, type, and conformation of his get.

Sodergreen Ranch is not a large breeding establishment, but a small place with the advantages of individual care for each mare. This means that every mare has her own pen, with no competition for food, or hazing by other mares. This also means that we must limit the number of mares that can come for breeding to the space we have available.

The number of straight Egyptian Arabians in this country is very small, only 1 percent of the total number of purebred Arabians registered. Although most straight Egyptians are used for breeding, the few who have been shown along with Egyptian crosses have taken as many as 28 percent of the national wins. The value of this breeding is proven. It can complement your own breeding program. We are members of the Pyramid Society, and Kamars Sharif's offspring are eligible for the Futurity for Egyptian Related Horses, with prize money in excess of $90,000, held at the Egyptian Event in Lexington, Kentucky, every June. We will contribute toward the E. E. futurity if the mare owner wishes to enter.

Pedigree:

		*Fadl, #896	Ibn Rabdan (EAO)
	Fabah, #6264		Mahroussa (EAO)
		*Bint Bint Sabbah	Bayyad (EAO)
			Bint Sabbah (EAO)
KAMARS SHARIF		Fa-Serr, #4482	*Fadl 896 (Ibn Rabdan × Mahroussa)
#112144			*Bint Serra I 897 (Sotamm × Serra)
Black	Rouffna	Aaroufa, #7892	Fay-el-Dine (*Fadl × *Bint Serra I)
15.1	#339988		*Maaroufa (Ibn Rabdan × Mahroussa)

Kamars Sharif is straight Egyptian, Pyramid Society, Al Khamsa, and Blue List.

You are cordially invited to attend our Pyramid Society-sponsored Open House on May 15, or on rain date, May 22, if the weather is bad the first date.

At present Ellie Prince has only one youngster available for sale, a jet black 1982 colt with beautiful conformation and presence. He has the quality to be a breeding stallion. He is out of a daughter of Fasaab, a black Babson-bred champion. Also for sale will be a bay Fasaab daughter bred to Kamars Sharif.

Kamars Sharif's stud fee for 1983 is $1,000. Mare care is $4.00 a day, and $4.50 a day with a foal. At present, previous breeders to Kamars Sharif may have a return breeding with a special discount.

Return the enclosed postcard for more information on Kamars Sharif, the black colt, or Sodergreen Horsemanship School's ten-day summer session.

Sincerely,

Co-owners:

Eleanor Prince
Sodergreen Ranch and Horsemanship School
Buford, WY 82052
(307) 632-7954

Dorothy Feldman
114 E. 28 Street
Cheyenne, WY 82001
(307) 632-4253

CHAPTER 11

BREEDING

STALLION MANAGEMENT

Facilities

Provide your stallion with as much freedom as possible. He should be able to see other horses and have an exercise area large enough so that he can trot and canter—ideally, one where he can run in or out of his stall to the paddock and have protection from insects, extreme heat, and cold.

Since most stallions are curious and innovative, take extra care for their safety: Electrical outlets should be inaccessible to them; fences and gates should be high, secure, and visible, and constructed so that a foot, head, or neck cannot be caught, even if he rears up against the fence. Double fencing discourages horses from leaning on the fence in an effort to reach their neighbors, as well as helping to prevent the spread of disease, since the horses cannot get together. When inside, some stallions constantly kick or paw the walls, and in extreme cases it may be necessary to run an electric wire around the inside, if it is a large stall. The stallion should be able to see other horses across the aisle, and there should be a window where he can see out.

The more that stallions can be treated as any other horses, the more likely they are to be well-mannered, healthy, and good performance horses. Since they do seem to have more energy than other horses, however, their quarters should be slightly larger.

Special equipment is necessary on the breeding farm, including a teasing and breeding area with a teasing wall approximately three and a half to four feet high and eight feet long. It should be of solid construction, so that the stallion and the mare can strike at each other without injury to either. If a regular fence is used, it is possible for one of them to catch a hoof when striking. When there are only a few mares to be teased each day, each mare can be taken to the stallion's stall; in this case, the stall must be constructed so that he can reach the mare with his head and nuzzle her.

The breeding area (shed or paddock) should be situated away from other activities and distractions, flat with good footing, protected from wind or drafts, and have sufficient space to avoid crowding in case either the mare or the stallion should become hard to manage. The breeding chute should be designed so that it can be opened immediately to release the mare, preferably toward the front. If the breeding operation is performed in a barn or other enclosed area, keep the doors open; if trouble starts, take the stallion out immediately. In large breeding operations, a palpation chute (closed stocks that immobilize the mare) restrains the mare during breeding preparations. A small, safe pen for a foal should be constructed adjacent to both the breeding chute and the palpation chute.

Stallion Behavior and Handling

Stallions have been both romanticized and vilified—as always, the truth about them lies somewhere in between. Although they should be treated like other horses in most respects, there are times when any stallion can be dangerous to people and other horses: proper training and handling are imperative.

Although we can alter or control his behavior by training and environment, a stallion retains his basic drives and instincts. His behavior has a basis in herd association. A young colt plays by experimenting with fighting and mating behavior; as a mature stallion, he will be possessive of his mares and interested in strange horses either as potential mates or rivals. The earlier nipping, biting, striking, and rearing in play can easily show up in the domesticated stallion by aggressive, nervous behavior at horse shows or when visiting mares arrive at the farm. Because of these factors, a stallion should be controlled and trained by a competent handler who can anticipate potential situations that could cause his horse or another's to act up, who can discipline the stallion properly, and who can be ever alert, capable, and responsible.

Unfortunately, a stallion never learns how to apply his basic breeding drives selectively; he will ignore fences, commands, and his own safety in his efforts to act as nature intended him to. Handling a stallion at breeding time requires an expert to avoid injury to the stallion, the mare, or other handlers, and to give the best chance of conception in the mare. Young stallions, especially, should be properly handled and trained so that they will not develop dangerous habits. They should respect and trust you at all times, and you should respect them.

Tack for stallions. Use one particular bridle or halter when handling your stallion for breeding or teasing a mare. All your equipment should fit correctly and be especially strong, as well as humane. Overly severe tack provokes rearing and fighting, and overuse of the whip can inhibit some stallions from breeding.

Some methods of control include the snaffle bridle with a stallion chain run under the chin and through the bit rings; a halter with a stallion chain run under the chin or over the nose; or the halter with chain run through the mouth or across the gums under the upper lip. The heavily weighted, superior type of rawhide bosal is effective as well. If a stallion bites excessively when

The chain lead, run under the chin and through the halter rings, provides firm control for a stallion. Kamars Sharif 112144, Arabian stallion owned by E. F. Prince and D. R. Feldman.

breeding, a dropped noseband can be used. The lead shank should be at least ten feet long; twelve feet is better. This allows the handler to give the stallion the room needed when rearing to breed and yet remain safely out of the way himself.

Safety tips in handling stallions.

1. Don't take risks with your stallion just because he is gentle and well trained.
2. Give your stallion close supervision, checking him often. Check your fences, gates, and latches daily; before closing your barn for the night, double-check for trouble.
3. Punishment for an unmannerly stallion (nipping, rearing, striking) should be just, immediate, and severe enough to be appropriate for that individual; then let him alone to think it over. If he is either abused or treated with nagging, "picky" correction, he will reciprocate with resentment. You do not wish to have your stallion fear or hate you.

4. A young stallion should be trained early and never teased, slapped, or permitted to perform "cute" tricks. The commands "whoa," "stand," and "back" should be taught while he is young, and they should be obeyed at all times. This helps when he comes of breeding age.

5. When transporting a stallion in a trailer, there should be a partition between him and any other horse (see the chapter on transportation).

6. When handling or riding a stallion with other horses, be sure that the other people know you have a stallion, so that they can avoid coming too close and can watch any belligerent mares or geldings. Do not ride a stallion close to a mare in heat. Stallions should be tied away from other horses with two ropes—a normal lead rope and also a neck rope tied with a bowline around the neck.

7. Domestic stallions can injure or kill each other if they get together, and separating them can be risky for humans. Your employees should be drilled in checking gates and fences and adhering to safety measures so that there is no chance for this to happen. In fights between wild stallions, one would drive the other off; however, with fences and paddocks, they cannot escape each other.

8. At horse shows, stallions (especially young ones) should not be stalled next to mares in heat, as they will fret and become very excited, often losing a great deal of weight. If they become excited during halter classes or where there are large groups of horses, put a small amount of Vicks ointment in each nostril to block out the smell of mares in heat. Also, at shows or public horse gatherings, do not let well-meaning people irritate your stallion by patting, tickling, and poking at him. He is already under some stress when at a show, and he deserves his privacy.

9. During breeding, the handler should take complete charge of the stallion and mares. The assistants should follow his directions explicitly. Hygienic precautions should be strictly observed to prevent infertility and infection.

10. Some breeding associations permit artificial insemination. Where AI is possible, it increases the chances of conception and reduces the risk of injury to stallions, mares, and handlers, as well as reducing chances of infection, if done properly. Hygienic precautions are especially necessary on farms where AI is practiced.

11. Stallions should be conditioned by proper exercise, feeding, and training, and be provided with veterinary care during breeding season. After breeding, the stallion should be washed and cooled out as though he were a performance horse—do not feed grain or cold water until he is cool and dry.

12. Handlers can compound a stallion's breeding problems by overusing him when he is two to three years old, by rough handling during breeding, by isolating him from other horses during the nonbreeding

season, by forcing him to breed a mare objectionable to him, by using him excessively as a teaser, and by using training methods and discipline that aren't consistent with good breeding management. A stallion should be relaxed, feel secure, and trust his handler.

Exercise, Feed, and Grooming

Feeding the stallion is discussed in the chapter on feeding. During the breeding season, it may be necessary to feed him three or more times a day to help him maintain his weight. However, do not feed him within an hour—before or after—of covering a mare.

Regular daily exercise is important and the best means to keep your stallion happy, thrifty, and virile. Ridable stallions are best exercised under saddle from thirty minutes to an hour daily, especially during breeding season. Other stallions can be longed, driven, or ponied. Exercise should not be hurried or hard; the walk and the trot are the best gaits. After exercise, he should be rubbed down and cooled if he is hot, but the exercise is more beneficial if he is brought in cool, brushed off, and turned into his corral. Paddock exercise alone is not regulated; some stallions may take too little, while others take too much. A stallion with adequate exercise and careful training will be well-mannered and free of vices.

Regular grooming contributes to a good hair coat, improves muscle tone, and keeps the stallion in a good, comfortable frame of mind. Any horse appreciates personal attention; some horses need it more than others. Finding a good farrier and taking regular care of your stallion's feet is essential. If he is not being ridden on hard ground, let him go barefoot as much as possible.

The Stallion's Reproductive System

In order to manage stallions successfully, you should know something about their reproductive anatomy. The organs involved in the male reproductive system are shown in the diagram.

The testicles produce the sex cells—spermatozoa (collectively, the sperm) and testosterone, the male sex hormone, which gives sex drive. They are responsible for male sexual behavior and masculine characteristics. The scrotum is the pouch of hairless skin that contains the testicles. The scrotum and its internal structures form a means of regulating temperature (in the cold, the scrotum contracts and pulls the testicles up closer to the warmth of the body; in hot weather, the muscles are relaxed, allowing the testicles to lie normally).

The vas deferens propels the sperm from the epididymis (part of the spermatic duct system connected with the testicles) to the ejaculatory duct in the

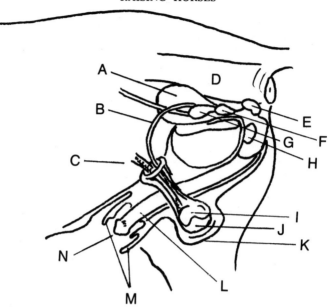

REPRODUCTIVE ORGANS OF THE STALLION
A. Bladder. B. Vas deferens. C. Spermatic cord. D. Rectum.
E. Prostate gland. F. Left seminal vesicle. G. Ampulla. H.
Bulbourethral gland. I. Epididymis. J. Left testis. K. Scro-
tum. L. Penis (containing urethra). M. Prepuce. N. Glans
penis.

urethra. The average effective life of spermatozoa inside the stallion is forty days, and they normally mature in about eleven days. In excessive use of a stallion, many immature spermatozoa can be found in the ejaculate, indicating a drop in fertility. The penis is the male organ of copulation. The brain and spinal cord are involved in the complicated system of nerve control. Erection is slow, but ejaculation takes only ten to fifteen seconds.

The ejaculate (a thick, adhesive fluid discharged by the seminal vesicles and prostate gland) acts as a transport medium for the spermatozoa down the urethra. It helps to activate and nourish them, as it contains electrolytes, citric acid, fructose, and other nutrients. During the service, the spermatozoa enter the uterus and travel in small numbers up the Fallopian tubes, where fertilization of the egg by one of them will take place. With age, the ability of the spermatozoa to fertilize the egg will decrease; two days is the approximate average length of time they remain active. Most stud managers, therefore, cover receptive mares every other day until they are out of season. The fewer the spermatozoa in the semen, the lower the fertility of the stallion. Some factors affecting the fertility of the stallion are as follows:

1. Seasonal variation in semen quality (spring and summer quality up; fall and winter quality down).

2. Overuse of the stallion. This is an individual thing, as some stallions can be used every day and sometimes twice a day for at least a month, while others may show signs of infertility if used as often as once a day.

3. Poor nutrition. A well-balanced ration will help maintain normal semen quality. Illness and infections (fever) affect semen quality.

4. Size of the testes. The size of the testicles has a direct bearing on a stallion's ability to produce and ejaculate sperm and is therefore an important factor in selecting and managing a stallion for the best reproductive efficiency. Size does change somewhat due to season—increasing during the breeding season—and older stallions have larger testes than younger stallions.

5. Adequate exercise is considered necessary, although it has not been scientifically shown to be responsible for good semen quality. Semen should be routinely evaluated before the breeding season or before a stallion is purchased, to be sure he is a good, fertile breeder.

THE MARE

The Mare's Reproductive System

The organs involved in the mare's reproductive system are the two ovaries, the two Fallopian tubes, the uterus, the vagina, and the vulva. The ovaries have two main functions: producing an ovum (egg) and producing hormones (estrogen and progesterone) for normal reproductive functioning. When the egg is expelled from the ovary (ovulation), it is called the heat period ("in season" or estrus)—the period when a mare is receptive to a stallion. Since ovulation usually occurs about twenty-four hours before the estrous period ends, a stallion should serve the mare about twelve hours before ovulation for a successful mating.

Diestrus is the period of the estrous cycle when the female will not accept the stallion (about fourteen days). The anestrous season is the period of quiescence during the winter months near the shortest day of the year, when only a few mares are cycling and ovulating. The natural breeding season occurs in late spring and summer, when the highest efficiency coincides with the longest day of the year. Temperature, length of daylight, and the type of feed or pasture are the environmental factors that control this cycle.

Studies put the average estrous cycle at 21.5 days, with the duration of estrus averaging 5.3 days; however, the range can go from 2 to 10 days or more. In the early part of the breeding season, mares tend to stay in heat for a longer time, and for less time toward the end of the breeding season. For successful breeding, mares should be inseminated at least every other day while in heat.

The uterus is the organ responsible for holding the developing fetus. There

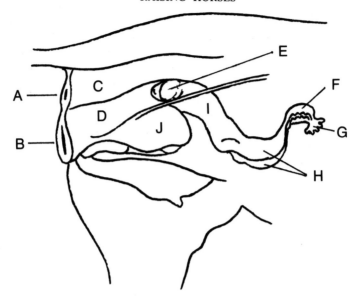

REPRODUCTIVE ORGANS OF THE MARE
A. Anus. B. Bulbal labia. C. Rectum. D. Vagina. E. Cervix. F.
Ovary and Fallopian tube. G. Infundibulum. H. Uterine horns. I.
Body of uterus. J. Bladder.

are three parts to the uterus: the body, the horns (cornua), and the cervix (neck). The cervix, a strong, smooth sphincter muscle, remains tightly closed except during heat and birth. The vagina and the vulva form the passageway for sperm during breeding and for the foal at birth.

Control of the Estrous Cycle

Synchronizing ovulation with the mating process is a challenge. The most common methods of ensuring that the mare is bred at the proper time (within twenty-four hours of ovulation) are rectal palpation and frequent breeding. Mares can also be treated with human chorionic gonadotropin (HCG), an ovulation-inducing hormone; even so, daily teasing, and breeding every other day, must still be done. Because the use of HCG reduces the duration of estrus and thus reduces the number of inseminations per cycle, it is a labor-saving device, as well as a way to save a busy stallion and let him breed more mares in a shorter period.

Other hormones administered to a mare to induce, speed up, or retard estrus for various reasons to ultimately aid in reproduction include FSH (follicle-stimulating hormone), LH (lutenizing hormone), progesterone, and prostaglandin.

Rectal palpation. The procedure of rectal palpation is valuable in predicting ovulation, especially in mares without a reproductive history, mares that have not developed a normal cycle, and problem mares. It should not replace sound teasing or management, however. Palpation also tells when a mare is in foal and determines whether there is an abnormality in the reproductive tract. Palpation is a delicate procedure; to avoid infection and internal damage, it must be done properly. The tail must be wrapped, the external genitalia cleaned and lubricated, and the palpation performed by an experienced, qualified person.

Teasing

The success of any breeding operation depends on knowing when a mare is in heat. An improper or inadequate teasing method is one of the primary causes of poor reproductive performance in mares. If a mare is cycling normally, she need be teased daily with only one stallion; if not, however, or if she was previously bred and is due to cycle, or if she is exhibiting the first day of diestrus, she should be teased with two stallions.

A mare indicates that she is in heat by laying her ears back, raising her tail, urinating and winking (contracting the lips of the vulva), kicking, striking, squatting, and squealing. A mare that is not in estrus will resist the stallion by kicking and biting and usually whipping her tail back and forth.

From our experience in a small breeding operation since 1960, giving adequate time to teasing is one of the most important considerations in making the mare receptive to mating and then completing an ultimately successful breeding. When a mare has been found in foal, she will sometimes wink when teased but almost never urinate. In our experience with Arabian stallions used on grade mares, registered mares of other breeds, and purebred Arabian mares, urinating and winking are the most reliable signs of heat.

There are several teasing methods:

1. Both mare and stallion can be led to a teasing area, where the stallion is allowed to call to the mare, nuzzle her, and push against the partition; control him with the chain lead or a light touch with a whip. Overuse of the whip and excessive jerking of the lead can make some stallions refuse to tease or breed. The whole operation of teasing and breeding should be kept as quiet and relaxed as possible.

2. Mares that do not show heat in obvious ways need a longer teasing period. We put mare and stallion in stalls next to each other with a solid partition at least eight feet high (and with safe bars above that) between them. Leaving them together for an hour or more will help the mare become more receptive if she is in heat. This may also help a fearful or reluctant stallion if he has previously had a bad experience with a mare. For safety's sake they should be watched. If the stallion has a busy

FLEHMAN RESPONSE
OF THE STALLION
This involuntary curling of the up-
per lip often occurs when a stallion
smells a mare in heat (and there-
fore is watched for when a stallion
is teasing a mare); however, the re-
sponse is triggered by other smells
also.

schedule, you may wish to use a substitute stallion (teaser) when you are only trying to find out if she is in heat.

3. If you have no teasing area, you can bring the mare to the stall or paddock of the stallion. Using a fifteen-foot lead rope on the mare's halter, you can run this rope through a large ring or around an upright (fixed so that the rope cannot go below five feet). Using this method, you can pull the mare close enough to tease her adequately, while remaining out of the way yourself and back far enough so that you can watch her hindquarters.

4. A stallion can be led by a pasture of mares, and the receptive ones will come to the fence. This will help cull a group quickly.

5. On large stud farms, a veterinarian can examine the mare (rectal palpation) and tell you if she is ready for covering.

BREEDING PRACTICES AND PROBLEMS

Pasture and Corral Breeding

Neither of these methods is practiced much today, since registered animals are considered too valuable to take the risks involved. However, the vast acreage and large numbers of horses in some Western operations might make the practice economically feasible.

In pasture breeding, the stallion is turned out with a band of mares for the breeding season. For foals to be registerable, mares must not be exposed to more than one stallion of breeding age; and there must be a thirty-day period between stallions if a different one is to be put in with those mares.

Advantages of pasture breeding include the comparatively high conception rate and the minimum time and work involved. Some range-raised mares conceive more regularly and do a better job of raising their foals when out on pasture in a natural situation; and after the foals are a few days old, the fresh air and exercise help them develop quickly and become strong and healthy. Both mares and foals should have adequate feed and supplements.

Disadvantages include the increased possibility of injury to a valuable stud and the difficulty of keeping exact records for predicting parturition dates. A stallion may become aggressive to people and especially to a horse and rider entering his pasture. This is minimized, however, if the stallion and mares are brought in each day for checking, supplementary feed, and handling. The stallion, especially, should have extra feed and supplements to keep his weight up when pasture breeding, and his band of mares should be kept small enough for him to handle. The pasture should be policed for hazards, and the fencing should be safe for horses and foals, with no horses pastured on the other side.

In corral breeding, stallion and mare are turned into a small corral or paddock together. The area should be rounded, and free of any danger spots where one of the animals could be cornered and kicked. This can be a good way for a shy, young, insecure stallion to "learn the ropes," if the mare is older, gentle, and will not kick. They can be watched to make sure no problems develop. The method is considered dangerous for the stallion, however, and is not recommended as a standard practice for valuable studs.

In-Hand Breeding

Preparation. When the mare shows signs of estrus, she will normally allow herself to be mounted and bred by the stallion. After teasing and being found in heat, prepare her for breeding: Wrap her tail, and clean her external genitalia thoroughly with a mild antiseptic solution, rinsing *thoroughly* afterward (antiseptics may have a spermicidal effect). When wrapping the tail, be sure all tail hairs are out of the way of the stallion's penis at the time of covering (a hair in the vagina can cause a small, painful cut and introduce bacteria). Lead the mare to the breeding area; restraints, if used, can then be readied or applied.

Breeding hobbles feature quick-release, panic snaps; they are applied either on the hocks or on the rear pasterns. Although most mares do not need these restraints, they are good insurance for the occasional mare that kicks. Many authorities suggest using both hobbles and a twitch for the ultimate safety of mare and stallion. Here, at Sodergreen Ranch, mares often arrive that may not be halter-broken, or more often, have learned to pull back on their halters. For more control, we use a special manila-rope halter (similar to a bull halter) that has headstall and lead rope all in one piece. This tightens around the nose and puts pressure on the poll when the mare pulls back. Her usual halter with lead rope is worn underneath and is not tied.

When the mare is brought into the breeding chute, the special halter rope is dallied around a sturdy post at the front of the chute and held by an assistant (anyone holding or using ropes should wear gloves). Have the stallion ready. The mare should not be expected to wait for any length of time after her restraints are in place.

Prepare the stallion by rinsing his abdomen, chest, and inside of forelegs with disinfectant. If he is being used heavily, we feel that washing his genitals thoroughly after service with mild soap and warm water, followed by rinsing with a reliable nonirritating disinfectant, is sufficient. In some cases—especially with young stallions—excessive cleaning of the genitals before servicing can reduce the sex drive. Use discretion and obtain your veterinarian's advice.

Covering the mare. For clarity in explanation, we will assume that you are handling the stallion and you have an assistant handling the mare. As soon as the mare is ready for service, lead the stallion to her near side (for his safety). Let him tease her for a minute or so until she stands with tail raised and legs well apart. She usually will urinate. When he is ready to mount, pull the mare's tail out of the way. The experienced stallion will swing himself from the near side around behind the mare as he jumps. The inexperienced stallion will often put both forelegs over the mare's back near the withers and have to work his way around. Try to correctly position the stallion. Stallions should not be allowed to mount until they are drawn (fully erected—penis out and slightly stiffened).

If the person handling the mare is not in a position to see well, give him any directions that may be necessary (such as "Hold her head up and still" or "Be ready to loosen the halter rope and lead her out"). The handlers should work as a team and know exactly what to do whatever the situation. Procure enough help for known problem mares.

There may be times when you will have to steady the stallion after he mounts (holding a foreleg or pushing against the barrel), or push against the mare's hindquarters to keep her in position. If the mare's chest is not against the bar in the breeding chute, she will move forward a few steps; if she has nothing solid across her chest, her handler may have to steady her. When a small stallion serves a large mare, it is more important to steady him, since he will be in a more upright position. You can also make a small mound for the stallion to stand on.

When the stallion ejaculates (releases the semen), his tail will move up and down (flagging). This is especially noticeable in breeds that have a high tail carriage (Arabians and American Saddlebreds). The stallion should not be allowed to kick or bite mares; do not reprimand him, however, for holding onto the mare with his teeth, as some horses steady themselves this way. If the stallion savages (bites) his mares, put a protective covering over their neck and withers. As he dismounts, the mare's handler should turn her to the left, causing her hindquarters to swing away from the stallion, saving him from being kicked.

After the covering, wash the stallion thoroughly with mild soap and disinfectant. It may be necessary to take him close enough to a mare that he will let down. Then take him to a secluded area and longe him at a walk or slow trot if he is still excited. Cool him out, and let him graze some green grass. This makes the whole breeding process as relaxed and pleasant as possible, while helping to keep his sex drive strong.

After breeding, remove the mare's restraints and tail wrappings; then loosen the breeding halter and slide it over her head. Have the handler lead her away from the sight of the stallion and longe or lead her quietly for about ten minutes. Although some breeders do not feel it is necessary to walk a mare after service to prevent her from straining, nevertheless it is relaxing for her; whenever possible, the breeding process should be made as pleasant as possible for all concerned.

When breeding a mare with foal, the foal should be confined in a safe pen adjacent to the breeding chute so that the mare will not worry; if she is tense and nervous, she will be less likely to settle.

When difficult mares must be bred, they should be tranquilized for the breeding process—especially those that panic if restrained. There are also some mares that have had unhappy experiences in breeding chutes, and it is impossible to get them in. For easy, successful matings, halter-break mares when young, and train maiden mares to enter the breeding chute and have their genitals washed and tail bandaged, before their first breeding experience. They should become used to restraints before the breeding process, since these in themselves panic some mares.

Visiting mares should be brought to the stud farm a few days before estimated estrus. This gives the mare a chance to adjust to the new surroundings and schedule. Some mares (especially maidens) can feel so insecure that they go off their feed and may skip a heat period due to stress.

Artificial Insemination (AI)

Artificial insemination is the depositing of the stallion's semen in the vagina or cervix of the mare by artificial means.

There are several advantages to the artificial insemination of mares. With proper hygiene, it controls reproductive infection. Clean surroundings and sterile equipment are absolute musts for the AI program to be successful. This is why AI was first recommended: to eradicate contagious equine metritis (CEM), a venereal disease imported from Europe.

Other advantages are that it reduces the possibility of injury to handlers and to small, shy, or nervous mares or stallions; it allows use of stallions when natural service is not possible (due to poor breeding habits or injury); it allows semen evaluation at each collection; and it identifies reproductive problems more easily. AI prevents stallion overuse, especially in the early part of the breeding season, and gives more effective use of older, valuable stallions. It also allows for a more accurate record-keeping system. Research has proved that the conception rate with AI is increased.

AI has its disadvantages also, ranging from technical and storage problems to those of abuse and fraud. The technicians or veterinarians who practice AI must be highly skilled, not only to prevent damage to the mare, but also because careless use of AI can increase the chance of disease.

Since it is an expensive program, the breeder must determine in advance whether AI is right for his operation. Although many breeds of horses allow AI, there are usually stringent, special rules set up by the registries. Before proceeding with artificial insemination, check with your registry for their approved conditions and procedures—failure to do so may mean that you cannot register the foal from AI matings.

Embryo Transfer

Embryo transfer involves implanting a fertilized egg from a donor mare into the uterus of a recipient mare, who carries the fetus and suckles the resultant foal. The host mare is only an incubator, providing the environment and nutrients for survival of the embryo. The foal receives all its genetic traits at the time of fertilization. The completion of a successful embryo transfer depends upon getting the donor mare (supplying the egg) and the recipient mare (receiving the egg) at or near the same phase in the estrous cycle; drugs can be used to synchronize the heat periods.

The advantage to embryo transfer is of course that foals may be produced out of mares that are able to conceive but cannot carry their foals to full term, especially older, valuable mares. On the other hand, the cost is high, especially since the chance for a successful transfer is low. And again, registries have special rules and restrictions on the program.

Common Breeding Problems and Diseases

Some *skin diseases* can be spread through breeding, but these are usually very evident in the form of lesions or active skin irritation, and breeding can therefore be avoided. The stallion owner has a perfect right to refuse to accommodate the mare until her skin problem has been resolved, especially any generalized infection caused by mange, mites, fungus, or lice.

Pox (coital exanthema) is not serious, in that it will not do permanent damage. However, it will throw a stallion out of service for two weeks, which is expensive and inconvenient. *Streptococcus* and *staphylococcus bacteria* are usually responsible for abortions in early pregnancy. Although they are normally present on the coat and skin of all horses and can gain entry easily during service, they generally are no problem in normal, healthy mares. The bacteria *Escherichia coli* and *Pseudomonas* are often responsible for abortions in the second half of pregnancy. *Uterine fungal infections* result in abortions or the birth of a weak foal.

Rectal damage. When the stallion is covering the mare, he may accidentally enter the rectum instead of the vagina and cause severe damage (rupture of the rectum or tearing of the anus, which can result in fatal peritonitis). If a veterinarian is called at once, he may be able to save the mare through surgery.

Masturbation is a vice that results in lower fertility and causes poor performance. It is usually done by stallions at night and when alone, and occurs less often in stallions allowed to see other horses. Because an accumulation of smegma or irritation encourages masturbation, periodic cleaning of stallions will help eliminate the problem. Physical devices used to control masturbation are the stallion ring (which fits on the penis about an inch behind the glans) and the metal stallion cage, which fits around the glans (physical devices must be removed before breeding). Masturbation can almost always be stopped.

Pregnancy Testing

There are several ways to determine pregnancy. Some small breeders consider a mare to be in foal if she shows no heat when teased during at least two regular cycles.

The manual test can determine pregnancy as early as nineteen days after service, but it is usually performed after forty days. This is the only test that will detect the presence of twins. For the blood test, a veterinarian collects thirty cubic centimeters of blood from the jugular vein between fifty and ninety days after the last service; seventy days is optimum. In order to use the urine test (which detects the presence of estrogen), the mare must be more than one hundred twenty days past the last service.

Two electronic tests—the Ovumeter and the Boveq—are promising, although research is continuing on these products. The accuracy of both tests depends upon the skill and experience of the user.

Caring for the Pregnant Mare

Although the average gestation period of a mare is 340–45 days, some mares go to 360 days with no problem. It would be wise to consult a veterinarian if your mare is over 360 days. Foals born five weeks or more too early will not survive. If the foal is born within four weeks ahead of time (the closer to full term, the better chance of survival), it may survive with veterinary assistance and good nursing care.

Table 3. MARE'S GESTATION DATES

DATE BRED	DATE DUE	DATE BRED	DATE DUE	DATE BRED	DATE DUE
Jan. 1	Dec. 7	May 6	Apr. 11	Sept. 3	Aug. 9
Jan. 6	Dec. 12	May 11	Apr. 16	Sept. 8	Aug. 14
Jan. 11	Dec. 17	May 16	Apr. 21	Sept. 13	Aug. 19
Jan. 16	Dec. 22	May 21	Apr. 26	Sept. 18	Aug. 24
Jan. 21	Dec. 27	May 26	May 1	Sept. 23	Aug. 29
Jan. 26	Jan. 1	May 31	May 6	Sept. 28	Sept. 3
Jan. 31	Jan. 6	June 5	May 11	Oct. 3	Sept. 8
Feb. 5	Jan. 11	June 10	May 16	Oct. 8	Sept. 13
Feb. 10	Jan. 16	June 15	May 21	Oct. 13	Sept. 18
Feb. 15	Jan. 21	June 20	May 26	Oct. 18	Sept. 23
Feb. 20	Jan. 26	June 25	May 31	Oct. 23	Sept. 28
Feb. 25	Jan. 31	June 30	June 5	Oct. 28	Oct. 3
Mar. 2	Feb. 5	July 5	June 10	Nov. 2	Oct. 8
Mar. 7	Feb. 10	July 10	June 15	Nov. 7	Oct. 13
Mar. 12	Feb. 15	July 15	June 20	Nov. 12	Oct. 18
Mar. 17	Feb. 20	July 20	June 25	Nov. 17	Oct. 23
Mar. 22	Feb. 25	July 25	June 30	Nov. 22	Oct. 28
Mar. 27	Mar. 2	July 30	July 5	Nov. 27	Nov. 2
Apr. 1	Mar. 7	Aug. 4	July 10	Dec. 2	Nov. 7
Apr. 6	Mar. 12	Aug. 9	July 15	Dec. 7	Nov. 12
Apr. 11	Mar. 17	Aug. 14	July 20	Dec. 12	Nov. 17
Apr. 16	Mar. 22	Aug. 19	July 25	Dec. 17	Nov. 22
Apr. 21	Mar. 27	Aug. 24	July 30	Dec. 22	Nov. 27
Apr. 26	Apr. 1	Aug. 29	Aug. 4	Dec. 27	Dec. 2
May 1	Apr. 6				

Based on 340-day average

Gestation time is influenced by sex and season: stud colts are generally carried one to three days longer than fillies, and winter foals are usually carried a few days longer than late-spring or summer foals. Disease can also influence the length of gestation (an unusually long gestation time may indicate a diseased or abnormal foal).

Up to the sixth month of pregnancy, your mare should be fed and handled like any other mare. Regular worming and a proper vaccination program are essential, as well as proper hoof and teeth care. Mares that have difficulty keeping weight on, perhaps due to timidity or temperament, need a special feeding program.

The last three months of pregnancy are the most important in terms of exercise and nutrition, since the foal gains 70–80 percent of its birth weight and size then. See the chapter on feeding. Stress of any kind should be kept to a minimum. Such things as trailering, changing stablemates, or leaving her out in a cold rain without protection, can have a detrimental effect.

Six weeks before foaling, boost your mare's antibody level for all major vaccinations so that the colostrum will provide adequate antibody level for the foal. Light work will help both muscle tone and general condition. However, overexertion and heavy work or work over rough, slippery terrain may result in abortion.

The pregnant mare should have her environment protected—she should not be pastured with frisky geldings, yearlings, or other aggressive horses. She will appreciate being pastured with other matrons in foal. If she is very timid (low on the totem pole in her pasture), take care that you never put her in a situation in which she could get squeezed going through a gate or cornered in a shed. When feeding hay and grain in a group, be sure that the timid mare receives her share and can eat without being hassled.

CHAPTER 12

FOALING

NORMAL FOALING

Facilities for Foaling

Prepare your facilities several weeks before foaling is due. We like a twelve-by-twelve-foot or larger foaling stall that is well ventilated but free from drafts. It should be sturdily constructed, with no gaps under the door, well lighted, and free from projections (hay mangers, nail points, pails, and so on).

Basic hygiene in the case of the foal and foaling stall is essential, as navel ill is the most common cause of death in foals. Before bedding the stall, hose down and disinfect the walls, ceiling, and floor, with careful attention to cracks and corners. Apply disinfectant again a week or so later with a pressure sprayer, and keep out people, dogs, and other animals. The foaling stall should be deeply bedded with super-clean straw (avoid sawdust and shavings, as they can irritate the sensitive membranes).

Even if you plan for the mare to foal in paddock or pasture, you should have a stall available in the event of bad weather or complications in foaling. A pasture or paddock should be fenced in safe wire (V-wire is preferable) or with poles or boards. Provision should be made so that the foal cannot get under the fence. A foaling mare that lies next to a fence may have the foal come under it or on the other side, and young foals that lie down next to a fence may maneuver themselves under in the process of getting up. This is especially dangerous if the adjoining pasture contains rambunctious geldings or other hazards, or if the fence borders a busy highway.

Another hazard is a creek or irrigation ditch. A mare may have a slight fever or feel too warm during labor and lie down near water, where she feels cooler. She may foal directly into the water and cause the foal to drown. Or the baby may fall in, while still weak, in its bumbling attempts to stand and move.

The footing in paddock or pasture should be firm and stable. Don't turn your mare out when icy, slippery, or muddy conditions exist. If she needs to drink at a water hole, be sure that it is a safe place (not slippery or where another horse could corner her).

How long can a mare in foal be ridden? If she is in good condition, she can be ridden up to thirty days before foaling and started again thirty days after foaling. Do not ride hard or on uneven, slippery ground, jump, or ride the mare under stressful conditions. Using your mare carefully and keeping her in good condition help her to foal easily. Be sure to cool her out thoroughly.

Foaling Supplies

Prepare your foaling supplies well before the expected event. Pack them in an easily carried bag or suitcase, arranged so that you can quickly find any item. Some of the supplies should be sterilized and kept separately in plastic sacks (we use Ziploc bags, or clean plastic bread bags with snap-clothespin closures—if you use wire closures, care must be taken that they are not lost in the bedding, where they could be accidentally ingested by foal or mare). Some suggested supplies:

1. Stainless-steel bucket with Ivory or castile soap (or new two-gallon plastic buckets).
2. Wide-mouth plastic bowl with sterilized funnel (if necessary, the mare can be milked into the bowl and the milk poured into a feeding bottle).
3. Baby's feeding bottle or sterilized (older-type) pop bottle with lamb nipple that fits tightly over the end. You should test the flow through the nipple; if not adequate, make a larger hole.
4. Small jar of Vaseline.
5. Cotton gauze roll and Vetrap (or similar bandages).
6. Obstetrical cord or chain (sterilized).
7. Oxygen cylinder.
8. Double-strength or 7 percent iodine—mixed half and half with glycerine—and a small jar or whiskey shot glass.
9. Flashlight.
10. Antibiotics and tetanus toxoid.
11. Needles and syringes (sterilized).
12. Sterile surgical scissors and forceps.
13. Surgical gloves.
14. Several turkish towels.
15. Enema can with 4–5-inch tube, 3/8 inch wide.

Ask your veterinarian about obtaining items you can't find elsewhere.

Signs of Imminent Foaling

Although there is no way of forecasting the exact time of birth, we do have some signs that say a birth is imminent. Some mares may show all the signs, others none, but usually one or more are present.

1. The udder grows, is hard, and looks more round and shiny.
2. Wax-like drops form on the nipples (waxing), usually lasting twenty-

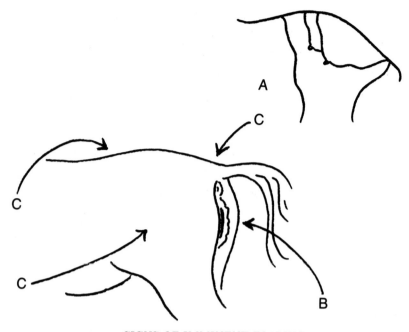

SIGNS OF IMMINENT FOALING
A. Large, hard, shiny udder, with "wax" appearing on the nipples. B. Swell-
ing, softening, and moist vagina. C. Softening and sinking of muscles.

four hours. This sign can occur from two hours to one week before foaling.

3. Milk drips or runs (birth will occur at any time or up to one week). Two or three weeks of running milk may indicate a problem, plus the fact that the colostrum, with necessary antibodies, will have been wasted. Your veterinarian may want to collect and freeze some of this too-early milk; a foal without colostrum will need special veterinary attention.

4. Muscles around the base of the tail soften and sink.

5. One of the most reliable signs is the relaxation and softening of the vaginal lips.

6. Restlessness, pawing, pacing, sweating, and making many small piles of droppings, and lying down and getting up repeatedly, indicate birth is imminent.

7. Breaking of water bag.

Mare Surveillance

How you handle the "night watch" is up to you. Some folks sleep in the barn until the blessed event occurs, while others wait until morning to see

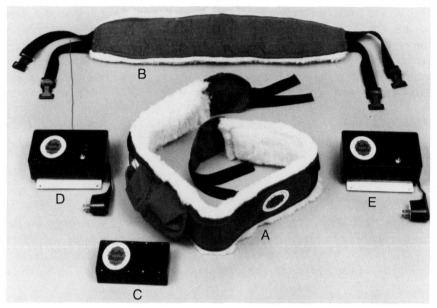

The Baby Buzzer, invented by Dr. Leonard Skeggs, is designed to warn the horse breeder that a mare is about to foal. As she lies down to foal, the alarm sounds in your bedroom, office, or wherever you choose. This gives you time to monitor the birth, give assistance if needed, or call a veterinarian immediately if a major problem develops. A. Washable, Kodel-padded surcingle with unbreakable Lexan tree, worn over withers. B. Padded girth that secures surcingle. C. Radio transmitter contained in small plastic box that slides into pocket on side of surcingle. D. Primary receiver, which is plugged into 110-volt outlet. E. Remote station wired to primary receiver to enable buzzer to be heard at a distance. (Courtesy Locust Farms Arabians)

what has happened. Most of us go on hourly checks to the barn and try to catch our mare in the process. Two other alternatives are an intercom system (can alert the horseman to unusual sounds or the absence of sound), and the Baby Buzzer—a patented transmitter "foaling alarm." The mare wears a surcingle with the Baby Buzzer attached; when she goes down to foal, the alarm goes off in your bedroom. Closed-circuit television is the ultimate in mare surveillance and of course the most expensive.

Mares usually foal between 7 and 11 P.M. Be as unobtrusive and quiet as possible when you are on night watch.

Preparing the Mare for Imminent Birth

Your mare should be used to being touched on her udder (especially the maiden mare). Stroke her gently several weeks before foaling so that she will not reject her foal. When foaling is imminent, wash her udder and vagina with a mild soap such as Ivory. You can wrap her tail if she is used to it, but be sure the bandage is clean and very secure so that it cannot come undone during foaling. Your mare should be barefoot (no shoes) and without a halter. Although leaving a halter on her may be convenient, if you should miss the foaling, the foal could put a foot in the halter and become caught while thrashing around after birth—a potential death trap! If you have a gentle mare and she trusts you, you can halter her if and when there is a need.

Mares that have had Caslick's operation (stitching the vagina closed) should have the stitches removed.

The Foaling Sequence

Stage I. This stage is characterized by restlessness, patch sweating, increase in skin temperature, and looking at the flanks. Colostrum may drip or spurt and the insides of the hind legs may be wet with milk. The mare will deposit small piles of manure around the stall. Small contractions may have begun in the uterus. The lips of the vulva will swell out and there may be a copious slimy discharge. Your mare may lie down and rise repeatedly. Stay in the background; do not disturb her, as she does have the power to delay the foaling process (some sources say up to two weeks!). At this stage, the hormone cortisol is being released, which helps the mare deal with the stress of foaling.

Stage II. The first signal that the second stage of labor has begun is the rupture of the placenta—"breaking water"—which precipitates the foal on its way into the world. Two to five gallons of fluid will be expelled, usually followed by ten to fifteen minutes rest. Shortly thereafter, more violent contractions begin (birth pains). Only about 1 percent of foalings are difficult, since the mare is more conveniently shaped for foaling than the cow for calving. Once the mouth of the womb has opened a little way, then it rapidly widens out under the pressure of the water bag and the foal. The mare is usually lying down at this point, but occasionally a mare gets up and walks around with the foal's feet sticking out. The foal is wrapped in two membranes—the outer bag of waters, and the inner membrane, or caul (surrounding the foal at the time of birth)—which help stretch the mouth of the womb and lubricate the birth canal. Normally the foal is presented with its head between its forefeet (we see first one front foot, then the other foot, four to six inches behind). The soles of the feet should point downward. The nose of the foal will appear about even with the knees. From this point, the complete birth usually takes from five to twenty-five minutes.

If the mare seems to be taking too long (perhaps because the foal is large), you may need to assist. Taking the sterilized chains or clean cloths around the forefeet, pull firmly and steadily *down toward the mare's hocks*—but only when she strains. You pull when she strains and rest when she rests. This help should *only* be given when the foal is presented normally. If there is any question at all, or if this is one of your first experiences with foaling, do not attempt to help, but get veterinary attention immediately. After the foal has been presented beyond its shoulders and starts to slip out, stop pulling. The foal will come quickly and usually suddenly. The mare will rest.

The foal will have a wet coat, draped in the placental veil (caul). *Do not cut or disturb the umbilical cord.* The caul should be immediately stripped away from the foal's nose, if it has not broken away naturally, but there is no hurry to remove it from the rest of the body, since the foal is still gaining nourishment from the umbilical cord, which is a part of it. The foal can receive up to one pint of rich, oxygenated blood from the placenta (which is ten to fifteen pounds in weight and contains twelve to fifteen hundred cubic centimeters of blood) through the attached, still-pulsing umbilical cord—extra energy to help him in this new world.

Clear the nostrils (press a thumb and forefinger on the bridge of the foal's nose). If he has trouble breathing (seems weak), pump the forelegs back and forth alternately. Raising the hindquarters slightly and pressing the ribs in and out also helps. Giving oxygen in this case is beneficial. In cold weather, it will help to massage and rub the foal vigorously with turkish towels to dry him and encourage circulation and warmth.

Immediate care of the new foal. When you are satisfied the foal is breathing normally, leave the mare and foal alone for a few minutes to socialize and rest. Any licking the mare gives the foal contributes to their well-being, not only helping the foal but also helping her to secrete milk and pass the afterbirth quickly. Bonding—the establishment of a close relationship—seems especially important in horses, and this process should not be interfered with.

When the foal tries to stand or the mare rises, the umbilical cord will break at a naturally weak point inches from the foal's navel. Swab the stump with iodine (or iodine-glycerine mixture) to block bacteria from entering the foal's system. We generally fill a shot glass (or small jar such as pimentos come in) and saturate the whole stump. Bring the glass up under the stump all the way to the belly, gathering it into the glass and sloshing the iodine around the base of the cord on the belly.

The foal is generally on its feet within thirty to forty minutes and will make many bumbling attempts before standing successfully. If your baby still has problems "putting it together" after two hours, milk the mare into a wide plastic bowl and pour into a feeding bottle via the funnel. This colostrum milk should give him the energy he needs to renew his efforts (as well as giving him passive immunity to diseases until his own immune system can take over). Or you may be able to hold and steady the foal so that he can suck from his dam.

Your foal can best absorb the antibodies in colostrum within the first four hours after birth. After that time, the value of the mare's colostrum diminishes (even though she may continue to produce it for several days) and the ability of the foal to utilize it diminishes rapidly. After twenty-four hours, the structure of the foal's intestinal tract changes and the antibodies can no longer pass through to the blood system. Colostrum also has a laxative effect and helps the foal pass the meconium (fecal waste) accumulated during gestation. Colostrum is vital for your foal—make sure he gets it, and the sooner the better! It may be wise to freeze some extra colostrum if you have several broodmares (warm it up to room temperature to use—never put it in boiling water).

The normal foal will get up within an hour. He will respond to light in ten minutes, have a suck reflex within twenty minutes, and upon rising, quickly show a desire to nurse. Deviations in any of these normal signs—or their absence—may indicate partial or permanent brain damage.

The first four days of the foal's life is an adjustment period imposing stress factors on him. Being susceptible to infection is of primary concern, and only through the antibodies of his dam's milk will he have a natural defense. Some veterinarians suggest giving the new foal antibodies and a tetanus antitoxin; others, however, think that if nothing is wrong with the foal, such measures are not necessary and using antibodies indiscriminately may lead to resistance.

If the foal has not passed meconium within eight hours, give an enema with one pint of warm, soapy water. Insert the hose very gently not more than a few inches into the rectum.

Your mare should be given tepid water to drink; if she was sweating during foaling, a warm blanket will keep her from chilling, especially if it is cold or damp.

The stall should be cleaned completely (it will be wet due to the breaking of the bag of waters) and new, clean straw put down, especially deep in corners to help keep the foal from injuring himself during attempts to stand and nurse.

Stage III. Your mare will experience some contraction pain a few hours after the birth of her foal. These contractions should expel the afterbirth—a process referred to as "cleaning." Usually its own weight (hanging from the vulva) is enough to supply the force to assist the contractions. Never pull the placenta; it must peel away from the uterus of its own accord.

In maiden mares and spooky mares, it may be wise to tie the amnion (placental veil) in a knot so that it does not drag on the ground and scare the mare—do not tie it to the tail.

After she passes the placenta, you should examine it carefully to make sure it is all there. If even a small piece is missing or if it is very bloody, call a veterinarian immediately. Leaving pieces of afterbirth in the mare can result in metritis (infection of the uterus) or acute foaling founder (laminitis). Some signs of problems in the mare are sweating, heat in the feet, shivering, nervousness, and anxiety. Your veterinarian will also look for tears in the vagina.

When the afterbirth is not expelled in six hours (retained placenta), call

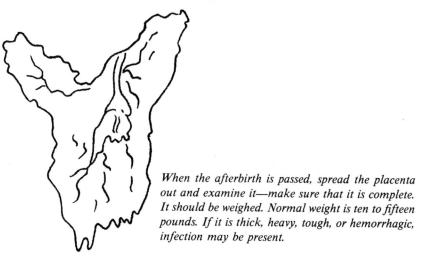

*When the afterbirth is passed, spread the placenta
out and examine it—make sure that it is complete.
It should be weighed. Normal weight is ten to fifteen
pounds. If it is thick, heavy, tough, or hemorrhagic,
infection may be present.*

your veterinarian—do not delay! Serious complications are caused by a retained placenta in mares—much more so than in cattle. Usually oxytocin is
administered to stimulate contraction of the uterus. Your veterinarian will
check the afterbirth and perhaps flush the mare and administer antibodies;
treatment must continue a week or more.

It is normal for the mare to discharge (from the vagina) a viscous, choco-
late-brown liquid for about six days. This discharge takes place even if the
placenta has been passed cleanly.

FOALING PROBLEMS

Causes of Difficult Birth (Dystocia)

The major causes of a difficult birth are a malpositioned foal, an unusually
large foal, twins, a premature foal, or a diseased, contracted, or dead foal.
Some misalignments may include:

1. The forelegs are present, but the head is not visible—the chin may be
   caught on the rim of the pelvis, or the head may be turned back.
2. A common breech birth: the soles of the feet are facing up and no head
   is visible—the foal is either upside down or coming hind feet first.
3. One forefoot and the muzzle of the foal are visible—an elbow may be
   caught on the rim of the pelvis, or a foreleg may be held back. A severe
   puncture can occur if the missing foot is caught by the roof of the
   vagina.
4. The tail of the foal is visible, but no legs or head—this is an abnormal

breech birth—the foal must be pushed back in and the hind legs straightened and pulled out.

5. The head is visible but no legs or feet—this is the worst position the foal can be in, since the forefeet are caught on the mare's pelvis.

Treat any of these situations as an emergency as soon as it appears. You will need veterinary assistance immediately. While waiting for the veterinarian to come, get the mare up and walk her slowly around. The foal will slide back into the uterus and will stay as long as thirty to forty minutes, provided that the mare stays on her feet. Your veterinarian will probably give the mare an intravenous drug to help relax the uterus and birth canal, enabling him to reposition the foal for a normal delivery.

Misaligned foals can produce lacerations of the cervix, uterus, vagina, and rectum. Without immediate veterinary help, there is not only a threat to your mare's future reproductive health, but also to her life.

Birth Defects

The percentage of birth defects is rather high in horses. Congenital defects are not necessarily inherited. Viruses or radiation can alter the formation of the embryo and can cause a congenital defect that is environmental, rather than genetic (such as a cleft palate brought on by drugs or infective organisms).

Inherited defects are usually produced by a single gene mutation but can also happen as a result of chromosomal defects. With chromosomal problems, defects can easily be identified as to the carrier. Gene mutations are often carried in a recessive form: only if the defect is received from both parents will the problem crop out.

Genetic defects can be classified as either lethal or nonlethal. A lethal defect causes death sooner or later. A delayed lethal (such as a heart defect) will eventually kill the average horse, and a partial lethal is a defect that causes death only under certain circumstances (such as predisposition to ruptured blood vessels in a racehorse—the rupture may occur only under the stress of racing).

Other problems include *weak foals:* anoxia (lack of oxygen) can result when a foal has a difficult birth (long, slow labor or pinched umbilical cord) or premature rupture of the umbilical cord. Oxygen can be administered under veterinary supervision. *Sleeper syndrome* is a fatal condition caused by the bacterium *Actinobacillus equuli.* The foal shows signs of weakness (is unable to stand) and has a subnormal temperature, with severe diarrhea.

Navel ill, or *joint ill,* is a bacterial infection, often fatal, circulating through the bloodstream to almost every organ.

Dummy foal syndrome (wanderers, sleepers, barkers) is a condition characterized by disturbed behavior including convulsions, lack of suck reflex (will not nurse), muscle spasms, wandering, and fast breathing rate accompanied by "barking" noise. It is caused by a lack or cutoff of oxygen during birth, pressure during birth, premature birth, or disturbed fetal development. If treated with sedatives, anticonvulsant drugs, oxygen, tube feeding, and good nursing, the foal may recover, or he may die.

Premature foals. The mare may have an intrauterine infection or hormonal failure, producing a small or weak foal. Oxygen should be administered at birth, the foal placed in a warm place, and antibiotics given.

Wobbles (foal atoxia) is an injury to the vertebrae (characterized by incoordination and aimless gait). There is no known treatment.

Simple constipation. Fecal matter is small and hard; signs are tail switching and straining. Treat with a mild-soap-and-water enema. *Severe constipation* (retained meconium). The large fecal mass cannot be reached by enema; signs are rolling, thrashing, and lying on back. Treatment consists of a mixture of mineral oil, milk of magnesia, and castor oil. When very severe, IV fluids and sedation are used.

Hernias (umbilical, scrotal, irreducible) are caused by accident or from an enlarged opening in the abdominal wall. Some hernias close, but others need manual or surgical aid.

Eye injuries. Irritation of the surface of the eye due to hay, straw, or wind. The eye will water, the foal will rub it, and the cheek will be wet with tears. Use ophthalmic ointment or drops and keep the foal out of wind or dust. *Entropion* (inversion of eyelids). The lower lid folds in, usually due to dehydration; characterized by tearing, blinking, and the avoidance of light. The eye and lids should be lubricated and the lower eyelid pulled out hourly. Surgery is needed in extreme cases. This should be diagnosed and treated early, as it can lead to blindness.

Ruptured bladder can be caused during birth or by a jerk on the umbilical cord after delivery. The foal will become weak, with distended abdomen; he will strain and be short of breath, but no urine is produced. Toxicity, fever, and uremic poisoning can result in death. Surgery must be performed immediately to close the hole in the bladder.

Pervious urachus ("leaky navel"). The umbilical stump fails to close, becoming wet and soiled, and constantly dribbling urine. The stump must be cauterized with silver nitrate or 7 percent iodine. Occasionally surgery is required.

Foal pneumonia is often caused by a bacterium that is thought to exist in some soils and is contracted through open wounds such as the umbilical stump. It appears not to spread from animal to animal. Foal pneumonia has a high mortality rate (see also Chapter 8).

Viral pneumonia can clear up by itself unless compounded by bacterial invasion or immune deficiency. The most common cause of the disease is streptococcal infection. For pure viral pneumonia, a broad range of antibiotics are used, usually with four to ten days of intensive therapy, then a month of follow-up therapy.

Pneumonia in a foal should never be taken lightly. Immediate help is needed. Careful management and control of the foal's environment can prevent the conditions that lead to any respiratory disease. Good ventilation and keeping foals dry and free from drafts and extremes in temperature are good preventatives.

Foal Rejection

Usually the rejection of a foal by its dam is temporary. However, until the foal is accepted, the baby must be considered an orphan.

Possible causes:

1. A first-time dam may have pain in the udder, which is aggravated by the foal's pushing; she may resent—or not recognize—her foal.
2. A mare that is moved into strange surroundings and subjected to an unusual environment prior to foaling may suffer so much stress that she rejects the foal.
3. It may be that a certain temperament would make a mare predisposed to rejection, and this quality might be inheritable.

Rejecting mares may be savage, indifferent, or fearful. Savage mares will kill their foals and can severely injure their handlers. It has been found that the early environment of the mare plays an important role in this abnormal behavior: almost all were spoiled, pampered, and reared with a special bond to their owners. Mares that had serious injuries as young horses and needed prolonged care seem to fall into this category. The savage mare can be rehabilitated—though perhaps not with the first foal. Shortly before the second foal, the mare is given a stilbestrol injection; immediately after foaling, hormone shots (to increase lactation) and tranquilizers are administered.

A fearful mare may not recognize her foal and attack out of terror.

There are mares that simply abandon or ignore their foals. Such a mare will tolerate the presence of the foal until it tries to nurse or approach her. She will try to hold up her milk even when tranquilized. Mares that are uncomfortable from the third stage of labor contractions, or in pain from the pressure of a full udder, should be tranquilized or twitched until the pressure is relieved. Hand milking may be necessary in some cases. It is also possible that the mare is ill, the foal unhealthy, or she may not have enough milk. Foals that nurse continually may not be getting enough milk and the dam may need hormone injections. In severe cases, a nurse mare or goat may be tried, or the foal treated as an orphan.

Postfoaling Problems in the Mare

Hemorrhaging does not occur very often, but when it does it is serious and can be fatal. The clinical symptoms occur anytime from within hours of foaling up to two to three days after. Pain, uneasiness, sweating, weakness, and paleness of membranes are some signs, although they are variable. In older mares, after a sufficient number of pregnancies and slight damage each time to the weakened uterine arteries, the total damage to the arterial wall may be so great that it breaks and bleeding starts. Some mares survive, since clotting occurs, but for others, the clotting is insufficient and the mare dies. Call your veterinarian immediately and keep the mare quiet.

Recto-vaginal fistula. During foaling, the strong contraction of the mare's muscles may cause one of the foal's feet to push through the vaginal wall into the rectum. The foal's foot may return to the vagina before another contraction, but a recto-vaginal fistula (passageway between rectum and vagina) has been made. If the foot does not return before another contraction, there will be a ripping and tearing of the vaginal and rectal tissue, and surgical correction is required. The mare must be put on antibiotics for some time before surgery, due to contamination from the fecal material, and surgery must be delayed for about thirty days to allow time for the tissue to return to normal.

Prolapse of the uterus. When the uterus turns itself inside out and protrudes from the vagina, it is called a prolapse—fortunately relatively rare in the horse. However, this is a life-threatening situation, and your veterinarian must be called immediately—he will attempt to replace the uterus. The prolapse can occur in the mare any time up to twenty-four hours after foaling. In some cases, only the vagina is seen outside the walls of the vulva, and in other cases the whole uterus appears, hanging down as a large, fleshy mass. When the whole uterus is involved, it must be kept clean, warm, and moist. Great care should be taken that it is not damaged. Support the organ in a clean sheet and sprinkle it with clean warm water to keep it from drying. Keep your mare standing and as quiet as possible while you await your veterinarian.

Colic. Mares will often show signs of colic (pawing, lying down, looking at their abdomen) shortly after foaling. Since these pains are produced by uterine contractions (expelling the afterbirth), this is not a true digestive colic. If the pains persist longer than thirty minutes, however, you should call your veterinarian.

A true digestive colic may be seen six to eight hours after foaling. It is usually due to an impaction in the intestines caused by the straining the mare experienced during foaling. Call your veterinarian immediately. Do not walk the mare out of the colic as you would ordinarily do, since signs of colic after foaling may indicate rupture of the uterine artery. Take care that the foal is not injured by the mare's pawing and thrashing.

If at all possible, find a foster-mother for your orphan foal.

MANAGING MARES AND FOALS

Orphan Foal Care

Orphan foals or foals from mares that cannot suckle them should be given a foster-mother if possible. To help the foster-mother accept the new foal, sprinkle it with her milk before presenting the baby to her. If a foster-mother cannot be found, you must hand-feed the foal. If a horse farm near you has a colostrum bank, get colostrum for the foal if he was unable to nurse. If the mare died when the foal was born, she should be milked immediately, even though dead.

To help the new foal drink, dip your fingers in milk and rub his mouth. He should be fed at first every hour (day and night!) with a cup of formula or a little more. Overfeeding, even when the foal seems very hungry, is a mistake —colic and diarrhea can result.

Another way to teach the foal to drink is to offer him milk in a shallow pan containing one or two ice cubes, after first withholding feed for several hours. Evidently the change in temperature helps him learn to drink, since he can feel that his lips are in contact with something.

The earlier your orphan will eat hay and crushed oats, the easier hand-feeding will be and the sooner your foal will gain weight and energy. To induce the baby to eat grain, put a little in the side of his mouth. Do this several times a day when you feed him his formula. The protein level of the grain ration should not be less than 16–18 percent. When young foals are growing rapidly due to added protein and energy, increase the calcium to 1 percent and the phosphorus to 0.8 percent of the grain ration.

Since mare's milk has a different composition from cow's milk (low butter-fat and high sugar content), you will have to either make up a formula or use a commercial product such as Foal-Lac (Borden Chemical, Pet Products). Here are some formulas:

1. 1 pint low-fat cow's milk (1–2 percent butterfat)
   4 oz. limewater
   1 teaspoon sugar

2. 1 pint low-fat cow's milk
   2½ oz. limewater
   2 teaspoons lactose
   2½ oz. water

3. 1 13-oz. can evaporated cow's milk
   1 can water
   4 tablespoons limewater
   1 tablespoon sugar or corn syrup

The orphan foal should be fed every hour for the first two or three days, about one-half pint each time. Then he may be fed every two hours for a week, increasing the amount. By three weeks of age, feed three pints of formula every four hours, and if he is eating well, you can stretch the night feedings a bit. If your foal starts to lose weight, "up" the formula feedings. Watch his bowel movements to see whether your formula should be adjusted —if there is diarrhea, you may have too much water (but if it continues, call your veterinarian); if he strains, your formula may be too rich—not enough water. After the first week on formula, along with hand-feeding grain, introduce a creep feed (see the chapter on feeding).

Your orphan foal should be gentled and trained early. Put a halter on and off often, but do not leave the foal unattended with a halter on. The especially strong need for bonding in horses can make problems for the orphan foal. Lacking the discipline their mothers would normally mete out, they become sassy and show little respect for their owners. If they bond strongly with their owners, they apparently think they are "people." It will help them to have an animal friend—an old, gentle mare is an excellent choice (perhaps you can lease or borrow one if necessary).

You don't wish a spoiled-brat foal, but you do want a youngster that likes, respects, and trusts people. An orphan foal will become bored, especially if kept confined. Provide him with a few toys, such as an empty bleach bottle tied to a pole (at head height), a beach ball, and an empty grain sack.

Twins

Twinning is not desirable in horses and is not common. Usually both foals die, or one lives and the other mummifies. Only one in ten diagnosed twinning mares can carry both foals to term. If both foals live, they will be small, one usually smaller than the other. One may have to be raised as an orphan, or the mare may be able to raise both if they are supplemented with extra milk. The mare and foals will need extra attention for some time.

The Foal Heat

The mare owner must decide whether or not to re-breed the mare on the first heat period after foaling (foal heat, or nine-day heat). This foal heat lasts about twenty-four hours and is not necessarily on the ninth day; it can occur from three to eighteen days. It is usually the easiest heat period to detect, but if the mare needs eighteen to twenty-four days to repair and rest, it would be better to wait the extra time. If the mare foaled easily, expelled the placenta within two to four hours after foaling, is normal in all respects, and exercises regularly, she can safely be bred on her foal heat.

The decision should take into consideration the time you wish the mare to foal. If you have an early foal, in January or February, it would be better to wait, whereas in June and July, the foal heat would put the foal in a month where there would still be time to re-breed if she didn't settle the first time.

Growth of the Foal

The weight of a foal at birth is 8–10 percent of the mare's weight, and its height (at the withers) is 60 percent of its mature height. Foals about double

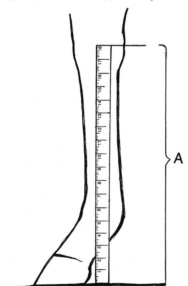

HOW TALL WILL YOUR FOAL GROW?
Studies done on Arabian and Quarter Horse youngsters showed that, by six months of age, the distance (A) from the midpoint of the knee to the ground attains 97 percent of its ultimate length; this distance averages three tenths of the horse's mature height at the withers. To find how tall your foal will be, 1) have your six-month-old stand squarely on a level surface, 2) set a ruler on the same surface against the outside of the foreleg, and measure to the midpoint of the knee (subtract for shoes or overlong hoofs). 3) Multiply the result by ten and divide by three to find the approximate height when mature.

their weight in the first month (four pounds per day)—thus the importance of the mare's being a good milker and the foal's receiving creep-feeding supplementation. After three and one half months, the growth rate decreases and the foal's height is about 80 percent of his mature height. This shows the rapid rate of bone growth during this period and emphasizes the need for proper nutrition.

Studies at Cornell University found that colts were heavier than fillies at birth, and the difference increased with age. Dams under seven years of age and older than eleven had foals of lighter weight at birth than mares seven to eleven years of age. Dams under seven had shorter foals, with smaller cannon bones, than mares seven to eleven. Foals born in January, February, or March were lighter and shorter and had smaller cannon bones than foals born in April, May, and June. The difference continued throughout the study period (January 1958 to June 1976).

Weaning

Breeding farms have their individual ideas on when foals should be weaned, running anywhere from three months to six or seven months. Because weaning is one of the most traumatic experiences in a horse's life and the one most likely to invite injury, you should make it as easy as possible for them. In making your judgment on when you wean your foals, keep these considerations in mind:

1. Has the mare been re-bred? If so, and if the foal is in good health and growing well, earlier weaning (four to five months) is better for the mare.
2. Was the foal born late and the mare not re-bred (August and September)? A late foal not having the advantages of several months of green grass and having the trauma of a northern winter, may need his dam for a longer period (six to seven months), not only for physical reasons but for mental well-being as well. Late foals usually do not have any foal friends of the same age and must be weaned alone, which is even more traumatic. When they are older, they can handle it better.
3. You have several foals to wean. They are all healthy and growing well; one or two are four months old, the rest are five to six months. Weaning them all together may be advantageous to all, especially for their emotional well-being.

If your foal must be weaned alone, put an old, gentle mare in with him. She will have a calming effect, as well as being company. However, when feeding, separate them or provide creep feeding so that the foal gets the nutrients he needs.

We do not advise weaning a foal before four months unless there are abnormal circumstances. Foals weaned prior to four months seem to lack aggressiveness and do not respond to training as well as those weaned at a later age.

Broodmares in poor condition—often older mares—can get back into good condition sooner and easier if their foals are weaned early. Experience makes it seem preferable to separate the mares and foals completely, since the foals may try to get at their dams and perhaps injure themselves. Prolonging the total weaning will make it more difficult to dry up the mare as well.

Foals of poor-milking mares almost invariably develop and grow best when weaned early (four months), provided that they are ready to wean (from a maturity standpoint).

Methods of weaning foals:

1. Completely separate the foal from its dam all at once—out of sight and sound.
2. Separate the foals from their dams starting out for a short time (three hours) the first day, four hours the second day, and so on, letting mares and foals keep in sight of each other. This takes more time and labor.
3. Separate foals all at once from dams across a safe, high fence—mares have access to pasture but can visit foals.
4. If you have several foals to wean, remove one or two mares at a time, beginning with the dams of the oldest foals. In a few days, remove the next mare, and so on. The drawback here is that the foals without their dams may get kicked while trying to nurse from a remaining mare.

Your facilities will have some bearing on the method you use to wean your foals. The different methods have varying advantages and disadvantages, and the success of any of them may depend partly on the temperament of mare and foal.

There is an old wives' tale about weaning foals by the new moon—as some breeders say, it can't hurt, and anything that may help is welcome.

When first weaned—and for the first twenty-four to forty-eight hours, the foal may be too upset to turn his attention anywhere but to his missing mother. As soon as possible, however, give the foal some attention several times a day. This is the time he will appreciate human companionship, and it will be a good time for him to learn the basics of leading, standing, and perhaps showing at halter. Make the most of your time with him before he is again turned out to pasture to grow and develop.

Proper management of weanlings and their dams is very important:

1. Foals need protection from inclement weather; a pasture with a run-in shed is ideal.
2. Foals need exercise. Take care that any enclosure is carefully inspected for protruding nails, wood splinters, and other hazards. Never use barbed-wire enclosures for foals. Dutch doors on stalls invite injury as well.
3. Do not wean a foal by himself; he should have company, and usually an old, gentle mare is most convenient. Give the foal time to get attached to the old mare before turning them out in a pasture with other horses.

4. Foals should be healthy and eating grain and hay well before weaning. Do not wean just before or just after deworming (about two weeks after worming is ideal).
5. Do not wean a foal if he has a cold or any other indications of sickness.
6. Keep any changes such as deworming, trimming feet, or any other stressful practice to a minimum until the foal gets used to being without his mother.
7. This is also a stressful time for mares. Some will run a fence and become hot and upset. In cold, damp, or windy weather, they can develop a chill which leads to other, more severe complications. Watch them closely.
8. Especially in early weaning, feed a high-protein ration (at least 18–20 percent) and good-quality pasture or legume hay.

To dry up the mare, cut the grain ration way down, starting several days before weaning. If she has good pasture, grain can be completely removed until she dries up—about ten to fourteen days. Because exercise is very important in the drying-up process, pasture is ideal; if she is kept confined, riding, longeing, or ponying can furnish the necessary exercise.

Mares that are very heavy milkers, or mares with a history of mastitis, may benefit from hand milking two or three times a day for a few days after weaning. Do not "strip" the udder (milk out the last drop), as this would counteract the drying-up process—merely relieve the worst of the pressure. If she runs a temperature, consult your veterinarian; she may be developing mastitis.

A period of at least two to three months is necessary before turning the weanling back into the same pasture with his dam.

Handling Foals

During the first twenty-four hours after birth, your foal will have no fear of people, perhaps because his eyes do not focus very clearly and his nose cannot distinguish the difference between his dam and humans (or he has not yet bonded closely enough with his dam to make that difference significant). If the dam is distrustful of people, this quality will eventually influence the foal. In this case, it may be well to handle the foal within the twenty-four-hour sociable stage. Stroke him all over gently; hold him close to his dam (one hand in front of his chest; the other around his rump)—you may have to tie the mare to keep her quiet or have her held from outside the stall—and speak quietly to mare and foal to set up a recognition pattern.

Whenever communicating with the foal, keep as low to the ground as possible, sitting on a bale of hay or a campstool (if mare is gentle) or "hunkering down" so that you can spring out of the way if she objects. Because tall humans and other horses frighten a foal, your "low profile" will pique his inborn curiosity and encourage him to approach, rather than retreat.

Making friends: Hunker down and greet the new foal on his level. He'll be less likely to become frightened.

Do not handle very young foals excessively. The mare and foal should have some privacy, especially at first. Eventually even a nervous mare will become less wary when she becomes used to your presence. Letting her eat grain while you socialize with the foal will keep her mind on her stomach, rather than on you.

Do not become impatient in handling your foal by grabbing him or cornering him. Unlimited patience and understanding of foal behavior is very important, and the time you spend with mare and foal should be enjoyable to all concerned. Refer to *Basic Training for Horses: English and Western* for further information on training foals and older colts.

Mistakes to Avoid when Handling and Raising a Foal

Most mistakes that are made in raising foals do not seem serious when the foal is small, but when he is older and larger, these mistakes result in bad manners that may grow to vices and eventually injure the horse or his handler.

Teasing the foal. A foal has a natural tendency to nuzzle and suck. If people dangle their fingers in front of him and keep just out of reach, it is frustrating to the foal; he will try to grab the fingers and eventually may bite. What can start out as a normal reflex turns into a game and eventually a dangerous biting habit. Teasing a young animal is cruel and thoughtless. Do not poke at a foal, especially around the head and muzzle.

Playing with the foal. It is not wise to roughhouse with a foal by chasing him, playing hide and seek, jumping out at him, and so on. It is natural for foals to learn how to play together in a herd situation, since jumping, rearing, and kicking prepare them for becoming adults. Unfortunately, the foal does not distinguish between human and horse in this type of situation; he grows into a thousand-pound animal, he loses respect for his owner, and the human is bound to be injured. In general, do not run with a young horse, since it is a play activity, and running with him activates more aggressive behavior.

Excessive work with the foal. It is better not to longe a young foal at all. Not only will speed on the longe line be detrimental to stifles and hocks, but foals do not have long attention spans, and working them steadily will sour them and tire them unnecessarily. After six months, a weanling can be worked ten to fifteen minutes a day at slow paces (longeing) or learning halter showmanship. Before that time, getting the foal used to being touched, having his feet picked up, wearing a halter, and leading willingly is enough handling. Be sensitive to the needs and mental attitude of your young horse, and don't overdo the training aspect.

Hand feeding. Letting a foal nuzzle your pockets and eat from your hand will lead to nipping and biting and a thoroughly spoiled animal. When a treat is withheld, the foal will naturally be disappointed and mad. When he demonstrates his sulky feelings, some owners feel guilty and reward the foal's poor behavior with a treat; thus the bad habit is reinforced and the owner loses the respect of his young animal. Giving food rewards in a carefully controlled manner is an acceptable method when training. Praise and petting are an adequate reward with young foals.

Rough, insensitive handling. Loud talk, impetuous action, exasperation, slapping, and yanking the foal around are actions that have no place around young foals (or any horse, for that matter). A foal subjected to rough handling will become aggressive and perhaps charge or kick, or become fearful and antisocial with all humans. Exhibit patience, quiet reassurance, and a genuine liking for the foal, and handle him so that he will reciprocate with desirable behavior.

Unsuitable environment. A poor environment can include everything from unsuitable, unhygienic facilities, to improper methods of feeding, exercise, and parasite control. If you must keep your mare and foal in a stall, do keep it clean and adequately bedded. Time should be given to both mare and foal for daily exercise in an area with enough room to run. If the mare tends to be lazy, she can be longed, but take care that the longe line does not trip or entangle the foal.

In paddock or pasture, barbed wire, trash piles, hidden obstacles, and strange horses pose a threat. When foals run, they usually make larger and larger circles around their dam, and they do not watch where they are going. Gopher and badger holes, as well as half-submerged rocks, can be hazards. When the foal is very young, deep pools in a creek, or separation when the mother crosses the creek, can make other problems. If your mares and foals

The beginning of a long and happy relationship.

are out on pasture, check them periodically during the day; it may be wise to either stall or corral them at night. In areas where violent storms occur, make provision for shelter—large hailstones can kill a young animal. It is not wise to overprotect your foal, but use common sense in the foal's protection.

Choosing the right time to handle the foal. We generally work with our foals several hours after they have been fed in the morning. Both mare and foal have their stomachs full and are relaxed and in a quiet mood. However, if the mare and foal have been stalled all night and the foal needs to express his high spirits, it may be well to let him run and play before asking for his attention to the business at hand.

When you work your foal at the wrong time, he will undoubtedly act up, and it will be difficult for you to achieve a rapport with him and to accomplish the task you had planned for the training session. Some poor times to ask for your foal's attention are when the stable is in commotion (horses and visitors coming and going), when you do not have adequate time to accomplish your task, when either the mare or the foal is not feeling up to par, or just before feeding time. You want your foal to feel positive and receptive toward his lessons.

Choose the right time to work with your foal, and give him love as well as the best of care. This may be the beginning of a long and happy relationship.

APPENDIX

CONFORMATION JUDGING SHEET 1
General Appearance

IDEAL	FAULTS
Breed type	Lacks type
Balance and symmetry	Lacks balance and symmetry
Sound in mind and body	Unsound in mind and body
Blending of parts—well proportioned	Parts do not blend together
Quality/refinement	Coarse—large-boned
Style (proud carriage)	Moves and stands without style / upstanding / leggy
Smooth muscling	Lacks smoothness of muscling
Stands square—legs well under or squareness of stance	Crooked legs / base wide or narrow
Deep-bodied	Lacks substance / shallow-bodied
Short-coupled (correct for breed type)	Long/weak coupling
Size	Too small/large for breed type
Substance (muscle and bone)	Light in bone and muscling
Uniform body lines	Not uniform in body lines
Vigorous "bloom," thrifty condition (glossy coat)	Unhealthy, rough coat
Sex character	Too masculine (mares) or feminine (stallions) for sex
Shows alertness and intelligence	Unintelligent/apathetic/sluggish/ lethargic
Flat bones	Round bones
Well-defined tendons	Tendons not defined
Lack of blemishes and unsoundnesses	Transmissible weaknesses / blemishes / unsightly
Good condition	Too fat / too thin / rough
Presence	No presence

CONFORMATION JUDGING SHEET 2
Forehand

IDEAL	FAULTS
Head	
Well-chiseled / refined features	Coarse / Roman-nosed
(dry) clean-cut about head and throatlatch	Thick throatlatch
Stylish	Plain
Breed type / correct profile for breed type	No breed type
Big, full nostril (capable of great dilation)	Small nostril
Head in proportion to body / with good head carriage	Head too large for size of body
Fine muzzle	Boxy muzzle
Broad forehead	Narrow forehead

IDEAL	FAULTS
Head	
Short-to-medium, fine ears with expression (stallions small, mares medium)	Set of ears indicates bad temper / coarse ears / mule-eared
Expressive, large, full, prominent eyes	Pig-eyes, dull eyes, set high
Low-set, wide-set eyes in broad forehead	High-set eyes, in narrow forehead
Jaw (jowls) deep, full and powerful	Weak jaws
Teeth meet correctly when biting	Parrot mouth / monkey mouth
Breadth under jaw (fist-width between jaws)	No breadth between jaws
Short distance between eye and muzzle	Long distance between eye and muzzle / eyes set too high
Neck	
Long, set on high, arched	Too short, upside down
Runs well back into withers	Ewe-necked
Clean, well-defined throatlatch	Thick, heavy throatlatch
Adequate crest (stallion)	Too feminine—weak
Well balanced	Too light / muscle-bound / thick
Fine, stylishly held	Low-set / coarse / staggy
Throatlatch width (clenched fist between branches of jaw)	Inadequate width
Shoulder, Chest, Withers	
Long, flat, deep-sloping shoulder, angle approximately 45 degrees, length important	Short, straight-angled shoulder
Well-laid-back shoulder	Straight, upright
Well-defined, prominent withers	Flat withers / mutton
Withers extended deep into back	Withers not deep into back
Withers moderately high	Low, coarse / mutton withers
Good width, deep chest, V's down well	Narrow / without substance / weak
Forelegs (Arm, forearm, elbow, knee, cannon, fetlock, pastern, hoof)	
Legs set parallel in front, straight from the inside, and toe set squarely ahead	Stands close, base narrow/wide
Arm long, oblique, and muscular	Arm short, straight, weak
Arm adequately (long-) muscled	Arm short-muscled
Smoothly muscled arm and forearm	Bunchy, fat muscle
Straight legs	Crooked legs / offset cannons / toe-in / toe-out / knock-kneed
Long, powerful forearm / short cannon	Forearm and cannon same length

IDEAL	FAULTS
Forelegs	
Forearm broad at elbow (long and muscular)	Forearm same width from elbow to knee
Elbow set away from body	Elbow set into body
Large, flat, square knees / clean	Small, round knees / meaty, fleshy / bow knees (hastens side bones) / buck-kneed (unstableness, stumbling) / knock-kneed (interfering) / calf-kneed (winging)
Short, clean cannon / flat bone	Long, round-boned cannon
Adequate width between forelegs	Narrow, not V'd down
Width of cannon-tendon sheaths (same width from below knee to just above fetlock)	Tied-in, bowed tendons
Strong, heavy tendons in cannons	Tendons in cannons not defined
Pasterns moderately long, elastic, and well sloped (approximately 45 degrees—same as shoulder/pastern)	Pasterns too steep, coon-footed, short
Fetlocks—clean, large, bold	Fetlocks small, meaty, weak
Feet (hard, adequate height at heel, heels open, large enough to carry bulk of body)	Splay-footed/ pigeon-toed (paddling, winging, tendency to interfere) / broken-angled / too small for weight
Hoofs round (forehand), tough	Hoofs narrow (in front) / contracted heels / cracked / angle too steep

CONFORMATION JUDGING SHEET 3
Body (back, loin, rib cage)

IDEAL	FAULTS
Length in underline	Short underline / wasp-waisted
Moderately short back (close-coupled)	Long, weak back (poor keeper)
Strong back	Long/weak back, swayback, roached back
Withers extend deep into back	
Widely ribbed	Shallow-bodied
Deep flank	
Proportional depth of body and heart girth in proportion to legs	Too short-backed for length of legs (contributes to forging)
Short, strong loins	Sagging loins
Ribs run to depth beneath chest and give room for great heart and lung capacity	Narrow or insufficient spread to ribs

CONFORMATION JUDGING SHEET 4

Hindquarters (croup, hips, stifle, gaskin, hock, cannon, fetlock, pastern, and hoofs)

IDEAL	FAULTS
Width through stifle	Stifles lack width / set into body (contributes to forging) / lack of muscling
Long, wide, rather level croup (according to breed type), sloping toward flat	Pear-shaped / apple-rumped / short croup, steep
Hip smooth	Rafter-hipped / rough over hips / high hips, too steep
Moderately straight, high tail-set (according to breed type)	Tail-set too low
Withers and croup same height after four years old	Croup higher than withers (after four years old)
Heavily muscled thigh, quarters, gaskins (inside and outside)	Pear-shaped quarters / dropping quarters
Long, smooth-muscled quarter and gaskin	Lacks muscles in quarters and gaskins
Sufficient angulation of hind legs	Insufficient angulation
Stands square and correctly, with legs set well under	Base narrow / base wide / too-straight hind legs (insufficient angulation / camped under / camped out
Hind feet more oval than front feet	Hind feet less oval than front feet
Hocks well let down (long line from hip to hock)	Short from hip to hock
Feet/pasterns same angle (approximately 45 degrees)	See faults in forehand / contributes to forging
Large, clean, strong, well-defined hocks	Cow-hocked / sickle-hocked / too close (interfering) / too wide / bowlegged
Cannons and hoofs (see forelegs)	See faults in forehand

CONFORMATION JUDGING SHEET 5

Aesthetic Qualities—Disposition/Attitudes

IDEAL	FAULTS
Beauty	Coarse, overly large-boned, not smooth, not pleasing appearance
Purity of breed	Shows no breed type
Classic type	Ugly head; shows no breed type; no definition of muscle, tendon
Sound in mind / stable	Unsound in mind and body
Free of vices	Unstable disposition—biting, charging, cribbing, weaving, bucking, kicking

IDEAL	FAULTS
Alert	Sluggish, lethargic
Intelligent	Backward, unintelligent
Shows courage	Unwilling
Has endurance	Unsound, "no bottom"
Affectionate	Shows enmity /animosity / has vices, is bad-tempered
Tractable	Intractable
Has personality	No personality
Capable of general utility	Not capable of performing general tasks (mind and body)
Willing	Balky, stale, bored, obstinate
Gentle	Wild, unpredictable, fierce

CONFORMATION JUDGING SHEET 6
Gaits and Action

SOME IDEALS	SOME FAULTS
Elegance of carriage	Goes stringy behind
Straight and balanced	Drags the hocks
Coordinated	Rotates the hocks
Long, true stride	Crosses over in front
Direct	Excess lateral movement (rolling)
Prompt	Walks the rope
Easy/free	Spraddles
Folds knees and works hocks	Goes short in front
Lifts knees and drives hocks	Dishes (wings in) in front
Knee and hock action good	Jerkiness
Style at walk and trot	Labored action
Fairly close hock action	Short
Collected	"Trappy"/dwelling
Balanced extension	Stiff-kneed/pounding
Correct flexion	Stumbling
Pushes off hocks, impulsion originating in hindquarters	Lame
	Wings
Spring	Paddles
Impulsion	Interferes, forges
Regularity	Goes too wide at hocks
Cadenced	Open in the hocks
Brilliance	Moves too close in front
Fire	Cuts the daisies behind
Natural dynamic action	Moves heavily on the forehand
Bold, confident stride	Crooked
	Uncoordinated

PURCHASE AND SALE AGREEMENT

THIS AGREEMENT is made between _____,
hereinafter referred to as "BUYER," and _____
_____, hereinafter referred to as "SELLER"; the
agreement is entered into between BUYER and SELLER for purchase and
sale of the horse(s) described below on the following terms and conditions of
sale:

DESCRIPTION OF HORSES: _____

A. Consideration: In consideration of the total sum of $_____,
SELLER agrees to sell BUYER the horse(s) described and BUYER agrees to
buy said horse(s) on the terms set forth.

B. Terms and Payment

    1. Cash price $_____

    2. Down payment $_____

    3. Time balance—amount of note $_____

    4. Finance charge, interest rate $_____, _____%

Time balance payable in ____ consecutive monthly payments of $_____ including
(plus) interest, or _____

_____. First payment due ____ day of _____, 19____. Should
BUYER fail to make _____ payments, SELLER shall have the option to declare
the balance of the note then owing to be due and payable. Time is of the essence.

C. Security: To secure the payments and duties of this obligation, SELLER retains the
registration papers until the horse(s) is (are) paid in full. SELLER agrees to execute
all necessary documents for breeding and registration required by the proper registration association, and to transfer title and ownership upon full payment.

D. Care: 1. BUYER agrees to keep described horse(s) insured in the amount of
$_____ until transfer of registration is completed.

    2. BUYER shall have the right to transport the said horse(s) in the usual course of
business of breeding, training, and exhibiting. However, BUYER agrees not to remove
said horse(s) in any permanent change from_____

_____ except where agreed in writing by SELLER.

    3. BUYER agrees to keep said horse(s) in good health and free from disease by
providing adequate feed, shelter, veterinary care, and farrier care.

    4. BUYER agrees to keep said horse(s) free of all liens and encumbrances.

E. Warranties: SELLER warrants that he has good clear title to said horse(s) and
guarantees said horse(s)'s breeding ability at the time of sale. Should said horse(s) fail
to meet this guarantee, SELLER agrees to refund BUYER'S monies, including all
interest paid to date.

EXECUTED this _____ day of _____, 19____, at _____

SELLER _____   BUYER _____

LEASE AGREEMENT

This lease, made the _____ day of _____, 19_____, between _____, hereinafter referred to as Lessor, and _____, hereinafter referred to as Lessee,

The parties hereto agree to and with each other as follows:

1. Lessor does hereby lease to Lessee the pure-bred Arabian mare _____, born _____. This lease is for the mutual benefit of both parties.

2. The Lessor has legal title to the above mare and the lawful right to make this lease.

3. Lessee hereby agrees to maintain and care for the mare, keeping her in good breeding condition. This includes but is not limited to proper feed, mineral supplements, and veterinarian and farrier services. Lessee shall make reasonable efforts to keep the mare in safe pastures and corrals and from accidents.

4. Lessee agrees to insure the above mare with full mortality insurance in the amount of $_____ with the cost of the insurance to be paid by

_____.

5. The term of this lease shall be _____ months, from _____ to _____. An option for renewal of this lease at the same conditions for an additional _____, or until Lessor is assured mare is safely in foal for a second time, may be granted in writing with consent of both parties.

6. Lessee agrees to breed this mare to _____ for Lessor's foal.

7. In consideration of parties' agreement herein contained, the Lessor and Lessee agree to divide the produce of this mare in the following manner: The first foal will belong to the _____, the second foal to the _____, and so on for the term and any extensions of the lease. In so far as possible, fillies shall be evenly divided between the two parties. When one party receives a filly, the next filly born shall go to the other party.

8. If lease continues past _____ months, Lessor agrees to take foal at weaning time. If Lessor cannot do so, Lessor agrees to pay costs of upkeep from time of weaning until such time as he can transport foal.

9. Lessor shall have the right to inspect the mare at any time. However, Lessor shall contact Lessee beforehand by phone or mail so that Lessee may be present if he so desires.

10. If the mare dies during the term of the lease, the Lessee shall be compensated for stud fees at the same rate that is charged to any outside mare as determined by published advertisements. This compensation shall be made from the insurance cover-

age. The remaining amount of insurance shall belong to the Lessor to compensate for the loss of the mare.

11. At the expiration of the lease or of any extension or renewal thereof, Lessee agrees to return above mare in good breeding condition, allowance being made for unavoidable accident or act of God. This return shall be by licensed carrier or transport approved by both parties.

12. Lessor and Lessee agree to promptly sign, fill out, or otherwise properly process all papers necessary for registration, insurance, and/or partnership records. Lessor will be responsible for filing a copy of this lease agreement with the Arabian Horse Registry.

13. Lessee has first option to purchase mare at the current market price if Lessor should desire to sell her.

IN WITNESS WHEREOF,

The parties have hereunto signed and sealed this lease in triplicate this _____ day of _____, 19____.

Witness

Witness

MINERAL CHART

SALT (sodium chloride)

Function: Regulates fluid balance in body; helps remove waste and is excreted in direct proportion to water excreted; helps transfer nutrients to cells; affects fluid intake by creating thirst; helps regulate cooling mechanism; acts as appetizer; involved in milk production.

Source. Keep salt available at all times for horses to eat free choice—they will eat what they need; salt blocks or loose salt can be used; feed iodized salt in iodine-deficient areas (trace mineral salt in mineral-deficient areas); plant foods are generally low in sodium and chloride.

Lack results in: Rough coat, depraved appetite, reduced growth, heat stress when working, reduced milk production, decreased energy, easy and quick fatigue.

Comments: A horse needs more salt if he sweats due to hot weather, exercise, work, or stress. Excess salt can be a problem only if adequate water is not available or if unlimited salt is given to an animal after long deprivation (fluid imbalance can occur and cause fatal poisoning). Salt poisoning causes colic, diarrhea, frequent urination, staggering, and paralysis of hind legs.

CALCIUM

Function: Necessary for bone formation, development, and repair; builds strong teeth; important during lactation; affects availability of phosphorus; 99 percent of body calcium is in skeleton and teeth.

Source: Molasses, ground limestone, calcium phosphate and dicalcium phosphate, steamed bone meal (unpalatable: so add to ration gradually), hay from calcium-rich soils.

Lack results in: Soft bones (osteomalacia), depraved appetite, reduced performance, rickets in young horses. *Excess* calcium over long periods can result in brittle bones and reduced availability of other minerals. Excess calcium interferes with phosphorus absorption.

Comments: CALCIUM-PHOSPHORUS RATIO. Calcium and phosphorus affect each other, and they are both affected by vitamin D. Problems occur when calcium and phosphorus are not in balance. The desired calcium-phosphorus ratio is 1.1 parts calcium to 1.5 parts phosphorus (1.1:1.5). A 2:1 ratio is acceptable, and as much as 5:1 may be acceptable in mature horses. In most areas of the country, especially where alfalfa hay is fed, the amount of calcium in the feed may greatly exceed the amount of phosphorus—even by ten times or more. Therefore, although the ideal calcium-phosphorus ratio is almost 1:1, it is often hard to obtain this. A wider ratio is acceptable as a horse matures, although it is always best to aim for the ideal when possible.

Both minerals should be increased proportionately for animals at work or experiencing stress, broodmares, and growing foals. If plenty of vitamin D is present, the calcium-phosphorus ratio is somewhat less important.

Some areas of the country, such as Wyoming, are high in calcium and low in phosphorus: add phosphorus, especially for broodmares, to prevent bone and leg deformities in foals. If pastures are deficient, use high-phosphate fertilizer (check with your county agent).

PHOSPHORUS

Function: Necessary for development of bones and teeth—80 percent of body phosphorus is in bones and teeth; necessary to metabolism of carbohydrates and fats, and for activation of enzymes.

Source: Cereal grains and especially bran (though much of the phosphorus is not readily available), monosodium phosphate, disodium phosphate, or sodium tripolyphosphate; steamed bone meal and dicalcium phosphate supply both phosphorus and calcium.

Lack results in: Same as for calcium. *Excess* phosphorus interferes with calcium absorption—results in lameness and enlarged facial bones (bighead disease, brain disease, or miller's disease).

Comments: See CALCIUM-PHOSPHORUS RATIO, under CALCIUM.

IODINE

Function: Controls metabolic rate (needed by thyroid gland to make thyroxin).

Source: Most parts of the country have adequate iodine in the soil, except for "goiter belt" areas. Use iodized or trace-mineralized salt in deficient areas or if you are in doubt (such salt will not produce an excess).

Results of lack: When mares are deficient in iodine, their foals may have goiter, be stillborn, weak, or hairless, and have a higher than normal percentage of navel ill. Stallions: decreased semen quality. *Excess:* May also produce goiter, weak foals, leg weaknesses—and foals may die shortly after birth.

MAGNESIUM

Function: Reduces stress and irritability; essential for bones and teeth. *Source:* Normally adequate where forage is nutritious; magnesium sulfate, magnesium oxide. *Results of lack:* Under stress, horses become nervous, jumpy, and high-strung; muscle incoordination, glazed eyes, tetany, and collapse.

Comments: Excess magnesium upsets calcium-phosphorus ratio metabolism; excess calcium or phosphorus reduces magnesium digestibility. Problem horses are sometimes found to be magnesium-deficient; adequate magnesium improves disposition.

POTASSIUM

Function: Necessary for maintaining proper acid/alkali balance in cells, muscle activity. *Source:* Molasses, potassium chloride; most diets have adequate potassium—especially those with at least 50 percent forage; however, availability of potassium decreases with advancing forage maturity.

Lack results in: Permanent disorders of heart and kidney, decreased appetite. *Comments:* In severe illness (intestinal disorders such as excessive fluid excretion, as in diarrhea and kidney problems), potassium level can quickly be lost. Blood test can determine level.

IRON

Function: Necessary for healthy blood formation—an essential component of hemoglobin of red blood cells; important to some enzyme systems. *Source:* Supplied by normal diet, cane molasses, trace-mineralized salt.

Lack results in: Anemia—with fewer than normal red cells, and red cells having less than normal hemoglobin. *Excess:* Too much iron might be harmful. *Comments:* Loss of blood due to a wound or heavy parasite load is primary cause of iron loss. Milk is deficient in iron, and feeding iron to a mare does not increase iron content in milk—creep-feed foals as soon as they're old enough.

COPPER

Function: Necessary for healthy blood formation; important to normal bone development. *Source:* Supplied by normal diet except in some copper-deficient areas (see comments); trace-mineralized salt with copper sulfate or copper carbonate. *Results of lack:* Deficiency in foaling mare might result in hemorrhaging; anemia; thin, weak bones in foals.

Comments: Milk is low in copper. Excess molybdenum will tie up copper, creating a copper deficiency. Can be a real problem with feeds grown on soils high in molybdenum. In this case, copper supplementation is suggested. Check with county agent or have feed tested from your area, as it tends to be an area (or even ranch) problem.

COBALT

Function: Synthesizes vitamin B_{12}. *Source:* Supplied by normal diet except in cobalt-deficient areas; cobalt salt (salt with cobalt chloride, cobalt sulfate, cobalt oxide, or cobalt carbonate). *Results of lack:* Anemia; cobalt deficiency plus copper deficiency results in "salt sick" (Florida).

MANGANESE

Function: Necessary for growth, reproduction, and formation of good bones; important to some enzyme systems. *Source:* Hay is high in manganese—requirements easily met. *Lack results in:* Anemia, poor growth; lameness, enlarged joints, deformed legs;

impaired reproduction. *Comments:* Too much phosphorus interferes with absorption of manganese.

ZINC
Function: Needed for normal protein synthesis and metabolism, good growth, normal hair development. *Source:* Zinc carbonate, zinc sulfate. *Lack results in:* Poor growth; skin lesions (parakeratosis); loss of appetite; rough, dull hair coat. *Comments:* Imparts gloss to hair coat; too much calcium may reduce utilization of zinc.

SELENIUM
Function: Necessary for adequate utilization of vitamin E. *Source:* Sufficient amounts present in normal diet, except in selenium-deficient soils. *Lack results in:* Muscle degeneration in foals (white muscle disease). *Excess:* Too much selenium results in toxicity (alkaline and desert climates where levels in forage are high). Symptoms are loss of hair and development of ring around hoof. Horses on selenium pastures are especially liable to poisoning after rain-spatterings from ground deposit more selenium on plants. *Comments:* There are reports from Wyoming of performance horses "tying up" (stress-related). An injection of selenium and vitamin E eliminated the problem.

FLUORINE
Function: Not known to be essential to horses. *Source:* Water and hay. *Comments:* Excessive amounts can be toxic—causes irreversible damage to teeth (mottles and stains); bones of nose may become thicker, producing Roman-nose effect.

SULFUR
Function: Not known to be essential to horses.

LEAD
Function: Not known to be essential to horses. *Comments:* Lead poisoning can occur when horses are pastured near smelters with lead emission, or horses chew on wood coated with lead paint. Causes bone lesions, poor growth, anemia, muscular weakness, paralysis of pharynx and larynx.

VITAMIN CHART

VITAMIN A
Fat-soluble. Found through its yellow pigment, carotene (masked by chlorophyll, but the greener the plant the more carotene available).

Function: Essential for good vision and for healthy skin, hair, hoofs; promotes growth; helps in reproduction and lactation; stimulates appetite; provides resistance to infection of epithelia and keeps mucous membranes healthy.

Source: Green grass—leaves contain more carotene than stems; green hay not over one year old; grass or legume silage; stabilized vitamin A; vitamin A supplements such as vitamin A cake and wheat-germ oil. When pastures are dry and bleached during droughts, or bleached hays are fed throughout a long winter, or green hays are stored for six months or more, vitamin A deficiencies are likely to occur.

Deficiency results in: Infertility, poor hoof growth, digestive and respiratory problems, night blindness, chronic tearing (lacrimation), nerve degeneration, lack of appetite, incoordination. *Excess:* Results in same symptoms.

Comments: Horses are inefficient in converting carotene to vitamin A. Surplus vitamin A is stored in the liver (of mature horses) for up to six months.

Vitamin A content of forage deteriorates rapidly with age; when roughage is dry or weathered, little carotene remains. Regardless of green color, hay over one year old has little carotene or vitamin A. Vitamin A added to feeds and supplements can be destroyed by air, light, and heat—careful storage is essential.

Vitamin A deficiencies show up quicker in younger animals. If pasture or hay is poor, bred mares will need supplementation to help prevent resorption of the fetus and ensure good growth of the foal. Supplementation will reduce problems of tendons, joints, and lameness in stressed horses.

B-COMPLEX VITAMINS

These are synthesized by bacteria in the intestines and have separate functions. They should probably be supplemented to young, growing horses; stressed horses; heavily worked horses; and high-producing horses. Also, horses on poor-quality forage should be considered as candidates for supplementation. Absorption efficiency of B vitamins from the cecum and large intestine is questionable. Horses on green, lush pasture are probably okay.

THIAMIN (Vitamin B_1)

Function: Required for normal carbohydrate metabolism; promotes good appetite; helps in reproduction and growth. *Source:* Cereal grains; green pastures and well-cured, leafy, green hay; brewer's yeast; thiamin hydrochloride. *Deficiency results in:* Nervousness, loss of appetite, loss of weight, incoordination (especially hindquarters), enlarged heart. *Comments:* Synthesized by bacterial action—may not be sufficient. Deficiencies may occur during stress and physical exertion (carbohydrate metabolism is increased) and when green pastures and high-quality roughage are not available.

NIACIN (Nicotinic acid)

Function: May not be essential for horses, according to some sources; however, it seems to have some function in the metabolism of carbohydrates and protein.

Source: Green alfalfa, animal by-products, synthetic niacin. *Deficiency results in:* Reduced appetite, poor growth, skin rashes, diarrhea, nerve disorders. *Comments:* If niacin is insufficient, the amino acid tryptophan can be converted into niacin by the horse; however, the horse is then short of this essential amino acid.

RIBOFLAVIN (Vitamin B_2)

Function: Essential for proper energy release; essential to proper function of nervous system; important in protein metabolism; important for synthesis of ocular vitamin C. *Source:* Green hay and pasture, silages, synthetic riboflavin, milk and milk products. *Deficiency results in:* Periodic ophthalmia (moon blindness), although lack of vitamin B_2 is not the only factor in this disease. *Comments:* This is a stable vitamin, not affected by heat and air.

PYRIDOXINE (Vitamin B_6)

Function: Necessary for metabolism of protein and fat. *Source:* Grains; and synthesized in lower digestive tract. *Comments:* Deficiencies are not likely, since vitamin B_6 is synthesized by the horse.

FOLACIN (Folic acid)

Function: Necessary for cell metabolism; related to vitamin B_{12} function; necessary for normal blood formation. *Source:* Green, leafy grass and hays; synthetic folacin. *Deficiency results in:* Anemia, poor growth. *Comments:* Rarely deficient.

BIOTIN, CHOLINE, and INOSITOL

Function: Work together and combine with other substances to aid certain enzymes; essential in formation and maintenance of cell structure; essential in transmitting nerve impulses. *Source:* Content in normal feeds is generally sufficient. *Deficiency results in:* Slow growth (choline); loss of hair and loss of appetite (biotin). *Comments:* Horses on a normal diet synthesize these vitamins adequately in the intestine without supplementation.

VITAMIN B_{12} (Cobalamin)

Function: Function linked with folic acid; important to some enzyme systems. *Source:* Animal protein supplements; fermentation products; synthetic B_{12}. *Deficiency:* Horses in poor nutritional condition with anemia respond to vitamin B_{12}. *Comments:* Requirements are small—usually met with good diet.

VITAMIN C (Ascorbic acid)

Function: Not considered essential for horses. *Source:* Horses appear to synthesize adequate amounts. *Results of deficiency:* Deficiency of vitamin C might be linked with deficiency of vitamin A. *Comments:* Some horsemen believe that adding vitamin C (1,000 mg daily) will help fertility.

VITAMIN D

Fat-soluble.

Function: Essential for proper absorption, transportation, and metabolism of calcium. *Source:* Sunlight, sun-cured roughages, fish liver oils, irradiated yeast. *Deficiency results in:* Rickets in foals, osteomalacia in mature horses; toxicity could appear as calcification of lungs, heart, and other organs. *Comments:* Less vitamin D is required when calcium-phosphorus ratio is in balance.

VITAMIN K

Fat-soluble.

Function: Promotes normal blood coagulation; prevents hemorrhaging. *Source:* Green, leafy hay and pasture (horses synthesize vitamin K from this in the intestines); fish meal; menadione (vitamin K_3). *Deficiency results in:* Bleeding—increased clotting time; deficient animal may bleed to death from injury or bruise that ruptures a blood vessel. *Comments:* A factor in moldy hay and some clover pasture destroys vitamin K. May be supplemented, especially during foaling, when postparturient hemorrhaging is possible.

PANTOTHENIC ACID

Function: Necessary to some enzyme systems. *Source:* Fish solubles, calcium pantothenate, normal diet of good-quality roughage. *Deficiency results in:* Poor growth, nervous disorders, skin rash, loss of appetite. *Comments:* Synthesized in intestines—unlikely to be deficient.

VITAMIN E

Fat-soluble.

Function: Insures against destruction of vitamin A, improves reproduction, prevents anhidrosis (dry, dull coat). *Source:* Good-quality hay and forage, cereal grains, wheat germ, wheat-germ oil, alphatocopherol (stable form of vitamin E). *Deficiency results in:* Infertility myositis, muscular dystrophy of foals, degeneration of muscle tissue, mild form of azoturia. *Comments:* Vitamin E appears to be destroyed or used up rapidly during stress. Combined with selenium, it is effective in treating white muscle disease. Foal survival rate increases if mares have vitamin E during late gestation. When E levels are sufficient, vitamin A is used more efficiently, so not as much is needed.

HOW TO BALANCE A RATION

Many people never actually go to the trouble of balancing a ration: figuring the exact amount of grain, hay, and supplements needed to provide proper nutrition for each animal. They feed pretty much "by guess and by golly," and provided they keep a close eye on their individual horses and keep various feeding considerations in mind, they do very well.

To balance a ration properly, you must know the nutritional content of what you are feeding. Tables and charts can only be approximate, since in any year, in any given area, at various growth stages, this content will differ. If you wish to balance a ration accurately, you must first have your soils, pastures, and hays analyzed—as well as the grain you are feeding—if the analysis is not shown or available. Ask your county extension agent or agricultural college to help you obtain these analyses.

If you don't have your own analyses made, at least ask your county agent or veterinarian for averages or special conditions in your area; if you know that your area is generally low in phosphorus, for example, you can plan to supplement more highly in phosphorus than is indicated on the charts. Remember also to adjust for weather conditions and other considerations.

First set down the daily requirements for your horse (we'll take a 760-pound yearling as an example):

From Table	Daily feed lbs.	Crude protein %	Digestible protein %	TDN %	Calcium %	Phosphorus %	Vitamin A IU
A	14	12.3	7.7	60	0.43	0.29	30,000

By multiplying each of the given percentages by fourteen, you find the number of pounds needed of each requirement:

Daily feed lbs.	Crude protein %	Digestible protein %	TDN %	Calcium %	Phosphorus %	Vitamin A IU
14	1.72	1.08	8.4	0.06	0.04	30,000

Next, find the analysis for the roughage you are feeding (Table B), and set it below the requirements (we'll assume a fairly good-quality prairie hay):

Table A   APPROXIMATE NUTRITIVE REQUIREMENTS OF HORSES[1]
Feeding for Age, Reproduction, and Work

	Daily pounds of dry feed	% of live weight	Crude protein %	Digestible protein %	TDN* %	Calcium %	Phosphorus %	Vitamin A* IU daily
MATURE HORSES 1,100 pounds								
WORK								
IDLE	13.0	1.2	10	5.3	50	0.33	0.25	50,000
LIGHT WORK	17.5	1.6	10	5.3	54	0.25	0.18	50,000
MEDIUM WORK	23.0	2.1	10	5.3	60	0.20	0.15	50,000
HARD WORK*	22–26	2.2	10	5.3	70			50,000
REPRODUCTION MARES								
FIRST TWO-THIRDS OF PREGNANCY	13–15	1.2	10.7	6.0	52	0.33	0.25	50,000
LAST NINETY DAYS	14.0	1.3	11.5	6.9	58	0.38	0.29	50,000
PEAK OF LACTATION	22.0	2.0	13.1	8.3	60	0.47	0.37	50,000
STALLIONS* during BREEDING SEASON	16–22	1.6–2	14.0		68			50,000
AGE GROWING HORSES mature weight 1,100 pounds								
FOALS 250 lbs.	10.0	4.0	19.0	14.1	70	0.69	0.44	30,000
WEANLINGS 500 lbs.	12.5	2.5	13.4	9.6	65	0.82	0.51	35,000
YEARLINGS 725 lbs.	13.5	1.9	12.3	7.7	60	0.43	0.28	40,000
LONG YEARLINGS 900 lbs.	14.0	1.6	11.3	6.7	55	0.37	0.26	45,000
3½ YEARS 1,100 lbs.	13.0	1.2	10.0	5.3	50	0.34	0.25	50,000

Note: Information unavailable for areas left blank
1. From "Nutrient Requirements of Horses," National Research Council, 1973, except as noted by *, where information has been extrapolated from other sources. Some sources suggest that requirements shown by NRC are low, and should be considered as constituting a bare minimum.

Table B APPROXIMATE COMPOSITION OF COMMON HORSE FEEDS[1]

	crude protein %	digestible protein %	crude fiber %	TDN %	nutritive ratio	calcium %	phosphorus %	Vitamin A IU/lb.	good source of vitamin
ROUGHAGES									
ALFALFA HAY	15.3[2]	10.9	28.6	50.7	1:3.7	1.47	0.24	33,833-4,500[3]	A, D, E
CLOVER HAY	14.2	8.1	29.5	53.2	1:5.6	1.15	0.23	18,333-3,000	A, D, E
TIMOTHY HAY	6.6	3.0	30.3	49.1	1:15.4	.35	.14	15,333-4,167	A, D, E
ALFALFA/BROMEGRASS HAY	11.8	7.6	32.5	47.9	1:5.3	.77	.20	11,167 av.	A, D, E
PRAIRIE HAY	6.0	2.0	29.7	45.1	1:21.6	.33	.12	15,167-6,000	A, D, E
CONCENTRATES									
OATS	12.0	9.4	11.0	70.1	1:6.5	.09	.33	83	B, E
CORN	8.7	6.7	2.0	80.1	1:11.0	.02	.27	2,167	A, B, E
BARLEY	12.7	10.0	5.4	77.7	1:6.8	.06	.40	333	B, E, niacin
WHEAT BRAN	17.0	13.1	11.2	71.0	1:4.4	.10	1.30	2,000	B, E
20% PROTEIN CAKE	20.0		max. 10.0					20,000	A
MILO	10.9	8.5	2.3	79.4	1:8.3	.03	.28	167	
SUPPLEMENTS									
SOYBEAN MEAL	44.0	37.0	5.9	77.9	1:1.1	.27	.63		riboflavin, thiamin
MOLASSES (CANE)	3.0	00.0	00.0	53.7	—	.66	.08		B, E
LINSEED MEAL	35.2	30.6	8.9	75.5	1:1.5	.37	.86		
COTTONSEED MEAL	43.3	35.9	11.0	72.6	1:1.0	.23	1.07		
BONE MEAL (STEAMED)	7.5	—	1.5	—	—	30.14	14.53		

1. The source for this table is *Feeds and Feeding*, by F. B. Morrison, 22nd edition (see Recommended reading). Since sources vary widely, and any figures can only be an approximation in any case, the figures given have value mainly for comparison. By glancing at the chart, you can see that oats have more protein but less energy value than corn, or that cottonseed meal is especially high in phosphorus. For a valid study, have your own analyses made, and write the figures in the space provided.
2. An average; very leafy, prebloom alfalfa may have 18.6 percent, while stemmy, late-cut hay may have only 12.3 percent.
3. The variation is so wide that some extremes are shown, rather than the average. Late-cut, weathered hay loses a tremendous amount of vitamin A.

From Table	Crude protein %	Digestible protein %	TDN %	Calcium %	Phosphorus %	Vitamin A IU
B	6.0	2.0	45.1	0.33	0.12	10,000/lb.

Again, find the number of pounds of each in 14 pounds of hay:

Daily feed lbs.	Crude protein %	Digestible protein %	TDN %	Calcium %	Phosphorus %	Vitamin A IU
14	.84	.28	6.31	.05	.017	140,000

When compared to the requirements above, this falls short, especially in phosphorus (although the vitamin A appears more than adequate, remember how quickly it deteriorates). By trial and error, adjust the ration to increase the nutrients (first we'll try feeding half prairie hay and half alfalfa):

	Daily feed	CP	DP	TDN	Cal	Phos	Vitamin A IU
Prairie hay	7	.42	.14	3.16	.023	.008	70,000
Alfalfa	7	1.07	.76	3.55	.103	.017	105,000
	14	1.49	.90	6.71	.126	.025	175,000

This is better, but still falls short. Let's add some grain:

	Daily feed	CP	DP	TDN	Cal	Phos	Vitamin A IU
Prairie hay	5.5	.33	.11	2.48	.018	.007	55,000
Alfalfa	5.5	.84	.60	2.79	.080	.013	82,500
Oats	2.0	.24	.19	1.40	.002	.007	—
Soybean meal	1.0	.44	.37	.78	.003	.006	—
	14.0	1.85	1.27	7.45	.103	.033	137,500

This is much better but is still short in phosphorus and could be improved still more, perhaps by adding some corn for higher TDN, or cottonseed meal to improve phosphorus. It is important to watch the calcium-phosphorus ratio, which is much too wide; more phosphorus is needed to narrow it to at most 2:1 (in this ration, it is over 3:1). A commercial vitamin-mineral supplement or commercial pre-mix may be the best answer.

Chances are you'll do just fine by following the recommendations outlined in the chapter on feeding, adjusting them to the individual by your own observation and common sense. However, it's well to know *how* to balance a ration. Then, if you do run into feeding problems, you can have the proper analyses made and see if you have any deficiencies. Balance the ration accordingly. The results may surprise you!

COMMON UNSOUNDNESSES, DISEASES, AND AILMENTS
(See also, Chapters 7, 8, and 12.)

Problems by Part, Including Skeletal and Muscular Systems

HEAD AND NECK: *Bent neck.* Mild or severe injury causing lowered head, carried bent to one side. *Goiter.* Swelling of the thyroid gland, usually due to lack of iodine. *Lampas.* Swelling of the hard palate behind the front teeth. *Warts.* Virus-caused nodules on lips and nose of young horses, usually disappearing in two to three months. *Strangles (distemper).* Contagious, pus-forming abscess of lymph nodes, caused by bacteria. It is accompanied by fever, cough, and heavy nasal discharge. *Sinusitis.* Any infection or inflammation of the nasal sinuses. *Conjunctivitis.* Inflammation of the membrane that lines the eyelid and covers part of the eyeball. *Periodic ophthalmia (moon blindness).* Inflammatory disease of the eye—most common cause of blindness in horses. *Other eye disorders,* such as corneal injuries, corneal dystrophy, disorders of the iris, cataracts, or glaucoma. *Poll evil.* Bacterial infection of bursa in poll area involving painful swelling and drainage.

SHOULDER: *Sweeny.* Atrophy of shoulder muscles. *Bursitis.* Inflammation of the bursa, restricting movement in shoulder joint. *Arthritis.* Inflammation of the structures of the joint, including changes in the joint capsule and bony changes of the joint surfaces. *Dislocation* of the shoulder joint.

FETLOCK: *Windpuffs* (wind galls, road puffs). Small, puffy swellings on each side of the tendon just above the fetlock joint. *Osselets.* Inflammation of the fetlock joint capsule. *Sesamoiditis.* Inflammation of the proximal sesamoid bones, involving the bone, its covering, and associated ligaments. *Suspensory ligament injuries:* strains, sprains, ruptures.

PASTERN and CANNON: *Scratches* (grease heel). Similar to chapped hands in humans; can become raw, cracked, and painful. *Bowed tendon.* Inflammation of the tendon, or of tendon and its sheath. *Ringbone.* Bony growth on either or both sides of the pastern, which may involve the joint. Rachitic ringbone: a fibrous tissue enlargement of the pastern on young horses. *Contraction of the digital flexor tendon.* A shortening of the tendon due to inheritable characteristics, malposition of the fetus, or nutritional deficiency. *Splints.* A bony enlargement on the inside upper part of the front cannon bone.

FOOT and HOOF: *Canker* and thrush (see Chapter 7) have a similar description: odor, foot appearance, and the fact that it is found in stables where there are urine, feces, and mud-soaked bedding. The specific cause is still an unidentified infection, and lack of frog pressure is a factor. Canker is different from thrush in that it involves the horn tissue (which loosens easily, and when removed reveals a foul smell).

Keratoma. An abnormal cylindrical growth on the hoof wall starting at the coronary band and working down. It pushes the white line toward the center of the sole, thus eventually pressing on the sensitive laminae and sometimes causing lameness.

Gravel. An infection that enters at the white line into the sensitive tissues; when drainage occurs at the heel area and coronet, lameness will cease. Soaking in Epsom salts reduces the swelling and promotes drainage. Apply tincture of iodine to the drainage area and bandage the foot until it is healed.

Seedy toe. A separation of the wall from the sensitive laminae.

Sidebones. An ossification of the lateral cartilages of the foot (usually the forefeet).

Sidebones in themselves are not considered very serious, as the horse is usually not lame, but they do predispose to corns and contracted heels.

Quittor. A chronic, deep-seated, pussy inflammation of the lateral cartilages, characterized by a drainage of pus through the coronary band. Sores periodically break out, then rupture, break, drain, and seem to heal over. Lameness is intermittent, showing when the pressure builds up.

Pedal osteitis. The coffin bone becomes inflamed, characterized by rarefication of the bone (a demineralized state sometimes called "eats-away"), making it rough, porous, and less dense. *Pyramidal disease* (buttress foot), a form of low ringbone, is new abnormal bone growth on the upper front of the coffin bone due to a fracture or inflammation of the bone. When the inflammations heal, they manufacture excessive bone growth.

Fractures in the foot require prompt veterinary attention.

KNEE, FOREARM, and ELBOW: *Big knees* (knock-knees) in young horses: inflammation of the growth plate of the bones above the knee. *Capped knee.* A swelling filled with fluid over the front surface of the knee. *Carpitis* (popped knee). Acute or chronic inflammation of joint capsule, or bones of knee. *Radial nerve paralysis* in forearm is caused by injury; mild case may cause stumbling, severe case may involve atrophy of leg muscles. *Capped elbow* (shoe boil). A fluctuating, soft, flabby swelling over the point of the elbow, due to injury.

WITHERS, BACK, and BARREL: *Fistulous withers.* As with poll evil, an inflammatory disorder of the bursal sac, with pain, fluctuating swelling, and drainage. *Saddle sores* (galls). Friction-caused sores that may swell, blister, and develop pus, leading to bursitis or fistulous withers if not treated. *Dislocation* of the sacroiliac joint. *Umbilical hernia.* The protrusion of any internal organ through the wall of the containing cavity, forming a swelling or lump at or near the navel.

HINDQUARTERS: *Dislocation of hip joint. Myopathy.* Disease of a muscle. *Lathyrism.* Gradual progressive paralysis of the hind legs caused by toxic reaction to eating large amounts of plants of genus *Lathyrus.* STIFLE JOINT: *Stifling.* Upward fixation of the patella. *Gonitis.* General term referring to acute or chronic inflammation of the stifle joint. *Dislocation* of the stifle joint, accompanied by tearing and stretching of the ligaments. GASKIN: *Rupture* of muscles or tendons.

HOCK: *Capped hock.* A swelling (soft when fresh, firm when fibrous) on the point of the hock. *Stringhalt.* A nervous disorder regarded as a gross unsoundness; an involuntary flexion of the hock which jerks the foot up much higher than normal. *Curb.* A hard, firm swelling of the ligament on the back surface of the rear cannon. *Thoroughpin.* A soft, puffy, spherical swelling just above the point of the hock that can be hand-pressed from one side of the hock to the other. *Bog spavin.* A large, soft, fluctuating swelling on the hock. *Bone spavin.* A bony growth on any of the bones of the hock.

Problems of the Respiratory System

Because of the similarity of symptoms in some respiratory diseases, it is important to have your veterinarian diagnose the problem, which may have to be done with the help of laboratory tests. Avoid do-it-yourself guesswork. Early diagnosis, correct diag-

SKELETAL SYSTEM

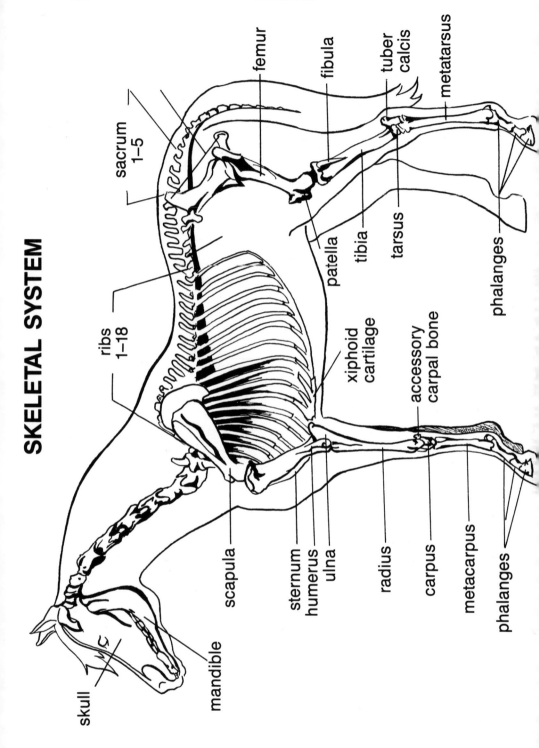

skull

mandible

scapula

sternum
humerus
ulna

radius

carpus

metacarpus

phalanges

ribs
1–18

sacrum
1–5

femur

fibula

tuber
calcis

metatarsus

patella

tibia

tarsus

phalanges

xiphoid
cartilage

accessory
carpal bone

MUSCULAR SYSTEM

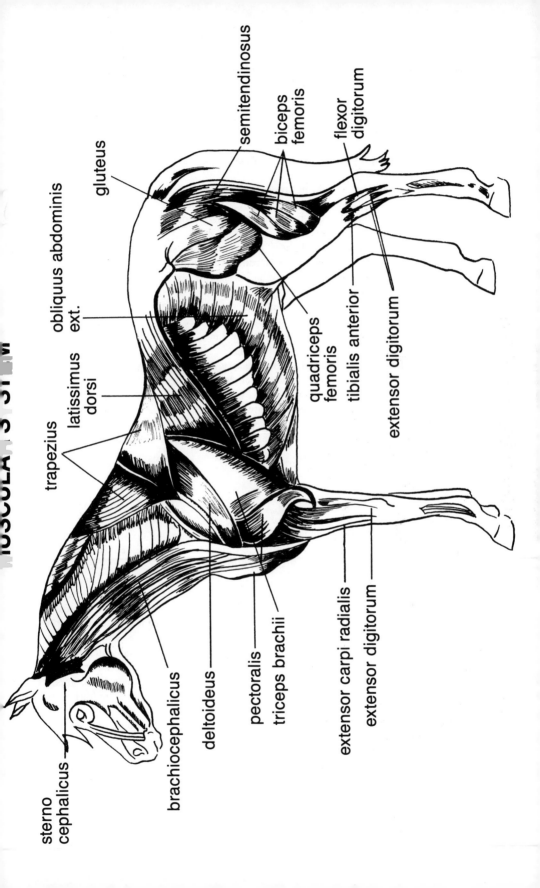

sterno cephalicus

brachiocephalicus

deltoideus

pectoralis

triceps brachii

extensor carpi radialis

extensor digitorum

trapezius

latissimus dorsi

obliquus abdominis ext.

gluteus

semitendinosus

biceps femoris

flexor digitorum

quadriceps femoris

tibialis anterior

extensor digitorum

nosis, and proper treatment may be critical, if widespread contagion or permanent damage is not to result.

Treatment will include use of specific drugs selected to combat the specific infections. Vaccines are available for protection in some cases. One aspect of treatment in most respiratory diseases is an extended period of complete rest, even for three to six months after symptoms disappear; forced exercise during the disease may do permanent damage or be fatal.

Obstructions may be partial or complete, giving the horse discomfort or becoming severe enough to make breathing impossible. Symptoms include nasal discharge; reduced efficiency; difficulty in breathing; loud respiratory sounds; irregular, labored breathing, especially when exercising.

Roaring. A sign of paralysis of one or both intrinsic muscles of the larynx, occurring on inspiration (taking in air); can be accompanied by difficulty in breathing. Symptoms include a harsh, dry cough, retching, or gagging; excitement and exercise aggravate the condition.

Pleurisy. Inflammation of the membrane that encloses the lungs. First signs are moderate fever, depression, lack of appetite, reluctance to move, and an anxious expression; then painful breathing, fluid in the lungs, and a shallow, painful cough. Leads to pneumonia and collapse of the lungs.

Viral arteritis. An infection of the respiratory tract, frequently causing abortion in pregnant mares. Symptoms are similar to other respiratory diseases; however, degeneration of arterial walls occurs, sometimes with hemorrhage and blood clots.

Adenoviral infection. An upper-respiratory disease, with symptoms similar to others; reported cases so far have all involved Arabian foals under three months of age; all have died. *Strangles* (distemper): see Problems by Part . . . , Head and Neck.

Problems of the Circulatory System

Nosebleed may be due to injury, or may be indicative of other problems such as tumors, parasites, EIA, or congestive heart failure. If bleeding does not stop quickly, call your veterinarian. If bleeding is profuse, the nostril can be packed with a tampon. Walk the horse slowly until the veterinarian arrives.

Heart problems include heart murmurs, enlarged heart, various heart diseases, congenital defects, and damage due to strongyles. Suspect heart problems when your horse reacts to exercise and hard work with difficulty in breathing and exhaustion, when there is a rapid and irregular heartbeat, when there are incoordination, stumbling, and lameness, and if the horse collapses after exertion.

Piroplasmosis (horse-tick fever, equine malaria, Texas fever, red-water fever). A contagious protozoal disease carried by bloodsucking ticks found in the tropics and subtropical parts of such states as Florida. Symptoms include depression, appetite loss, swollen eyelids, mucous discharge from the nose, sometimes fever, reddish-brown urine, and weakness in hindquarters.

Phenothiazine toxicity. A toxic reaction to phenothiazine, a common element in many horse wormers. Symptoms are the same as for anemia.

Jaundiced foals (similar to Rh factor in human infants). Foal is healthy when born, but antibodies in the mare's colostrum attack and destroy the foal's red blood cells.

The foal becomes dull and weak within twelve to thirty-six hours, mucous membranes develop, yellowing within twenty-four to forty-eight hours, and the foal dies if it does not quickly receive large-volume transfusions of whole blood.

Purpura hemorrhagica involves extensive collections of fluids and blood in the tissues beneath the skin, usually on the head and legs. Symptoms include variously sized swellings of the head and legs, stiffness, difficulty in urination, loss of appetite, and death.

Problems of the Nervous System

Congenital hydrocephalus. Excessive amounts of cerebrospinal fluid in the cranial cavity at birth, causing abnormal enlargement of the cranium and compression of the brain; death. *Meningitis* (caused by the bacterium that causes strangles) is inflammation of the membranes enveloping the brain or the spinal cord. Symptoms include incoordination, circling, head-pressing, convulsions, high but fluctuating temperature. Treatment must be given early to save the horse.

Epilepsy. Functional disorder of the brain, recognizable by the sudden, repeated characteristic seizure. *Injury of the central nervous system* may not be immediately apparent on the surface. Brain injuries can cause paralysis; hemorrhage anywhere in the system can affect organs and muscles. Symptoms may include convulsions, head-pressing, impairment of reflexes, drowsiness, coma, spastic movements, lack of sensation. Get immediate attention from your veterinarian.

Electric shock. Although animals can tolerate high voltage if the amperage is low, most stables are wired with 15–30 amperes and 110 volts—enough to kill a horse if he is well grounded. Lightning is estimated at 1 million volts. Severe electric shock is usually fatal but may result in temporary unconsciousness. Nervous damage can vary from hyperexcitability to complete paralysis, with dizziness and affected vision. Horses may recover but need good nursing care.

Shivering is a chronic neuromuscular disease usually affecting heavy workhorses. The muscles of the hind limbs suddenly jerk, flex, and pull in toward the abdomen while backing, quivering as they do so.

Various chemical and plant poisons affecting the central nervous system include *chlorinated hydrocarbon poisoning, strychnine poisoning, antu* (alpha naphthyl thiourea) *poisoning, fluoroacetate poisoning, thallium poisoning, creosote poisoning, lead poisoning, encephalomalacia* (moldy-corn poisoning), *nicotine poisoning, locoweed poisoning, bracken fern poisoning,* and *yellow star thistle poisoning.* The extent of damage and chance of survival depend largely on the amount consumed. Treatment is often possible in milder cases, or the horse may recover spontaneously if the source of the poison is removed. Absorption through the skin may be as toxic as ingestion.

Problems of the Digestive System

Dysphagia is a difficulty in swallowing due to pain, mechanical obstruction, brain damage, or other cause. Symptoms include food and saliva coming from the nostrils, loss of weight and condition, pneumonia.

Trichomoniasis is an infectious intestinal disease, usually affecting colts two to three years old, characterized by sudden, severe, greenish, watery diarrhea and abdominal pain.

Salmonellosis is a mild or severe enteritis caused by the bacterium *Salmonella typhimurium.* (A strain also causes abortion in mares, testicular lesions in males, and septicemia in newborn foals.) Symptoms include disinterest in food but frequent drinking of water, fever (103–108 degrees), diarrhea with mucus in the feces, abdominal pain, straining. Surviving horses are carriers.

Hyperparathyroidism involves a calcium-phosphorus imbalance. Symptoms include mild lameness and creaking joints, loss of weight, and anemia. If diagnosed early, the condition can be cured by correcting nutritional imbalance.

Peritonitis is inflammation of the membrane lining the walls of the abdominal cavity, due to penetration of the abdominal wall (accidental wound), leakage of material through gastrointestinal wall (rupture, parasites), or systemic disease. Symptoms include abdominal pain, shock, fever, high pulse rate, low blood pressure, and constipation followed by acute diarrhea and dehydration.

Atresia coli is a birth defect involving incomplete formation of the small colon, with little chance of correction. In a related condition, *atresia ani,* the foal has no opening from the small colon to the rectum; this can usually be corrected surgically.

Castor bean poisoning. Horses can be killed by eating as few as twenty castor beans (source of castor oil). Dullness, sweating, spasms, and strong heartbeat are symptoms. *Arsenic poisoning* from dips and sprays, weed killer, rodent poisons, sometimes feed additives, may be incurred from eating the substance or absorbing it through the skin. It is usually fatal unless the veterinarian can treat it immediately. Symptoms include restlessness; acute colic; diarrhea; rapid dehydration; fast, shallow pulse; increased thirst; no appetite; convulsions.

Selenium poisoning (blind staggers) may be acute or chronic. Symptoms when acute: signs of blindness, head-pressing, colic, fever, eventual paralysis, and death. Chronic: dullness, loss of condition, hair loss, stiffness, lameness—contributes to abortion and hoof abnormalities.

Organophosphate poisoning occurs in horses that are exposed to insecticides and some other pesticides, and also dewormers. Death can occur quickly, depending on the substance, though effective treatment by your veterinarian is often possible. Symptoms include diarrhea, colic, difficulty in breathing, constricted pupils, excess salivation, tremors, sweating, and death.

Liver diseases. Jaundice is a yellowish discoloration of the mucous membranes and the white part of the skin, indicating further disorder. *Hepatitis* describes the liver's reaction to a foreign agent in the body: infectious hepatitis, to an infectious organism; toxic hepatitis, to a poison in the system, whether chemical, plant, or metabolic; and serum hepatitis, reaction to injected serums or antitoxins. *Cirrhosis* is a liver disease characterized by loss of the normal lobe structure and fibrous regeneration, resulting in death.

Enteritis is inflammation of the intestines, often secondary to an infectious disease. Symptoms include diarrhea with foul odor and color range from black to white, abdominal pain, depression, increased thirst. Foals may die within a few hours. The cause may be a sudden change in feed, eating damaged feed or toxic substances, unsanitary conditions in a foaling stall, among others.

Colitis X is a disease of unknown cause that sometimes affects horses under stress. It is not contagious but is usually fatal. Symptoms include sudden severe diarrhea, rapid (100-per-minute) pulse, depression, abdominal pain, difficult breathing, rapid dehydration. The onset is so rapid that treatment is generally not possible.

Choke. See the chapter on feeding.

Problems of the Urinary Excretory System

Sore kidneys. When your horse has a soreness over the loin area, it is often thought to be caused by "sore kidneys," which in actuality is rare. Soreness and stiffness in the loins that is not due to bruising or muscle strain may indicate "tying-up" syndrome and azoturia.

Nephritis is inflammation of the kidneys, a rare disease in the horse. Symptoms include edema caused by accumulation of fluids within the body tissues, a fast heart rate, and difficulty in breathing after exercise; the horse passes little or no urine—retention of urine has toxic effect.

Cystitis is inflammation of the bladder, usually involving the urethra and usually caused by bacterial infection. Symptoms include frequent, painful urination with blood and pus, and continuing strain to pass more urine. Sudan-grass pasture seems to be involved, although Sudan hay does not bother horses.

Nephrosis is inflammation and degeneration caused by toxic substances brought to the kidney by the circulating blood.

Disorders of the Skin and Hair

Pigmentary disorders. Albinism is a total lack of pigmentation; leukoderma is loss of pigmentation due to a wound or lesion (saddle sore); vitiligo is a color loss because of age. *Anhidrosis* (dry coat) is loss of the ability to sweat. *Seborrhea* is a chronic skin disorder with dry scales, oily crusts, or irritation and inflammation. *Ventral midline dermatitis* is inflammation along the middle of the chest (behind forelegs) and abdomen, with scaly lesions and loss of hair, due to parasitic worm larvae or biting insects.

Allergic dermatitis (summer itch) is an allergic skin irritation, usually in hot weather, due to flies or other irritants. *Summer sores* are wounds that do not heal in the summertime, due to stomach worms. *Sarcoid* is the most common tumor appearing on horses. *Urticaria* (hives, nettle rash) is an allergic reaction, usually to some substance in the diet, resulting in flat-topped swellings and sometimes involving other symptoms. *Photosensitization* is a skin allergy caused by sensitization to sunlight, affecting hairless and unpigmented parts of the skin.

Systemic Disorders Affecting the Body as a Whole

Malignant edema is an acute infection caused by bacteria that are attracted by wounds, the umbilical cords of newborn foals, and the vaginal mucosa of mares after foaling. The infection appears twelve to forty-eight hours after injury, with swelling, high fever, froth oozing from a wound, depression, weakness, and lameness. Immediate emergency treatment by your veterinarian is imperative.

Leptospirosis. Horses affected with periodic ophthalmia usually have leptospirosis bacteria in the blood. Lepto is contagious, and the organisms rest in the kidneys for years, spreading infection through the urine. A veterinarian must diagnose through blood or urine samples.

Brucellosis (Bang's disease) is found in the lesions of poll evil and fistulous withers of horses running with affected cattle. Symptoms include variable temperature, dullness, stiffness, and difficulty in moving.

Aspergillosis is a fungal infection appearing on plants and feed as white fluffy mold, which horses inhale. Horses that have been extensively treated with antibiotics seem most susceptible. Symptoms vary according to which system is affected (respiratory, nervous, etc.); it can be fatal.

Anthrax is an old disease affecting man and animals. In the horse, it is a fatal septicemia occurring suddenly and rapidly. It is spread by spores that are eaten (they remain in the soil for years), or transmitted by insects. Convulsions and death usually appear within forty-eight to ninety-six hours. Vaccination and quarantine are effective in controlling the disease.

Snakebite, usually from rattlesnakes, copperheads, or moccasins in the United States, is rarely fatal for horses unless it occurs on the nose, where swelling could shut off breathing. If possible, do not move the horse (exercise helps disperse venom throughout the body). Give first aid as for humans, and call your veterinarian immediately.

Insect venoms. Bee and wasp stings can be especially injurious when occurring on the head, since resultant swelling can interfere with breathing. If a horse is attacked by a great number of insects, a general systemic reaction can occur.

GLOSSARY

ACTION. The way a horse moves his feet and legs; the "play" of the bit that causes the horse to flex his jaw.

AFTERBIRTH. Placenta and fetal membranes that are expelled from the mare after foaling.

AGE. Horses are considered to have been born on January 1 of a given year, no matter what day they were actually born.

AGED. A mature animal usually ten years or older.

AIDS. Signals by which the rider communicates with and controls his horse.

AMPULLA. Enlargement in the vas deferens.

ANESTRUS. Lack of estrus—a noncyclic period, usually during winter months.

ANTHELMINTIC. Dewormer, vermifuge.

ATAVISM (REVERSION). Terms referring to the reappearance of the type of remote ancestors or to certain features that suggest the type of remote ancestors (such as lineback and leg stripes).

BALANCE. Impulsion combined with suppleness and flexibility; correct weight distribution for the movement the horse is performing. When referring to conformation, a "well-balanced horse" would be one in good proportion, with substance and depth.

BALD FACE. A wide blaze covering most of the face, including the eyes.

BALLING. Method of administering a physic by use of a balling gun. Also, horses' hoofs "ball up," meaning that wet snowballs pack up on the soles, making movement difficult.

BARREN MARE. One that is not in foal.

BARS. That part of the lower jaw, devoid of teeth, where the bit rests.

BLAZE. A wide white stripe extending the length of the face and covering the nasal bones.

BLEMISH. A scar left by disease or injury that does not impair a horse's performance, although it may count against him in the show ring.

BLISTERING. Treatment used in chronic lameness; a counterirritant that produces severe inflammation for the purpose of drawing blood to the affected area and thereby encouraging healing.

BLOOD SERUM TEST. A test given to mares forty-five to ninety days after breeding to detect the hormone that indicates the mare is in foal.

BOLTING. Eating food very rapidly without proper chewing, due to greed. Also, running away uncontrollably: a serious vice.

BOSAL, BOZAL. The noseband of the hackamore (old Spanish type).

BREEDER. The dam's owner, who selects the sire of the foal.

BRIDLE PATH. Clipped area of the mane beginning at the poll and running two or more inches, where the crownpiece of the bridle rests. Keeps the mane from tangling in the bridle and contributes to a neater look.

BRIDOON. Small snaffle bit used in conjunction with the curb on the double bridle.

BROKEN KNEES. Knees showing scars or broken skin due to an open injury caused by a fall.

BROODMARE. A mare kept for breeding; that is, for the purpose of producing foals.

BROTHER (SISTER) IN BLOOD. A foal by the same sire out of full sisters, or by a full brother out of the same dam.

BRUSHING (interfering). To strike the lower leg (in the fetlock area) with the inner side of the opposite hoof or shoe.

BUCK-KNEED. Knee appears bent forward; opposite of calf-kneed.

BUCKLING OVER. The knee appears bent over; seen often in old horses due to hard work and strain in younger years.

BULBOURETHRAL GLAND. An accessory gland opening into the urethra.

BULK. Indigestible food fibers that are nevertheless necessary for proper digestion in the horse.

CAECUM. Cecum.

CALCIUM-PHOSPHORUS RATIO. The proportion of calcium and phosphorus in a horse's diet, vitally important to proper nutrition (see Mineral Chart, in the Appendix).

CALF-KNEED. Knee appears bent backward when horse is standing.

CAMP. Extending the forelegs out in front and the hind legs out behind—an indication of various health problems.

CAROTENE. A substance found in green and yellow plants that is converted to vitamin A in the body.

CARRIAGE. A horse's bearing: how he holds his head, neck, tail, and so on.

CASLICK'S OPERATION. Stitching the upper part of the vulva to prevent air from entering the vagina—sometimes necessary in mares having poor conformation.

CAST. When a horse has fallen or lain down (usually next to a fence or wall) and is unable to regain his feet without help.

CASTRATE. Remove the testicles (of a stallion).

CAUL. The inner envelope (seen around the foal when born); contains liquid to insulate from shock (fourteen pints).

CAVESSON. Noseband (or type of halter with noseband); a LONGEING CAVESSON has a metal ring at the top of the noseband, allowing the handler full control of the horse's head while longeing.

CECUM. Enlarged portion of the large intestine where fermentation takes place.

CERVIX. Narrow, outer end of the uterus.

CHECKREIN. A restraining rein, either overhead or to the side, that limits the movement of a horse's head.

COLIC. Abdominal pain—an emergency requiring immediate veterinary attention (see the chapter on health, ailments, and restraints).

COLLECTION. Shortening a horse's body length by pushing him into the bit, thus flexing at the poll, raising the action, lowering the croup, and bringing the hindquarters under him. A "well-collected" horse responds instantly to the aids, and performs any movement readily.

COLT. A male horse until the age of four.

COLOSTRUM. The mare's first milk after foaling (for twenty-four to thirty-six hours). It is laxative, rich, and nutritional, and it has immunization properties.

CONCENTRATE. A feed that is low in fiber and high in digestible nutrients.

CONCHA. Circular disc of leather or metal through which saddle strings protrude.

CONFORMATION. A horse's build.

CONGENITAL. Acquired during prenatal growth.

CONTACT. The "feel" between the rider's hands and the horse's mouth, through the bit and the reins.

CONTRACTED HEELS. The foot narrows at the heel, usually due to incorrect trimming or shoeing; can cause lameness.

COVER. A breeding term referring to the stallion's covering (breeding) the mare.

CREEP. An enclosure accessible only to the foal (not to his dam), where high-protein supplements are fed free-choice.

CROSSBREEDING. Mating of purebred individuals that are representative of different breeds.

CRYPTORCHID (RIDGLING, RISLING). A stallion that retains one or both testicles in the abdominal cavity.

CULLING. Removing the less desirable animals from a herd.

CUT PROUD. Said of a gelding that has had some, but not all, of a testicle removed; although sterile, he retains the characteristics of a stallion.

DAM. Female parent.

DIESTRUS. Period between ovulation and estrus when mare will not respond to teasing from a stallion or will respond antagonistically.

DISHING. Throwing the feet sideways in an outward arc; paddling.

DISTAFF SIDE. The female side of the pedigree.

DOURINE. A venereal disease more common in imported horses than in domestic ones.

EDEMA. Swelling caused by the accumulation of large amounts of body fluid in the tissues.

EJACULATION. Discharge of semen from the stallion.

ELECTUARY. A drug mixed with sugar, honey, or molasses to make it more palatable. See the chapter on health, ailments, and restraints.

EMBRYO. An organism during the first third of prenatal growth.

ENCEPHALITIS (SLEEPING SICKNESS). See *Encephalomyelitis,* in the chapter on health, ailments, and restraints.

EQUINE. Term relating to horses and to other Equidae (zebras, asses, etc.)

EPIDIDYMIS. A coiled tube, attached to the testicles, where the sperm cells are stored and matured prior to ejaculation.

ERGOT. Small callus at the back of the fetlock joint.

ESTROGEN. A female hormone.

ESTRUS. A mare's heat period (when she will accept the stallion), usually lasting four to seven days.

ESTROUS CYCLE. A series of physiological changes in the mare from one estrous period to the next.

EWE-NECKED. The crest of the neck is concave instead of convex—not desirable.

EXTENSION. The lengthening of the horse's body by causing him to reach forward with head and neck while forelegs and hind legs also extend forward—as opposed to collection.

FALLOPIAN TUBES. Ducts joining the ovaries to the uterus. Sperm swim up the tube to fertilize the egg.

FAMILY. The lineage traced through the sires or the dams.

FARRIER. Horseshoer.

FEATHER. Long hair running up legs from the fetlock joint.

FECES. Droppings, manure.

FECUNDITY (FERTILITY). Reproductive power; regularity with which progeny are begotten by sire and produced by mare.

FETUS. Unborn foal.

FILLY. Female of four and under (that has never produced a foal).

FLAT BONE. Good, hard, clean appearance; desirable.

FLEXION. Relaxation of the lower jaw, with head correctly bent at the poll in response to the bit.

FLOATING. Filing teeth that have sharp points to produce a better grinding surface so that a horse can better utilize his feed; often necessary on older horses.

FOAL. A horse of either sex, under one year old; sex is designated by "filly foal" or "colt."

FOAL HEAT. The mare's first heat, five to nineteen days after foaling, but usually nine days.

FOALING. A dam giving birth to a foal.

FOLLICLE. The bubble-like part of the dam's ovary, which contains the egg cell.

FORGING. Horse hits fore shoe with rear when traveling at a trot or pace.

FRESH. Spirited, excitable due to lack of exercise.

FULL BROTHER (SISTER). An individual having the same sire and dam.

GALLS. Sores caused by the rubbing of saddle or harness; untreated galls may result in white hair spots.

GAMETE. A mature sperm or egg cell.

GELDING. A castrated male horse.

GENE. The unit of inheritance, which determines a hereditary characteristic (anatomical, physiological, psychological).

GENOTYPE. The genetic constitution of a horse, especially as distinguished from its physical appearance (compare Phenotype).

GENOTYPE SELECTION. Selecting the best breeding animals to mate.

GERM PLASM. Constituent of germ cells, the basis of heredity.

GESTATION PERIOD. The amount of time that the mare carries her foal; it varies from 330 to 350 days, with an overall average of 340 days (certain breed averages may differ).

GET. Offspring; term used when referring to the stallion's offspring.

GLANS PENIS. Cap-shaped tip of the penis.

GRADE. A horse of unknown ancestry or unregistered in any breed registry.

GRADING UP. Mating a grade mare to a purebred stallion.

GREEN. Refers to a horse that has started his training but is still young and inexperienced.

HACKAMORE. A type of bitless headgear used instead of a bridle; control is achieved through pressure on nose and chin.

HALF BROTHER (SISTER). An individual having the same dam but a different sire, or the same sire but a different dam.

HALTER SHANK. Lead rope that attaches by means of a snap to the halter ring.

HAND. Four inches; a unit of measurement for determining the height of a horse (from withers to ground).

HAND BREEDING. Breeding the stallion and mare under carefully controlled conditions under the supervision of human attendants.

HEAT PERIOD. Four to seven days every twenty-one days on the average, when the mare will accept the stallion; estrus.

HEAVES. Broken wind (see chapter on health, ailments, and restraints).

HEAVY HANDS. Said of a rider who has no sensibility in his hands; one who rides by force.

HEMORRHAGE. Uncontrolled bleeding.

HEREDITY. The characteristics passed on from parents and ancestors.

HERMAPHRODITE. An individual in which the sexual organs of both sexes are more or less completely represented.

HETEROZYGOUS. Having unlike genes for one characteristic.

HOMOZYGOUS. Having like genes for one characteristic.

HORMONE. Chemical secreted into the bloodstream by a gland.

HORSE. A mature male, either a stallion or a gelding; may also refer to the whole species *(Equus caballus).*

HOT-WALKER. A mechanical exerciser.

HYBRID. Progeny resulting from crossing of representatives of different species, such as a jack and a mare, producing a mule.

IMMUNITY. Resistance to a specific disease.

IMPACTION. Blockage in the large or small intestine.

IMPORTING. Marking the certificate of registration to show the country of origin of a horse registered from another country. The certificate may be marked "Imp." or the name may be prefixed by an asterisk (*).

INBREEDING. Mating horses closely related, such as brother to sister or sire to daughter.

KEEPING QUALITIES. Ability of a horse to utilize his feed. A good keeper does well and maintains his condition on a minimum of feed. A poor keeper needs a larger-than-average amount of good-quality feed to maintain his condition.

LABIA. Lips of the vulva.

LACTATION. Milk production.

LATIGO. The long leather strap on the near side or the short leather strap on the off side of the Western saddle; used to fasten the cinch.

LEAD. Pattern of footfalls at the canter in which either the left foreleg (left lead) or the right foreleg (right lead) advances farther than the other.

LEUCODERMA. White patches that appear on hairless parts of the horse.

LINEBREEDING. Mating of individuals having a common ancestor a few generations back.

LOCKJAW. Tetanus (see text).

LONG YEARLING. An older yearling, close to his second year.

LONGEING. An exercise and training method in which the horse is controlled by a long line attached to the longeing cavesson or halter. The trainer stands in the center and directs the horse to walk, trot, canter, and reverse around him, using a whip and voice as directional aids.

LONGEVITY. Suggests procreational productivity over many years; a long and useful life.

MAIDEN MARE. Filly or young mare that has never had a foal.

MAKE A BAG. Gradual enlargement and filling of the mammary glands prior to foaling.

MALE TOAD (BUFO) TEST. Injecting a sample of the mare's blood into a male toad forty-five to one hundred twenty days after the mare has been bred, to determine if she is in foal.

MARE. A mature female horse, usually at least four years old.

MARTINGALE. A training aid or restraining device that affects head carriage of the horse. Kinds of martingales and their effects are discussed in the chapter on stable management and tack.

MASTITIS. Inflammation of the udder, usually with attendant spoilage of the milk, due to bacterial infection.

MATRON. A mare that has had a foal.

MECONIUM. The fecal matter in the foal accumulated during the prenatal period.

MEGRIMS (STAGGERS). Similar to fainting in humans; loss of balance; can be due to defective circulation, worms, indigestion, or brain problems.

MENDELISM. From the geneticist Gregor Mendel. The involvement of genes in inheritance.

METESTRUS. Follows estrus; mare not receptive to stallion.

MULE. The progeny of a jack and a mare. (The progeny of a stallion and a jenny is called a hinny).

MUSTANG. The wild horse found on the western plains of North America.

MUTATION. Changes in the genes resulting in a sudden variation.

MUTTON-WITHERED. Blunt, low withers, not well defined.

NAVEL ILL (JOINT ILL). A navel infection (see chapter on foaling).

NEAR SIDE. The left side.

NICK. A mating that results in a foal superior to both sire and dam.

OFF SIDE. The right side.

ORPHAN FOAL. A foal whose dam died or cannot suckle a foal.

OUTCROSSING. Mating members of the same breed but of no relation within the nearest four to six generations.

OUTER MEMBRANE. "Bag of waters" surrounding the fetus.

OVA. Female cells of reproduction; eggs.

OVARY. One of two egg-producing organs in the female.

OVERREACH. Indicates injury to the lower forelegs caused by the horse's striking himself with his hind legs.

OVULATION. When the follicle bursts and the egg is released.

OVUM. Egg.

PALATABLE. Pleasing to the taste.

PARASITE. Organism that grows and feeds in or on a living animal, at that animal's expense, such as a worm, mite, etc.

PARTURITION. Birth.

PASTURE BREEDING. Turning a stallion out into a pasture with a band or group of mares during the breeding season.

PASTERN. Area of the leg between the hoof and the fetlock joint.

PAUNCHY. An undesirable ballooning shape of the paunch (stomach) area, usually due to unthrifty condition.

PEDIGREE. Record of ancestry.

PEDIGREE BREEDING. Basing breeding on the worth of the parents and ancestors.

PENIS. Male organ of copulation.

PHENOTYPE. The observable appearance of the horse (or any organism), as determined by genetics and environment (compare genotype).

PIEBALD. A black and white pinto with large, distinct patches.

PINTO. A spotted or multicolored horse, also called a Paint.

PLACENTA. The membrane attaching the fetus to the uterus, through which nutrients pass from the dam. After birth of the foal, the placenta is expelled.

P.O.A. Pony of the Americas, a breed of pony or small horse derived from the Appaloosa.

POINTING. Extending one forefoot forward to take the weight off it; a symptom of navicular disease, lameness, or damage to foot or leg.

PONY. A small horse, 14.2 hands or under when mature.

PREPOTENCY. Breeding power of the stallion or mare, measured by its ability to pass its characteristics on to its produce, or get.

PREPUCE. Double fold of skin covering the non-erect penis.

PRODUCE. Offspring of a mare.

PROGENITOR. The originator or predecessor.

PROGENY. The offspring of the parents. A foal is "by" a sire and "out of" a dam.

PROSTATE GLAND. Accessory gland opening into the urethra.

PROUD CUT. See Cut proud.

PROUD FLESH. Unhealthy or excessive scar tissue that sometimes forms around a wound, especially on the legs.

PUERPERAL LAMINITIS (FOUNDER). Consequence of retention of afterbirth.

PULSE. Heartbeat.

PUREBRED. Having ancestors of the same breed even though they are not registered —no trace of alien blood.

QUALITY. A nobility of character and spirit; an attitude of majesty and fineness in appearance.

RAFTER-HIPPED. Peaked, poorly-muscled hips, reminiscent of rafters.

RECESSIVE. A characteristic that appears only if carried by both parents' genes.

REGISTRY. Pedigree record kept by associations of recognized breeds.

REVERSION. See Atavism.

RIDGELING (RISLING). See Cryptorchid.

ROUGHAGE. Feed that is relatively high in fiber content.

SACKING OUT. Rubbing the horse with burlap sacks, saddle blanket, slicker, or other material, letting it flap against him, to gentle him and teach him that such treatment is harmless and that he should stand quietly.

SCOURS. A type of diarrhea, usually occurring in newborn foals.

SCROTUM. The visible sack or pouch containing the stallion's testicles.

SCRUB. Mongrel.

SEASON. A mare is said to be in season (in heat) when she is ready to be bred by a stallion.

SEAT. Refers to the rider's position in the saddle. Also, the low part of the saddle between pommel and cantle.

SEMEN. Sperm and fluids from the prostate, the seminal vesicles, and Cowper's glands.

SEMINAL VESICLES. Accessory glands, opening into the urethra and providing nourishing fluid to carry sperm during ejaculation.

SEPTICEMIA. Diseased condition due to disease-causing bacteria or their toxins in the bloodstream; blood poisoning.

SERVICE. Act of breeding a mare.

SETTLED. Condition of having conceived and being in foal.

SEVEN-EIGHTHS BROTHERS (SISTERS). A horse's and his son's progeny produced out of the same mare.

SEX CELLS. The sperm and egg which unite to form life and to transmit genetic traits.

SICKLE HOCK. A conformation fault in which the hocks are too bent, thus weak.

SIRE. The male parent.

SKEWBALD. A horse with pinto markings of white and any color other than black.

SLEEPING SICKNESS. See *Encephalomyelitis,* in the chapter on health, ailments, and restraints.

SMEGMA. Discharge from the sheath of a stallion or gelding.

SNIP. A single small white marking in the area of the nose.

SOUND. In good condition, with no conformation problems or unsoundnesses to interfere with performance.

SPEED. Approximate speed of normal gaits: walk, 4 m.p.h.; trot, 9 m.p.h.; gallop, 12 m.p.h.

SPERM (SPERMATOZOA). Male sex cells produced in the stallion's testicles.

SPERMATIC CORD. Cord containing spermatic artery, veins, nerve, lymphatics, vas deferens, etc.

SPOOKY. Nervous and prone to shy.

STAG. Unsexed male; castration occurring later in life so that secondary sex characteristics are present.

STALLION. A male horse four years or older (five years or older for Thoroughbreds).

STAR. A white mark (of varied size) on the forehead.

STARGAZER. A horse that holds his head too high and thrusts his nose out and upward.

STERILE. Incapable of reproducing; not fertile.

STILLBORN. Born dead.

STRIKING. A dangerous vice in which the horse strikes out with his forelegs. Also, a form of brushing in which the horse strikes one leg with the toe or side of another leg.

STRIPE (STRIP). A narrow white mark running generally from a horse's eyes to his nose.

STUD. A breeding farm. Also, "stud" is often used interchangeably with "stallion"—however, technically this is correct only when the most important stallion on a breeding farm is referred to.

STUDBOOKS. The records in which the horses of the various breeds are registered.

STUD FEES. Fees that the owner of the stallion collects from the owner of the mare when she is bred.

STYLE. Usually refers to the way of going; distinct personal flair of an individual horse; involves presence and personal magnetism.

SUBSTANCE. Said of a horse whose conformation gives the impression of stamina and endurance.

SUCKLING. Foal receiving milk from its dam.

SURCINGLE. A strap (often of webbing) that goes around the horse's girth area and holds a blanket or saddle pad in place.

SYSTEMIC. In the bloodstream; affecting the entire body.

TDN. Total digestible nutrients; see the chapter on feeding.

TEASING. Process of allowing a teaser (may be a stallion, gelding, or proud-cut horse) to approach a mare to see if she is in heat and responsive to breeding.

TESTICLES (TESTES). The male's reproductive glands (there are two), which produce sperm and testosterone.

TESTOSTERONE. Male hormone from the testicles which gives masculinity and effectiveness to the reproductive system.

THREE-QUARTER BROTHER (SISTER). Individual having the same dam, with the sire having the same sires but a different dam.

TIED-IN (referring to knee and leg). Narrowed below knee. The cannon bone should be the same width (when looked at from the side) from the bottom of the knee to the top of the fetlock. When tied-in, the cannon is narrow at the top (the lower back of the knee).

TOP LINE. Refers to male line of ancestors (bottom line refers to dam's line); in conformation, refers to top of profile from poll to tail.

TOXEMIA. Diseased condition caused by bacterial toxins in the blood.

TOXIC. Poisonous; deadly.

TOXIN. Poisonous substance secreted by some disease-producing organism.

UNSOUNDNESS. Structural weakness that affects the normal use of a horse.

URETHRA. Tube from the bladder to the glans penis in the male (in the female, the tube that takes urine from the bladder to outside).

URETHRAL GLEET. Abnormal mucous discharge from the urethra.

URINE TEST. Sampling the mare's urine ninety days or more after breeding, to determine if she is in foal.

UTERUS. Female organ responsible for holding the developing fetus.

VAGINA. Passageway between the vulva and the cervix, part of the birth canal.

VAS DEFERENS. Duct carrying sperm from testes to urethra.

VERMIFUGE. Agent that removes or destroys intestinal parasites.

VULVA. External opening of the genital tract of the mare.

WALLEYE. Bluish eye surrounded by white, indicating a lack of pigment; it is not considered to be a blemish.

WAVE MOUTH. Grinding surface of the teeth has the appearance of gentle waves; upper and lower jaws do not meet properly.

WAXING UP. Sticky secretion that forms around the nipples of the udder (up to ten days before foaling); often means that birth is imminent.

WEANING. Removing the foal from its dam so that it can no longer nurse.

WEANLING. Foal under a year old that has been separated from its dam.

WEAVING. Rhythmic shifting back and forth from one forefoot to the other, usually because of boredom due to confinement and lack of exercise.

WIND SUCKING. Vice in which the horse arches his neck and swallows air; condition sometimes found in mares with poor conformation, allowing air and fecal matter to enter the vagina, sometimes causing infection. See Caslick's operation.

WINKING. Contracting the lips of the vulva; shown by mares in estrus.

WOLF TEETH. Rudimentary or underdeveloped teeth sometimes appearing on the bars and interfering with the bit.

WORMER. Dewormer; vermifuge.

YEARLING. A young horse from a year old to his second birthday.

YELD. A broodmare that is "open" for a year (not bearing a foal).

ZYGOTE. A fertilized egg.

RECOMMENDED READING

Basic Horsemanship: English and Western. E. F. Prince and G. M. Collier (Garden City, N.Y.: Doubleday, 1974).

Basic Training for Horses: English and Western. E. F. Prince and G. M. Collier (Garden City, N.Y.: Doubleday, 1979).

Buyer's Guide to Western Saddles. R. L. Sherer (Houston, Tex.: Cordovan, 1977).

Cavalry Manual of Horse Management. Frederick L. Devereux, Jr., ed. and rev. (Cranbury, N.J.: A. S. Barnes, 1979).

Equine Research Books (published by Equine Research, Inc., Tyler, Tex.):
  Breeding Management and Foal Development, 1982
  Equine Genetics and Selection Procedures, 1978
  Feeding to Win, 1973
  Illustrated Veterinary Encyclopedia for Horsemen, 1975, 1977
  Veterinary Treatments and Medications for Horsemen, 1977.

The Family Horse: How to Choose, Care for, Train, and Work Your Horse. Jackie Spaulding (Point Roberts, Wash.: Cloudburst, 1982).

Feeds and Feeding. F. B. Morrison (Ithaca, N.Y.: Morrison Publishing Co., 1956, 22nd edition).

Genetic Principles in Horse Breeding. John F. Lasley (Houston, Tex.: Cordovan, 1976).

Grooming to Win. Susan E. Harris (New York: Scribner, 1977).

Growth and Nutrition in the Horse. D. P. Willoughby (Cranbury, N.J.: A. S. Barnes, 1975).

The Horse-Breeding Farm. Larryann Willis (Cranbury, N.J.: A. S. Barnes, 1976).

A Horse of Your Own. M. A. Stoneridge (Garden City, N.Y.: Doubleday, 1980).

Horse Safety Handbook. Peggy Bradbury. (Houston, Tex.: Cordovan, 1977).

Horsemaster's Notebook. Mary Rose (London: Peter Barker, 1972).

The Horseman's Notebook. Mary Rose (New York: David McKay, 1977).

Horses and Horsemanship. M. E. Ensminger (Danville, Ill.: Interstate Printers and Publishers, 1977).

Horse's Health from A to Z (An Equine Veterinary Dictionary). Rossdale and Wreford (New York: Arco, 1978).

Horses, Hitches and Rocky Trails. Joe Back (Denver, Colo.: Sage Books, 1959).

How to Shoe a Horse. M. C. Manwill (New York: Arco, 1980).

Illustrated Glossary of Horse Equipment. California Polytechnic State University Foundation (New York: Arco, 1976).

Manual of Horsemanship of the British Horse Society and the Pony Club. (Kenilworth, Warwickshire, England: British Horse Society, 1971).

Mares, Foals and Foaling. F. Andrist (London: J. A. Allen, 1978).

Practical Horseman's Book of Horsekeeping. M. A. Stoneridge, ed. (Garden City, N.Y.: Doubleday, 1983).

Veterinary Notes for Horse Owners. M. Horace Hayes (New York: Arco, 1965).

Whole Horse Catalog. Stephen D. Price et al. (New York: Simon & Schuster, 1977). Magazines—there are many magazines with articles on horse care, including breed publications, local and regional publications that contain information adapted to that area, and other specialized periodicals. A few of the general, national magazines that carry up-to-date care and health information are listed here:

Equus (Fleet Street Corp., 656 Quince Orchard Rd., Gaithersburg, Md. 20878).

Horse Digest (same as above).

Horse and Rider (Rich Pub. Inc., P.O. Box 555, Temecula, Calif.).

Horseman (Cordovan Corp., Pub., P.O. Box 10973, Houston, Tex.).

Practical Horseman (Subscription Service Dept., P.O. Box 927, Farmingdale, N.Y. 11737).

Professional Horseman (same as *Equus).*

Small Farmer's Journal (3890 Stewart Rd., Eugene, Ore. 97402).

Western Horseman (Western Horseman, Inc., P.O. Box 7980, Colorado Springs, Colo. 80933).

INDEX

Italicized page numbers refer to illustrations

ELEANOR F. PRINCE grew up in New Hampshire and now lives on a ranch in Buford, Wyoming, where she raises and trains Arabian horses and teaches equitation at the University of Wyoming.

Originally from Long Island, New York, GAYDELL M. COLLIER lives in Sundance, Wyoming, where she and her husband operate the Backpocket Ranch.